Second Language Teacher Education

CAMBRIDGE LANGUAGE TEACHING LIBRARY
A series of authoritative books on subjects of central importance for all language teachers

In this series:

Teaching and Learning Languages *by Earl W. Stevick*

Communicating Naturally in a Second Language – Theory and practice in language teaching *by Wilga M. Rivers*

Speaking in Many Tongues – Essays in foreign language teaching *by Wilga M. Rivers*

Teaching the Spoken Language – An approach based on the analysis of conversational English *by Gillian Brown and George Yule*

A Foundation Course for Language Teachers *by Tom McArthur*

Foreign and Second Language Learning – Language-acquisition research and its implications for the classroom *by William Littlewood*

Communicative Methodology in Language Teaching – The roles of fluency and accuracy *by Christopher Brumfit*

The Context of Language Teaching *by Jack C. Richards*

English for Science and Technology – A discourse approach *by Louis Trimble*

Approaches and Methods in Language Teaching – A description and analysis *by Jack C. Richards and Theodore S. Rodgers*

Images and Options in the Language Classroom *by Earl W. Stevick*

Culture Bound – Bridging the cultural gap in language teaching *edited by Joyce Merrill Valdes*

Interactive Language Teaching *edited by Wilga M. Rivers*

Designing Tasks for the Communicative Classroom *by David Nunan*

Second Language Teacher Education *by Jack C. Richards and David Nunan*

The Language Teaching Matrix *by Jack C. Richards*

Second Language Teacher Education

Edited by

Jack C. Richards and David Nunan

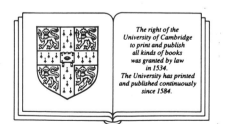

The right of the
University of Cambridge
to print and publish
all kinds of books
was granted by law
in 1534.
The University has printed
and published continuously
since 1584.

Cambridge University Press

Cambridge
New York   Port Chester
Melbourne   Sydney

Published by the Press Syndicate of the University of Cambridge
The Pitt Building, Trumpington Street, Cambridge CB2 1RP
40 West 20th Street, New York, NY 10011, USA
10 Stamford Road, Oakleigh, Melbourne 3166, Australia

First published 1990

Printed in the United States of America

Library of Congress Cataloging-in-Publication Data
Second language teacher education / edited by Jack C. Richards and
David Nunan.
p. cm. – (The Cambridge language teaching library)
ISBN 0-521-38384-6. (hardcover) – ISBN 0-521-38779-5 (paperback)
1. Language teachers—Training of. I. Richards, Jack C.
II. Nunan, David. III. Series.
P53.85.S43 1990
418'.0071'1–dc20   89-37286
                                                                CIP

British Library Cataloguing in Publication Data
Second language teacher education. –
(Cambridge language teaching library).
1. Modern language teachers. Professional education
I. Richards, J. C. (Jack Croft)   II. Nunan, David
418'.007

ISBN: 0-521-38384-6 hardcover
ISBN: 0-521-38779-5 paperback

Contents

Contents

Contributors

Kathleen M. Bailey, Associate Professor of Applied Linguistics, Monterey Institute of International Studies, California

Leo Bartlett, Senior Lecturer, Department of Education, University of Queensland

Roger Bowers, British Council, London

Susan Conrad, ESL teacher, Monterey Institute of International Studies, California

Richard R. Day, Professor, Department of ESL, University of Hawaii at Manoa, Honolulu

Fraida Dubin, Associate Professor of EFL/Education, University of Southern California, Los Angeles, California

Rod Ellis, Head, Department of EFL/ESL, Ealing College of Higher Education, London

John F. Fanselow, Professor, Teachers College, Columbia University, New York

Donald Freeman, Senior Faculty, Master of Arts in Teaching Program, School for International Training, Brattleboro, Vermont

Stephen Gaies, Professor, Department of English, University of Northern Iowa

Sergio Gaitan, Head, Resource Center, Teachers College, Columbia University, New York

Jerry G. Gebhard, Associate Professor of English, Indiana University of Pennsylvania

Lynn M. Goldstein, Assistant Professor, M.A. TESOL/TEFL, Monterey Institute of International Studies, California

Robert Keith Johnson, Senior Lecturer, Department of Education, Hong Kong University

Dale L. Lange, Professor, Second Languages and Culture Education, University of Minnesota

Judith Leatherman, EFL teacher and teacher trainer, San Francisco, California

David Nunan, Associate Director, National Centre for English Language Teaching and Research, Macquarie University, Sydney

Robert Oprandy, Coordinator, Master's TESOL Program, Columbia University, New York

Contributors

Patricia A. Porter, Associate Professor of English, San Francisco State University

Martha C. Pennington, Assistant Professor, Department of ESL, University of Hawaii at Manoa, Honolulu

Jack Richards, Professor and Head, Department of English, City Polytechnic of Hong Kong

Nina Spada, Assistant Professor, Department of Education in Second Languages, McGill University, Montreal

Rita Wong, Assistant Director, American Language Institute, San Francisco State University

Tony Wright, teacher and teacher trainer, English Language Teaching Unit, Christ Church College, Canterbury, England

Preface

This book is an examination of major issues and practices in second language teacher education. It is designed as a state-of-the-art account of current approaches to second language teacher education, as well as a source book for those designing programs and activities in classroom observation, supervision, teacher self-evaluation, teaching practice, and related components of either preservice or inservice teacher education programs.

The field of teacher education is a relatively underexplored one in both second and foreign language teaching. The literature on teacher education in language teaching is slight compared with the literature on issues such as methods and techniques for classroom teaching. Few of the articles published in the last twenty years are data-based, and most consist of anecdotal wish lists of what is best for the teacher. "Minimal attention is paid to the development of teachers in second languages either conceptually or research-wise" (in Lange, this volume, p. 252). Little data have been gathered on the kinds of programs that work and don't work, and there has been a reluctance to subject assumptions behind current approaches and practices to critical scrutiny.

As we move from a period of "teacher training," characterized by approaches that view teacher preparation as familiarizing student teachers with techniques and skills to apply in the classroom, to "teacher education," characterized by approaches that involve teachers in developing theories of teaching, understanding the nature of teacher decision making, and strategies for critical self-awareness and self-evaluation, teacher educators need to reassess their current positions and practices and examine afresh the assumptions underlying their own programs and practices. This book is designed to provide the data for this kind of self-reflection and examination. Its specific goals are:

- to help define the conceptual base upon which the design of teacher education programs in language teaching is based;
- to report on significant and innovative practices in teacher education;
- to describe research issues and research findings in second language teacher education and to identify areas for further research;
- to provide a source of information for teacher educators to use in designing teacher education programs;

– to serve as a text for use in courses on second language teacher education.

The need for such a comprehensive overview of issues in teacher education in second language teaching is prompted by the fact that the field of second and foreign language teaching is constantly being renewed both by different claims as to what teachers need to know, as well as by different approaches to the process of developing this knowledge base in future teachers. In planning this book, we therefore invited a representative group of teacher educators from around the world to address major issues in second language teacher education, in order to provide a focused exploration of issues of both content and process in teacher education. Although the contributors were invited to address a range of diverse issues and practices, including the areas of observation, supervision, practice teaching, and self-observation, and to document successful practices in many different kinds of teacher education programs, a number of themes nevertheless recur throughout the collection:

– a movement away from a "training" perspective to an "education" perspective and recognition that effective teaching involves higher-level cognitive processes, which cannot be taught directly
– the need for teachers and student teachers to adopt a research orientation to their own classrooms and their own teaching
– less emphasis on prescriptions and top-down directives and more emphasis on an inquiry-based and discovery-oriented approach to learning (bottom-up)
– a focus on devising experiences that require the student teacher to generate theories and hypotheses and to reflect critically on teaching
– less dependence on linguistics and language theory as a source discipline for second language teacher education, and more of an attempt to integrate sound, educationally based approaches
– use of procedures that involve teachers in gathering and analyzing data about teaching.

The teacher education program and the teacher educator are seen to be sources of knowledge, experience, and resources for student teachers to use in exploring and developing their own approach to teaching. Such a program needs to be firmly grounded in both theory and practice, informed on the one hand by an understanding of what we know about the nature of classroom second language teaching and learning, and on the other by a scrutiny of classroom data, either in the form of direct or indirect teaching experiences.

Part I   Issues and approaches in teacher education

The chapters in this section of the book provide a context for the collection as a whole by overviewing the major issues involved in designing teacher education programs for second language teachers. They provide a rationale for a range of activities and processes in teacher education, directed both at skills and techniques as well as more abstract principles and theory.

Richards in Chapter 1 outlines the dilemma for teacher educators who wish to derive principles for successful practice from empirical data rather than from speculation and who wish to equip teachers-in-preparation with both low-inference, readily learnable classroom skills as well as higher-level principles and decision-making skills. The dilemma as Richards sees it is that while low-inference techniques and teaching behaviors can be readily taught, their aggregation does not necessarily result in good teaching. Rather, good teaching is a complex, abstract phenomenon comprising clusters of skills, such as those relating to classroom management and lesson structuring. These cannot readily be atomized into discrete skills to be mastered separately. The chapter concludes with the suggestion that a balance needs to be struck between holistic and atomistic approaches to teacher preparation.

In Chapter 2 Gebhard, Gaitan, and Oprandy also consider the limitations of prescriptions on how to teach. They propose a multiple-activities approach to teacher preparation through which student teachers are provided with opportunities to investigate their own teaching and the teaching of others, to carry out investigative projects in their own classrooms, and to discuss teaching in a range of contexts. The multiple-activities approach is particularly effective in developing decision-making skills. To be fully effective, however, it is necessary for the teacher educator to be sensitive to interactions between teaching, observation, and investigation, and to make connections between these different activities.

Ellis examines activities in teacher education in more detail in Chapter 3, and provides an analytical framework for describing and developing activities. He distinguishes between *experiential* and *awareness-raising* practices, and illustrates the use of a wide range of activities that focus on different dimensions of teacher awareness and skill.

Despite difference in focus, all three chapters share some underlying themes. All three point out the inadequacy of a prescriptive approach to teacher development in which a set of imperatives for practice are imported from outside the classroom. While the shortcomings of the prescriptivist approach are aired most comprehensively by Richards, they are also dealt with by Gebhard et al. and by Ellis. Given the inadequacies of prescriptivism, it is incumbent upon teacher preparation programs to work toward the ideal of the autonomous practitioner, that is, someone who is able to draw on knowledge and skills in making on-line decisions to solve problems that are unique to a particular teaching situation. In practical terms, these three chapters underline the importance of providing teachers-in-preparation with a range of experiences. Each provides a unique perspective on classroom action and interaction, while reinforcing the others to provide a much richer picture than if the classroom were explored from a single perspective.

1 The dilemma of teacher education in second language teaching

Jack C. Richards

One indication of the degree of professionalization of a field is the extent to which "the methods and procedures employed by members of a profession are based on a body of theoretical knowledge and research" (Carr and Kemmis 1983: 12). In second language teaching, teacher education programs typically include a knowledge base, drawn from linguistics and language learning theory, and a practical component, based on language teaching methodology and opportunity for practice teaching. In principle, knowledge and information from such disciplines as linguistics and second language acquisition provide the theoretical basis for the practical components of teacher education programs.

One interpretation of the development of second language teaching in the last twenty years or so is that a substantial degree of professionalization has taken place. Thus, the theoretical basis of the field has moved from the study of phonetics and grammatical theory – once considered a necessary (and sometimes sufficient) basis to launch a student into a career as a language teacher – to include the study of pedagogical grammar, discourse analysis, second language acquisition, classroom-based research, interlanguage syntax and phonology, curriculum and syllabus design, and language testing. Language teaching has achieved a sense of autonomy, with its own knowledge base, paradigms, and research agenda.

Yet if a primary goal of graduate teacher preparation programs is the preparation of effective language teachers, this claim to professionalism may be misplaced. While there has been an expansion of the theoretical concepts, research issues, and subject-matter content which constitute much of the field, few who are engaged in developing this knowledge base or research agenda would claim any direct relation between their work and the preparation of language teachers. Research or theory that deals with the nature of second language teaching per se is scant in the professional literature. While there is a body of practice in second language teacher education – based almost exclusively on intuition and common sense – until recently there has been little systematic study of

Reprinted from "The dilemma of teacher education in TESOL" by J. Richards, 1987, *TESOL Quarterly 21*, pp. 209–226. Copyright 1987 by Teachers of English to Speakers of Other Languages. Reprinted by permission.

second language teaching processes that could provide a theoretical basis for deriving practices in second language teacher education.

To prepare effective language teachers, it is necessary to have a theory of effective language teaching – a statement of the general principles that account for effective teaching, including a specification of the key variables in effective language teaching and how they are interrelated. Such a theory is arrived at through the study of the teaching process itself. This theory should form the basis for the principles and content of second language teacher education, which is thus dependent upon the following sequence: (a) Describe effective language teaching processes; (b) develop a theory of the nature of effective language teaching; and (c) develop principles for the preparation of language teachers.

This chapter examines two approaches to the study of teaching from which theories of teaching as well as principles for teacher preparation programs can be developed. The first, a *micro approach* to the study of teaching, is an analytical approach that looks at teaching in terms of its directly observable characteristics. It involves looking at what the teacher *does* in the classroom. The second, a *macro approach*, is holistic (see Britten 1985a, b) and involves making generalizations and inferences that go beyond what can be observed directly in the way of quantifiable classroom processes. Both approaches can be used to develop theories of effective teaching and to derive principles for teacher education. However, they lead in different directions, and this is the dilemma of teacher education.[1]

The micro approach to teaching and teacher education

The principles of the micro approach to the study of teaching were developed from the study of the teaching of content subjects and were only subsequently applied to the study of second language teaching. In content-matter teaching, there is a long tradition of research into what teacher and teaching variables account for higher levels of learner achievement. This research began by examining teacher characteristics such as the teacher's interests, attitudes, judgment, self-control, enthusiasm, adaptability, personality, or degree of training to see how these factors influenced learning outcomes. Teachers were often evaluated according to how they matched profiles of good teachers derived from the opinions of experts, despite the fact that there was no evidence that teachers having these characteristics were actually successful in bringing

---

1 The terms *teacher education* and *teacher preparation* are used synonymously throughout this book.

about higher levels of learning in their pupils (Peterson and Walberg 1979; Ornstein 1985).

In the 1950s, a different dimension was added when research began to examine teaching rather than the teacher. The focus was on what the teacher *does* rather than what the teacher *is*. Systematic analysis of teacher–student interaction in the classroom, as well as other aspects of teacher and learner behavior, led to the development of systems for the coding and analysis of teaching in real time. The focus was on how effective teachers achieved their instructional goals and the kinds of processes they employed. Systematic observation of teachers indicated that

when teachers are visited by observers trained to record their behavior accurately and objectively, appropriate analysis of the records reveals stable differences between the behaviors of teachers who are more effective in helping pupils grow in basic skills, as well as in some affective areas. (Medley 1979: 16)

Effectiveness was generally measured in these studies by higher-than-predicted gains on measures of achievement in math and reading. The emphasis had thus shifted to the behaviors of effective teachers and the relationship between teacher behavior (what the teacher does) and pupil learning. This became known as *process-product research*.

By the 1970s, after a decade of systematic observation of teachers, a number of aspects of effective teaching had been described and used as the basis for models of effective teaching (Joyce and Weil 1980). Once identified, effective teaching strategies could be incorporated into various kinds of training packages and pre- and posttraining differences assessed (Mohlman, Kierstead, and Gundlach 1982).

One characteristic of effective teaching that was soon identified was the teacher's use of questions. Questioning is one of the most commonly employed techniques in the teacher's repertoire. Elementary school teachers may ask as many as 150 questions per hour when teaching science or social studies (Gall 1970). Researchers were consequently interested in finding out how teachers use questions and what constitutes effective use of questions in the classroom.

Among the aspects of question use that have been investigated are (a) the frequency of low-level and high-level questions (low-level questions require recall of facts; high-level questions require synthesis, analysis, and critical thinking) (Winne 1979); (b) the degree to which students are encouraged to ask questions (Graesser and Black 1985); (c) the amount of wait-time teachers allow after a question (i.e., the length of the pause before which a student is called upon to answer a question) (Rowe 1974); (d) the amount of multiple-response questions used (questions to which at least three or four students may each provide a response) (Gallagher and Aschner 1963); and (e) the number of times teachers repeat their own or student questions (Orlich et al. 1985).

The quantity and quality of questioning that teachers engage in is thought to influence the quality of classroom learning (Orlich et al. 1985). For example, higher-level questions are thought to facilitate better learning (Redfield and Rousseau 1981). The use of student questions rather than teacher questions orients instruction toward students. Increasing the wait-time after questions can lead to increased length of student responses, a greater frequency of student questions, a greater degree of student involvement in lessons, and more participation by slower students (Rowe 1974). Multiple-response questions encourage student participation in learning, while repetition of questions wastes class time.

The study of teachers' use of questions during instruction and the effects of different patterns of question use on student learning thus enables effective and ineffective question strategies to be distinguished. This information can then be used to teach teachers how to use more effective questioning strategies. A variety of training formats can be employed to modify a teacher's use of the desired instructional feature.

For example, the Far West Laboratory for Educational Research and Development developed a minicourse designed to improve teachers' questioning skills. The components are a film, which explains the concepts, and training, which includes modeling, self-feedback, and microteaching. In field tests with forty-eight elementary teachers, there was an increase in redirection questions (those requiring multiple student responses) from 26.7% to 40.9%; thought-provoking questions rose from 37.3% to 52.0%; and the use of probing or prompting questions increased from 8.5% to 13.9%. At the same time, teachers' repetition of their own questions decreased from 13.7% to 4.7%, and the answering of the teacher's own questions by the teacher decreased from 4.6% to 0.7% (Borg et al. 1970: 82).

Other dimensions of the instructional process that have been found to make a significant contribution to student learning include time-on-task and feedback. Time-on-task, or *engaged time,* refers to time during a lesson in which learners are actively engaged in instructional tasks (Good and Beckerman 1978). For example, Teacher A and Teacher B are both teaching the same reading lesson. In Teacher A's class, learners are actively engaged in reading tasks for 75% of the lesson, the remaining time being taken up with noninstructional activities such as taking breaks, lining up, distributing books and homework, and making arrangements for future events. Students in Teacher B's class, however, are actively engaged in reading for only 55% of the lesson. Not surprisingly, studies of time-on-task have found that the more time students spend studying content, the better they learn it. In one study (Stallings and Kaskowitz 1974), the students with the highest levels of achievement in a reading program were spending about 50% more time actively engaged in reading activities than the children with the lowest achievement gains. Relatively simple procedures can be used to train teachers to monitor their own teaching (e.g., audio recording of their lessons) and to help them increase the ratio of engaged time to classroom time.

How the teacher gives feedback to students has also been examined. Feedback can include praise, picking up an idea suggested by a student and developing it, suggestions that something should be corrected, or criticism. Berliner (1985: 147) suggests that "the first three forms of feedback have been associated with more effective teachers." These kinds of strategies can therefore be used as models in teacher preparation programs.

While studies of this kind have identified some of the strategies employed by successful teachers in content classes, such information does not necessarily help us identify what it takes to be an effective second language teacher. The goals of instruction in language classes are different from those of content classes, and as a consequence, the strategies adopted by teachers to achieve these goals will vary. Long and Crookes (1986) point out the need for psycholinguistically motivated studies of instruction in second language classrooms – that is, studies that are informed by constructs drawn from second language acquisition theory.

A pioneering project of this kind (Long et al. 1984) focused on ESL teachers' question patterns and wait-time. These were selected as independent variables on the basis of their assumed contribution to the quantity and quality of classroom language use, both of which are essential to second language acquisition. The dependent variable was the kind of input and interaction that resulted from manipulating question patterns and wait-time. A simple training module was developed in which teachers were taught the differences between display questions (those for which answers are known in advance) and referential questions (those for which answers are not known) and the advantages of providing longer wait-time after questions. Teachers' question use and wait-time before and after training were measured, and "it was found that the training modules affected teaching behaviors, and that the new behaviors affected student participation patterns in ways believed to be significant for these students' language acquisition" (Long et al. 1984: vi).

A basic assumption of process-product approaches to the study of instruction is that teaching can be characterized by recurring patterns of behaviors. The teaching process is viewed in terms of the repertoire of strategies (e.g., control of question patterns and wait-time) employed by the teacher during instruction. The goal of teacher preparation is to impart these strategies as competencies to teachers-in-preparation. This is sometimes referred to as competency- or performance-based teacher education, which "assumes that the effective teacher differs from the ineffective one primarily in [having] command of a larger repertoire of competencies – skills, abilities, knowledge, and so forth – that contribute to effective teaching" (Medley 1979: 15). Teaching is viewed as a kind of technology, and the teacher educator's task is to get the teacher to perform according to certain rules.

In second language classrooms with instructional goals in the domain of oral proficiency, the relevant behaviors are verbal phenomena. In order for the researcher to be able to characterize and quantify these behaviors in a micro approach of the kind described here, phenomena are selected that can be readily operationalized. These are referred to as low-inference categories, that is, categories whose definitions are clearly enough stated in terms of behavioral characteristics that the observers in a real-time coding situation would reach high levels of agreement, or reliability. Question types and wait-time, for example, are unambiguous categories that are easy to identify and quantify because they reflect a straightforward form-to-function relation. Recognition of examples of the categories does not depend on making abstract inferences. These low-inference categories can be contrasted with a category such as "indicating a lack of interest in a topic," in which the relationship between form and function is less direct. This is a "high-inference category," the recognition of which depends on more abstract inferences.

The microanalysis of teaching depends on the identification of low-inference categories of teacher behavior that are believed to contribute to student learning (G. Brown 1975). While categories of this kind relating to oral language proficiency are fairly readily identifiable (e.g., teachers' questioning patterns, the ratio of teacher talk to pupil talk), it is not clear from current second language acquisition research or other research that these same categories would also be relevant to the study of instruction in second language reading, writing, or listening comprehension.

However, even if it were possible to identify relevant categories of teacher behavior in different kinds or aspects of second language programs, would the nature of effective teaching have been identified? As many observers have noted, effective teaching cannot be described only in terms of low-inference skills or competencies (G. Brown 1975). Higher-level categories are also necessary to a theory of teaching.

The notion of time-on-task, for example, is an obvious category for identification and treatment in teacher preparation programs: It is simple to identify and measure, and it is an aspect of teacher performance that should be easy to modify. But time-on-task is closely related to other dimensions of teaching, such as classroom management. A well-managed class is one in which time is well used and in which there are fewer distractions resulting from poor discipline or a poorly structured lesson.

Classroom management, however, is not a low-inference category but an aspect of teaching that has to be inferred by observing a teacher for a period of time in a number of different settings. It may take different forms, varying in nature from one teacher to another. Classroom management cannot be reduced to a few discrete components to be imparted to teachers in a short, one-shot training session.

Likewise, even a simple skill such as the use of referential questions versus display questions is dependent upon knowing when one kind of question might be appropriate. As Medley (1979) observes,

the ability to ask higher-order questions is a competency; clarity is not. There are times when higher-order questions are inappropriate, when the teacher who can ask them should not do so; there is no time when clarity is inappropriate. Research in teacher competencies must take account not only of how teachers behave, but when and why they behave as they do. (p. 16)

This essentially is the dilemma of teacher education. While low-inference behaviors can be taught effectively and efficiently to teachers-in-preparation, these competencies do not in themselves constitute effective teaching. They are linked to more complex aspects of teaching, categories in which it is much more difficult to train teachers but which are essential to a theory of teaching. Let us now consider these aspects of teaching.

The macro approach to teaching and teacher preparation

An alternative approach to the study of teaching and to the development of goals for teacher preparation programs is the examination of the total context of classroom teaching and learning in an attempt to understand how the interactions between and among teacher, learners, and classroom tasks affect learning. This can be called a holistic approach, since it focuses on the nature and significance of classroom events and involves both low-inference and high-inference categories. Such an approach implies different goals for teacher preparation:

Holistic approaches work towards training goals not all of which can be broken down into individually verifiable training objectives, and they stress the development of personal qualities of creativity, judgement and adaptability . . . The formulaic or prescriptivist nature of a mere "vocational training" approach to [teacher training in TESOL] is contrasted by holists with an "education" in more general principles. (Britten 1985a: 113)

This view of teaching is reflected in research on effective instruction. In a comprehensive survey of the research on effective schooling, Blum (1984: 3–6) summarizes effective classroom practices as follows:

1. Instruction is guided by a preplanned curriculum.
2. There are high expectations for student learning.
3. Students are carefully oriented to lessons.
4. Instruction is clear and focused.
5. Learning progress is monitored closely.
6. When students don't understand, they are retaught.
7. Class time is used for learning.
8. There are smooth, efficient classroom routines.
9. Instructional groups formed in the classroom fit instructional needs.
10. Standards for classroom behavior are high.
11. Personal interactions between teachers and students are positive.
12. Incentives and rewards for students are used to promote excellence.

This approach to the study of teaching – often termed direct, or *active,* teaching (the latter term is used here, since the term *direct teaching* has also been used in connection with the DISTAR program [Carnine and Silbert 1978], which treats only low-inference behaviors), is based on studies of effective teachers of content subjects, particularly at the elementary level. However, there is also evidence that the notion can be applied to certain kinds of second language settings as well (Tikunoff 1983). Rosenshine (1979: 38) describes active teaching as follows:

Direct instruction refers to academically focused, teacher-directed classrooms using sequenced and structured materials. It refers to teaching activities where goals are clear to students, time allocated for instruction is sufficient and continuous, coverage of content is extensive, performance of students is monitored, questions are at a low cognitive level so that students can produce many correct responses, and feedback to students is immediate and academically oriented. In direct instruction the teacher controls instructional goals, chooses materials appropriate for the student's ability, and paces instructional episodes. Interaction is characterized as structured, but not authoritarian. Learning takes place in a convivial academic atmosphere. The goal is to move the students through a sequenced set of materials or tasks. Such materials are common across classrooms and have a relatively strong congruence with the tasks on achievement tests. Thus, we are limiting the term "direct instruction" to didactic ends, that is, towards rational, specific, analytic goals.

According to the theory of active teaching, several dimensions of teaching account for the differences between effective and ineffective instruction (Doyle 1977; Good 1979). These include classroom management, structuring, tasks, and grouping.

Classroom management refers to the ways in which student behavior, movement, and interaction during a lesson are organized and controlled by the teacher to enable teaching to take place most effectively. Good managerial skills on the part of the teacher underlie many of the aspects of active teaching in Rosenshine's description. As noted previously, a category such as time-on-task is related to the teacher's managerial skills. In a well-managed class, discipline problems are few, and learners are actively engaged in learning tasks and activities; this contributes to the motivational level and expectations for success that the teacher creates in the class. Evertson, Anderson, and Brophy (1978) found that it was possible to identify teachers with managerial problems in the first few days of the school year, that such problems continued throughout the year, and that managerial skills were related to levels of student involvement.

A lesson reflects the concept of *structuring* when the teacher's intentions are clear and instructional activities are sequenced according to a logic and structure that students can perceive. Studies of lesson protocols indicate that sometimes neither the teacher nor the learners understood what the intentions of an activity were, why an activity occurred when it did, what directions they were supposed to follow, or what the relationship between one activity and another was (Tikunoff, Berliner, and Rist 1975); hence, it may not have been clear what students needed to focus on to complete a task successfully. Fisher et al. (1980: 26) conclude that students "pay attention more when the teacher spends time discussing the goals or structures of the lesson and/or giving directions about what the students are to do." Berliner (1984: 63) likewise suggests that "structuring affects attention and success rate: It is sometimes not done at all, sometimes it is done only minimally, and sometimes it is overdone."

Tasks, or activity structures, refer to activities that teachers assign to attain particular learning objectives. For any given subject at any given level, a teacher uses a limited repertoire of tasks which essentially defines that teacher's methodology of teaching (see Swaffar, Arens, and Morgan 1982). These might include completing worksheets, reading aloud, dictation, quick writing, and memorizing dialogues. According to Tikunoff (1985), class tasks vary according to three types of demands they make on learners: *response mode demands* (the kind of skills they demand, such as knowledge, comprehension, application, analysis/synthesis, evaluation); *interactional mode demands* (the rules governing how classroom tasks are accomplished, such as individually, in a group, or with the help of the teacher); and *task complexity demands* (how difficult the learner perceives the task to be).

Teachers have to make decisions not only about the appropriate kinds of tasks to assign to learners, but also about the *order of tasks* (In what sequence should tasks be introduced?); *pacing* (How much time should learners spend on tasks?); *products* (Is the product or result of a task expected to be the same for all students?); *learning strategies* (What learning strategies will be recommended for particular tasks?); *participation* (Should all learners be assigned the same tasks?); and *materials*

11

Jack C. Richards

(What sources and materials are available for completing a task?) (Tikunoff 1985).

The concept of task has been central to studies of active teaching; as noted earlier, the amount of time learners are actively engaged in academic tasks is directly related to achievement. Active teaching is thus said to be task oriented. Effective teachers also monitor performance on tasks, providing feedback on how well tasks have been completed.

A related dimension of active instruction is the *grouping* of learners to carry out instructional tasks and the relation between grouping arrangement and achievement. An effective teacher understands how different kinds of groupings (such as seat work, pair work, discussion, reading circle, or lecture) can impede or promote learning. Webb (1980) found that in mixed-ability groups, the middle-ability child suffers a loss of achievement while the low-ability child shows some gains in achievement, compared with what would be expected if both were in uniform-ability groups. Tikunoff (1985) cites Good's findings on groupings.

Good (1981) found that students in low-ability reading groups in the early grades received very little challenge, thus perceiving of themselves as being unable to read. In addition, a long-range result of interacting most frequently with only other students of low-ability in such groups was an inability to respond to the demands of more complex instructional activities. Ironically, Good pointed out that the very strategy used to presumably help low-ability youngsters with their reading problems – pull-out programs in which teachers worked with small groups of these students outside the regular classroom – exacerbated the problem. Demands in the special reading groups were very different from those in the regular classroom and at a much lower level of complexity, so low-ability students were not learning to respond to high level demands that would help them participate competently in their regular classrooms. (p. 56)

According to the theory of active teaching, effective instruction therefore depends on factors such as time-on-task, question patterns, feedback, grouping and task decisions, as well as on factors such as classroom management and structuring. Some of these can be categorized as low-inference and others as high-inference categories.

Although the concept of active teaching evolved from studies of content teaching, Tikunoff's (1983) major study of effective teachers in bilingual education programs has examined the extent to which the model can also be applied to other contexts. Tikunoff suggests that three kinds of competence are needed for the student of limited English proficiency (LEP): *participative competence,* the ability "to respond appropriately to class demands and to the procedural rules for accomplishing them" (p. 4); *interactional competence,* the ability "to respond both to classroom rules of discourse and social rules of discourse, interacting appropriately with peers and adults while accomplishing class tasks" (p.

4); and *academic competence,* the ability "to acquire new skills, assimilate new information, and construct new concepts" (p. 4). Furthermore, to be functionally proficient in the classroom, the student must be able to utilize these competences to perform three major functions: (a) to decode and understand both task expectations and new information; (b) to engage appropriately in completing tasks with high accuracy; and (c) to obtain accurate feedback with relation to completing tasks accurately (p. 5).

In the Significant Bilingual Instructional Features descriptive study, Tikunoff (1983) collected data to find out how effective teachers in bilingual education programs organize instruction, structure teaching activities, and enhance student performance on tasks. Teachers were interviewed to determine their instructional philosophies, goals, and the demands they would structure into class tasks. Teachers were clearly able to specify class task demands and intended outcomes and to indicate what LEP students had to do to be functionally proficient. Case studies of teachers were undertaken in which teachers were observed during instruction, with three observers collecting data for the teacher and for four target LEP students. Teachers were interviewed again after instruction.

An analysis of data across the case studies revealed a clear linkage between (1) teachers' ability to clearly specify the intent of instruction, and a belief that students could achieve accuracy in instructional tasks, (2) the organization and delivery of instruction such that tasks and institutional demands reflected this intent, requiring intended student responses, and (3) the fidelity of student consequences with intended outcomes. In other words, teachers were able to describe clearly what instruction would entail, to operationalize these specifications, and to produce the desired results in terms of student performance. (p. 9)

Tikunoff's (1983) findings confirm that the concept of active teaching can be used to account for effective teaching in bilingual education programs. These findings also suggest the value of extending this approach to the study of effective teaching to other kinds of language programs. What is the equivalent of active teaching in an on-arrival second language program, an advanced speaking class, or a secondary-level foreign language reading class? Once these questions have been answered, the issue arises of the application of the findings to teacher preparation.

Applications for teacher preparation

Although some aspects of effective teaching can be operationalized and presented to teachers-in-preparation as techniques to be mastered, there

Jack C. Richards

is more to teacher preparation than skills training. McIntyre (1980) observes that

> both managerial skills and direct instruction are defined only in terms of high-inference variables... If this is generally the case, its implication for teacher educators is that we cannot hope to *train* student teachers; whatever one's criteria of effectiveness, the components of effective teaching cannot be spelt out in operational terms, but are crucially dependent on the teacher's qualities. (p. 295)

For the development of these qualities, activities are needed that move beyond "training" and that seek to develop the teacher's awareness and control of the principles underlying the effective planning, organization, management, and delivery of instruction (Elliot 1980). Both the micro- and macrodimensions of teaching must be addressed (Larsen-Freeman 1983).

Activities and learning experiences in the first domain – the micro-perspective – reflect the *training* view of teacher preparation: Teaching is broken down into discrete and trainable skills, such as setting up small-group activities, using strategies for correcting pronunciation errors, using referential questions, monitoring time-on-task, explaining meanings of new words, or organizing practice work. Training experiences that can be provided for the novice teacher include the following:

1. Teaching assistantships – assisting an experienced teacher in aspects of a class, such as using classroom aids or administering tests
2. Simulations – participating in simulated classroom events, for example, to develop the ability to handle discipline and management problems
3. Tutorials – working as a tutor, for example, in a writing laboratory, to gain experience in the use of feedback techniques
4. Workshops and minicourses – participating in training sessions focusing on specific instructional techniques, such as use of wait-time
5. Microteaching – presenting structured mini-lessons using specific strategies and techniques
6. Case studies – observing films or videos in which desired teaching strategies and behaviors are demonstrated.

Activities in the second domain – the macroperspective – reflect a view of teacher preparation as *education* and focus on clarifying and elucidating the concepts and thinking processes that guide the effective second language teacher. Activities and experiences are needed that help the novice teacher understand and acquire the means by which the effective teacher arrives at significant instructional decisions. Learning experiences include the following:

14

1. Practice teaching – participating in a variety of practice teaching experiences that are closely supervised by a skilled teacher
2. Observation – observing experienced teachers in a focused way and then exploring with the teacher, in a follow-up session, why things happened as they did and attempting to determine the kinds of conscious or unconscious decision making that guided the teacher
3. Self- and peer observation – reflecting on self- and peer performance in actual teaching situations, through audio or video recordings, in order to gain a deeper awareness of the processes and principles being employed
4. Seminars and discussion activities – reflecting on the degree to which one's own experience as a student teacher relates to theory and to the findings of relevant research.

These and other activities are discussed in Chapters 2 and 3, and also in Part V.

Such an approach to teacher preparation requires changes in the role of both student teacher and teacher educator. The student teacher must adopt the role of autonomous learner and researcher, in addition to that of apprentice. The role of the teacher educator is no longer simply that of trainer; he or she must guide the student teacher in the process of generating and testing hypotheses and in using the knowledge so acquired as a basis for further development.

This approach rejects the philosophies of "teaching as a craft" or "teaching as common sense," both of which deny the significance of the principles on which good teaching depends. The view of teacher development described here attempts instead to use theory to guide and illuminate the meaning of observation and practical experience. In short, the intent of second language teacher education must be to provide opportunities for the novice to acquire the skills and competencies of effective teachers and to discover the working rules that effective teachers use.

2 Beyond prescription: the student teacher as investigator

Jerry G. Gebhard, Sergio Gaitan, and Robert Oprandy

Teacher educators are often viewed as authorities who are expected to prescribe what teachers should do to be effective. The role of the student teacher is to listen, accept, occasionally give an opinion, but ultimately to follow a prescription, or at least give this impression.

As Gebhard (this volume, Chapter 10) points out, there are several limitations to such a prescriptive approach to teacher preparation. Some teachers, especially those with some experience, do not want to be told how to teach, and may therefore resent the educational experience. Another problem with the use of prescription is the lack of convincing research evidence that there is a "best" way to teach. Although there are creative and effective ways to teach, as Dunkin and Biddle (1974) and Fanselow and Light (1977) point out, there is little proof that any one way of teaching is better in all settings than another.

A third and perhaps more immediate problem is that prescription keeps the responsibility for decision making with the teacher educator, thus lessening the likelihood that student teachers are being prepared to assume the responsibilities for what goes on in their classrooms. To assure that student teachers are being prepared to enter the real world of teaching, as Fanselow (1987) and Jarvis (1972) advocate, teacher educators need to shift responsibility for decision making to classroom teachers, providing them with investigative skills and methodology for making decisions about what and how to teach. In this chapter we are concerned with this third problem of how teacher educators can provide opportunities for student teachers in preservice foreign and second language teaching programs to gain the investigative skills they need to make decisions as responsible language teachers. Ongoing observation and Gebhard's (1985) research have shown that opportunities to gain these skills can be provided through a multiple-activities approach to teacher preparation. The activities discussed in this chapter include:

1. teaching a class
2. observing the teaching act
3. conducting investigative projects of teaching
4. discussing teaching in several contexts.

Reprinted with permission from the American Council on the Teaching of Foreign Languages, Inc. (ACTFL), publishers of *Foreign Language Annals*.

We are not suggesting that if teacher educators simply use these four activities, student teachers will automatically gain the ability to make decisions about what to do in their classrooms. As Gebhard (1985) points out, interaction within these activities between the teacher educator and student teachers, or between the student teachers themselves, can either provide or block opportunities for student teachers to gain the skills needed to investigate the teaching processes and make decisions about what to do next in the classroom. Thus, interaction between participants within any of these activities should be an ongoing consideration. Likewise, student teachers should have opportunities to relate their experience in one activity to that in another. It is through relating one experience to another that awareness of teaching behavior and teaching possibilities seems to evolve.

Activities

Teaching a class

Most teacher educators will point out the value of providing a "real" classroom setting for student teachers in which the students' goal is to learn the foreign language. Teacher educators may provide such a context through their own or an affiliated institution, or require student teachers to teach in a public institution.

If a real teaching context is not possible, one established way to provide classroom teaching experience is to use microteaching in which the student teachers themselves act as foreign language students. Since the student teachers are most likely invested in the language being taught, they can teach each other something that is beyond their present ability in using the target language. In this way the microteaching experience becomes a "real" as opposed to a "simulated" experience. Of course, time needs to be considered, especially for large classes. One way to work with a large class is to have several microteaching sessions going on simultaneously.

One obvious benefit of teaching a class is that opportunities are provided for student teachers to use their accumulated knowledge to make instructional decisions. The following example from an ESL class helps to illustrate this point (Gebhard 1985). In the first scene the student teacher, June, was not successful in her treatment of Anna's error. In the second scene, two weeks later, June was successful because she had changed the way she dealt with the learner error.

Scene 1
Anna: I have only two sister.
June: Uh-huh.

Anna: I have no brother.
June: Two sisters (*June uses rising intonation*)
Anna: Because my mother she dead when I was three years old.
June: She *died* when you were three?
Anna: Yes. She dead when I was three years old.

Scene 2.
Anna: When the house built?
June: When *was*.
Anna: When *was?*
June: When *was*. When was.
Anna: When was the house built?

June's change included treating the error directly after it was made, using shorter sentences, and stopping her sentence at the point of the error. However, the change June made appears to be unusual. As Hoetker and Ahlbrand (1972), Long (1983), and Shapiro-Skrobe (1982), among others, have discovered in their research, teachers, even with training, do not change the way they teach, but continue to follow the same pattern of teaching. Why, then, was June able to change the way she treated Anna's (and other students') errors?

We believe she was able to make these changes because she was not only given the opportunity to teach a class, but was also provided with complementary activities through which she could process her teaching and subsequently make decisions about her teaching behavior. In Fanselow's (1987a) words, June had the opportunity to "construct, reconstruct and revise teaching." Through teaching a class, she gained the chance to put her ideas about teaching into practice, but she also had opportunities to observe others teaching their classes, to examine how they worked with students in error correction, and to discuss her teaching, including when and how to treat errors, with peers and with the teacher educator. These activities gave her the freedom to reconstruct her ideas about what to do next in the classroom. She was doing what Barnes (1976) observed successful learners do, that is, she was developing her own ideas and making decisions as they relate to previous knowledge and experience.

Observing the teaching act

One activity in which June and other student teachers have participated is observation through classroom visitation and video recordings. Student teachers and teacher educators have reported two connected benefits of observing the teaching act. First, some student teachers have reported that observation allows them to see teaching differently. For example, one student teacher reported: "My training in observation has given me many different views of teaching. I used to look at only the content of a lesson. Now I look at and am aware of *how* that lesson is being taught, what teachers and students are doing, and what media are being used by the teacher." Second, student teachers have reported that observation gives them fresh ideas about what they can do in classrooms. As one student teacher pointed out: "Observation has made me realize that there are unlimited ways to teach. I can see that teaching is made up of behaviors and consequences of behaviors and that I am not limited in the behaviors I can use in the classroom."

However, other student teachers state that they are blocked from getting much out of the observation because, as one noted, "There is so much going on (in the class), I have no idea what to look at." In order to get a different perspective on observation, these and other student teachers say it is useful to learn a system of observation, and there are several approaches to the observation act. (Observation systems are discussed in detail by Day in Chapter 4.)

In the 1960s and early 1970s, Flanders's sign system was adapted by foreign and second language teacher educators such as Moskowitz (1971) and Wragg (1970). In the use of this system, observers place a tick every few seconds next to an observed behavior, such as "silence," "teacher asks question," "teacher praises student." However, as L. G. Bailey (1977) points out, this system has limited utility because it is teacher centered and carries with it the belief that a nondirective approach is the most effective way to teach. Since foreign and second language teaching methodology has become more varied, this instrument may fail to capture some classroom interaction, such as that which occurs during small-group activities.

Another instrument through which student teachers can systematically observe classroom interaction is a category system, which as its name indicates, contains lists of behavioral categories through which observed events are classified. One such system is COLT (the Communication Orientation of Language Teaching) by P. Allen, Fröhlich, and Spada (1984; see also Spada, this volume, Chapter 19). Another is Ullmann and Geva's (1982) TALOS (Target Language Observation Scheme). Another, which we have used over the past few years, is Fanselow's FOCUS (Foci on Communication Used in Settings).

The major categories in FOCUS allow the student teacher to identify the source and target of communication (teacher, student, group, book, map, movie, etc.), the purpose of communication (structure, solicit, respond, react), the media used to communicate the content (linguistic, nonlinguistic, paralinguistic, silence), the manner in which the media are used to communicate content (attend to, present, characterize, reproduce, relate, set), and the areas of content that are communicated (study, life, procedure).

Some student teachers state that this system of observation keeps their interest because they can study their teaching through any one category or across several categories and subcategories, as well as consider the consequences for student interaction of what and how they teach. Other teachers have found the use of an observation system distracting, especially if they have not been trained in its use. As one student teacher stated, "When I go to observe I can hardly make a decision. It's distracting to me. I can't even make myself begin to practice. Partly I don't want to do it, but it also feels like it gets in the way." When student teachers appear to lack knowledge and interest in how to use a system, we have found it useful to meet with these student teachers and provide them with special opportunities to describe teaching from videotapes of classrooms in process. It is possible that the more success student teachers have in recognizing categories of behavior through observation, the more interest they will gain in using an observation system to study teaching, including their own teaching.

Whether or not student teachers find the use of an observation system interesting is perhaps not as important as the benefit such a system appears to have for most student teachers, that is, as a metalanguage for discussion. During discussions of teaching, vague language such as "The students show enthusiasm" or "There is rapport" is replaced by a language of observation which allows participants to use specific terms through which communication can be easier and more effective.

As Long (1983) points out, classroom-centered research (CCR) offers another means through which student teachers can observe teaching, and we have discovered that some student teachers gain much from studying the research of others and using research observation categories and findings as a lens through which to observe their own and others' instruction. For example, some student teachers have used Rowe's (1986) research on "wait-time" as a means through which to view classroom interaction. Rowe studied the amount of time teachers waited for a response to their questions before repeating the same question or asking a new one, as well as the amount of time between getting a response to a question and reacting to it. She discovered that teachers generally wait less than one second, and that when the teacher increases wait-time to three or more seconds, the pattern of communication in the class changes. Students direct more questions to the teacher and to each other, and they react to others' responses more frequently. As a consequence of looking at wait-time, some student teachers have been able to examine their own use of wait-time and have successfully changed their use of it in their teaching. More importantly, they have also realized the importance of using others' research as a basis for investigating their own.

Conducting investigative projects

A system of observation also sets the groundwork for investigative projects, which can provide student teachers with the methodology for understanding their own teaching processes and behaviors. (See Part II of this book for fuller discussion.) One aim of investigative projects is to provide the opportunity for student teachers to gain new awareness of the interaction that goes on in their classrooms as well as to consider how they would approach a lesson differently. Topics student teachers have worked on include:

— What makes some directions I give in the target language clearer than others? Can I determine the features of clear directions and set guidelines for improving the directions I give?
— What are different ways I can facilitate classroom activities? How productive are group problem-solving activities in which the target language is used? How effective is pair work? What are the consequences of these activities for student interaction?
— How do I use classroom space? What different seating arrangements are possible? What happens when I change the seating arrangements?
— How much time in the classes I teach is spent "on task"? What can I do to get students to stay "on task"?
— How do I treat students' errors? What different ways exist for treating students' errors? How do I know if students pay attention to the corrections?

Teacher educators can make the process of conducting investigations easier for student teachers by providing them with guidelines. One set of guidelines, adapted from Fanselow (1987a), follows: (1) select an aspect of your teaching you would like to learn more about; (2) videotape or audiotape classroom interaction that centers on these aspects of your teaching; (3) transcribe the parts that are pertinent; (4) code the interaction using an observation system or through categories you have designed for the study; (5) study the coding for patterns and consequences of behaviors; (6) decide on a change in teaching behavior that will break the pattern; (7) implement the change while taping the classroom interaction, and again transcribe, code, and study the interaction for patterns and consequences; (8) finally, compare the consequences in the use of the old pattern with the new one.

Student teachers who follow these guidelines sometimes gain immediate insight into their teaching, much of which is, incidentally, not directly related to their investigative topic. For example, the student teacher who asked, "How productive are group problem-solving activities in the target language?" not only discovered that students solicit much information from each other in the target language related (and unrelated) to the problem-solving activity, she also found that when she wrote instructions down, students in her class would get into the task more quickly.

However, perhaps a more important benefit of this approach is the insight student teachers gain into how they can investigate their teaching, something they can continue to do after the teacher educator is no longer around. As Freire (1970) and Jarvis (1972) point out, this ability sometimes empowers teachers. They become free from oppression, knowing that they have the power to decide what and how to teach based on an awareness of classroom interaction and its consequences.

Possible insights into the process of investigation include the point that description of interaction, not judgments about it, is important; that much can be gained by studying the interaction for patterns, and patterns can sometimes be more easily recognized by coding the interaction through an observation system; that teaching and changes in teaching behavior require the teacher to make decisions, and these decisions can be made through investigation plus common sense.

Discussing teaching in several contexts

Discussion about teaching is the fourth component of a multiple-activities approach to teacher preparation, and it can take place in a number of required settings, such as in a seminar, during supervisory conferences, in an observation room, or through journal correspondence between the student teachers and the teacher educator. Discussions can also take place in less formal contexts, such as among student teachers over lunch, in the student lounge, or simply in the hallway. Such settings are important because they provide opportunities for student teachers to discuss not only their teaching, but also their observations, investigations, and other experiences. Through this process, they have the chance to relate their experiences to those of others, to gain awareness of possible teaching behaviors, and to consider their own teaching decisions.

To provide content for discussion, student teachers can be asked to supply their findings from classroom observations and investigations as well as share video- and audiotapes of their teaching, transcripts of short scenes from these tapes, and lesson plans. We have discovered that if discussion centers on a description of teaching rather than on judgments, it can be quite productive, often allowing student teachers to enter into a problem-solving process in which they share ideas about how to solve a problem and work together in a decision-making process.

For example, in an ESL practicum seminar, one student teacher, Monica, brought in an audiotape of her teaching. She gave the following background information: "I told them to go home and think of several things they like and several things they don't like about living in the United States. When they came in today I had them write them down on the board. I then went to the board and corrected each sentence."

The seminar group was then asked to listen to a section of the classroom interaction. Here is part of the transcription:

Scene 3
Monica: Jose, this is your sentence?
Jose: Yes.
Monica: (*Reads*) "United States people have much freedom." Here, ah,
          you should say, "American people." (*Writes the correction*)

Using FOCUS, the class studied the interaction. They decided that the teacher was the source of all the questions (solicitations) and that the students simply responded and then listened to the correction that the teacher presented. Monica then expressed her feelings about the experience: "It was such a bummer to have to go up and correct each sentence and to show each person where they were wrong. They were all just sitting there like, 'Oh, what mistake did I make?' How can I teach this lesson without laying this thing on them that their language is bad?"

In response, one student teacher suggested that Monica be silent and let the sentences on the board *structure* the activity. Students might start correcting them by themselves. Another suggested that she manipulate the *source* and *target* of communication by having students form groups to first decide if the sentences are correct and then to make necessary changes. In this way, students, rather than the teacher, *solicit* information from the teacher and from each other.

This same process of describing teaching and generating alternatives need not be done only in a seminar. During supervisory conferences the student teacher and supervisor can generate choices for the student teacher to try out in class. A clinical process of supervision (Abbott and Carter 1985) can be implemented in which both supervisor and student teacher determine the categories for observation. Based on a description of teaching the supervisor obtains through observation, the two can generate alternative ways to teach the same lesson or a part of it. Student teachers can implement small changes in their teaching based on the discussion and the supervisor can again observe the student teacher's class, followed by another discussion. In this way, the student teacher can become more aware of options in teaching behavior, share in the examination of purposes and consequences of particular choices, and gradually become an independent decision maker.

We have found that there are behaviors that the teacher educator or supervisor can use to promote opportunities for student teachers to share openly their ideas about teaching and gain new insights into teaching behaviors which allow them to expand their decision-making abilities. First, it appears that when teacher educators describe teaching, rather than make judgments about teaching or the student teachers, there is greater willingness on the part of some student teachers to share their ideas. When student teachers feel that they or their teaching are being constantly judged, they hold back their ideas. Second, the teacher educator's or supervisor's silence provides opportunities for discussion. Although some student teachers are at first uncomfortable with silence, most find that it provides them with chances to slow down and to consider their own and others' ideas without the threat of having to be constantly involved in talking or listening to talk.

Third, the teacher educator or supervisor can help student teachers to gain new insights into teaching by allowing them chances to reprocess ideas they have about teaching. This can be done by the teacher educator by remembering questions student teachers have raised in previous discussions and bringing them into the discussion at appropriate times. For example, June had shown concern over the treatment of student errors. During a discussion she had asked, "How can I get students to care about their language errors?" In order to provide June with more opportunities to consider her question and make decisions based on it, the teacher educator sometimes, as Gebhard (1985) observed, guided the discussion toward this topic, giving June the opportunity to bring in her teaching, observation, and reading experiences that had occurred since she had asked that question. This approach gave her the opportunity to consider decisions she had made about error treatment and to formulate new questions.

Conclusion

A multiple-activities approach to foreign-language teacher preparation provides student teachers in preservice programs with opportunities to gain the investigative and decision-making skills they need to function as responsible and autonomous teachers. Although each of the four activities discussed – teaching a class, observing the teaching act, conducting investigative projects of teaching, and discussing teaching in several contexts – is valuable in its own way, student teachers will possibly develop stronger decision-making skills if they are given chances to process their teaching through all the activities. Opportunities for student teachers to develop decision-making skills can be blocked as well as facilitated through the type of interaction that goes on within each activity. Teacher educators need to be aware of how the interaction within and across each activity can enhance or hamper opportunities for student teachers to gain the investigative and decision-making skills they need to become more creative, autonomous teachers.

3   Activities and procedures for teacher preparation

Rod Ellis

The last few years have seen a number of teachers' manuals for preparing teachers of English as a second or foreign language (e.g., Abbot and Wingard 1981; Gower and Walters 1983; Harmer 1983; Hubbard et al. 1983; Willis 1983). These manuals vary in their intended audiences and also in their approaches, but in their different ways they all provide information about both the theory and practice of second language teaching. This information is presented in a variety of ways. (1) There are *expositions* of theoretical principles and procedures for carrying out different kinds of lessons. (2) There are *examples* of lesson plans and of teaching materials. (3) There are *activities* for teachers-in-preparation to carry out in order to explore and evaluate different aspects of second language teaching. These manuals, then, not only inform us about the practice of second language teaching but also try to involve student teachers actively in the process of making decisions about what to teach and how to teach it.

The main purpose of this chapter is to examine in some detail what *teacher preparation activities* consist of. By providing an analytical framework for describing the various kinds of activities that can be used and the different procedures for exploiting them, I hope to encourage their use in teacher preparation courses and also provide practical information about how to devise and use activities.

There are three parts to this chapter. The first consists of a schematic outline of teacher preparation practices. This is intended to provide the context for the second part, in which a framework for describing teacher preparation activities is presented. This part also includes an example of an activity. In the third part, a list of teacher preparation procedures is given, together with a sample of a plan for exploiting an activity.

An outline of teacher preparation practices

Teacher preparation practices, in the first instance, can be divided into those that are *experiential* and those that *raise awareness*. *Experiential* practices involve the student teacher in actual teaching. This can occur through "teaching practice," where the student teachers are required to teach actual students in real classrooms, or in "simulated" practice, as when the student teachers engage in peer teaching. *Awareness-raising* practices are intended to develop the student teacher's conscious understanding of the principles underlying second language teaching and/ or the practical techniques that teachers can use in different kinds of lessons.

Two points need to be made about the distinction between experiential and awareness-raising practices. First, the two types are not mutually exclusive. Teacher preparation will often involve both kinds, although experiential practices are probably more common in preservice courses, while awareness-raising practices predominate in inservice courses. This, however, is perhaps more the result of convenience and tradition than principled decision making. Second, experiential and awareness-raising practices do not need to be separated; they can be combined in a single activity. This occurs, for instance, when teaching practice is used not only to develop the student teacher's practical classroom know-how, but also to develop understanding of particular issues through reflection and evaluation. The broken line in Figure 1 is meant to represent the potential integration of the two types of practices.

The purpose of this chapter is not to discuss the relative merits of the two kinds of practices. The assumption that underlies the use of awareness-raising practices, however, is that the practice of actual teaching can be improved by making teachers aware of the options open to them and the principles by which they can evaluate the alternatives. It is not known to what extent this assumption is justified. Do teacher educators, in fact, really influence what teachers *do* in the classroom by making them *think* about the principles and practice of teaching in sessions remote from the classroom? It is all too easy to assume that a better-informed teacher will become a better teacher. It would be comforting if there were some clear evidence to support this assumption.

The focus of this chapter is on awareness-raising practices. These involve the use of teacher preparation *activities* and teacher preparation *procedures*. Teacher preparation activities consist of the materials that the educator uses in his or her program; they correspond to materials for use in classroom language teaching. Each activity will give the student teacher a number of *tasks* to perform. These tasks are likely to be based on some *data*, which constitute the raw material of the activities. It follows that activities can be described by specifying the different ways in which data can be provided and the different kinds of operations that the student teacher is required to carry out in the tasks based on the data. Teacher preparation procedures constitute the teacher educator's methodology for using activities in teacher preparation sessions. Just as

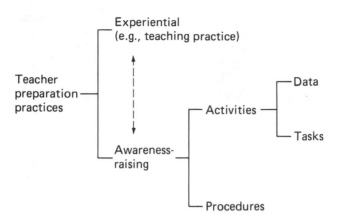

Figure 1   An outline of teacher preparation practices

the teacher needs to draw up a lesson plan for exploiting teaching materials, so the teacher educator needs to draw up a preparation plan incorporating appropriate procedures for exploiting different teacher preparation activities. Figure 1 diagrams the various teacher preparation practices that have been described.

A framework for describing teacher preparation activities

The purpose of a descriptive framework for teacher preparation activities is not to suggest what "good" activities consist of (i.e., no evaluative criteria are suggested), but to identify the various options available to the teacher educator. Teacher preparation activities can be described by detailing (1) the different ways in which data can be provided and (2) the different kinds of tasks that student teachers can be asked to perform.

Ways of providing data

1. *Video or audio recordings of actual lessons.* Recordings are potentially rich sources of data, as they can provide samples of real teaching. Ideally they should be made in the classroom contexts in which the student teacher will have to teach. There is, however, an excellent collection of video material, covering a variety of teaching contexts, available in the British Council's *Teaching and Learning in Focus*, and similar resources have been prepared by other institutions, such as the National Centre for English Language Teaching and Research in Australia. The British Council collection consists also of a number

of edited lessons and some thematic modules dealing with a number of key issues, such as class management and dealing with errors. The video materials are supported by handbooks that suggest different ways of using the materials. Teacher educators who wish to make their own video materials should consider who best to focus the camera on – the teacher, the students, an individual student, or a combination of these. The choice will be determined by how the material will be used (i.e., the tasks involved). Teacher educators will also need to consider whether the video or audio material is to consist of whole lessons or selected extracts.

2. *Transcripts of lessons.* Another way of presenting classroom data is by preparing transcripts of lessons, in part or in whole. One advantage that transcripts have over video or audio material is that they permit detailed inspection and analysis more easily. There is, of course, nothing to prevent the teacher educator from using video or audio materials in conjunction with transcripts.

3. *Classroom teaching.*

4. *Peer teaching.*

5. *Microteaching.*

Activities 3, 4, and 5 are all experiential. That is, they can be used to give the student teacher direct experience of teaching and do not need to be accompanied by awareness-raising tasks. However, they can also serve as further ways of providing data about teaching for analysis and evaluation.

6. *Readings.* Student teachers can be provided with readings from articles and books on second language teaching as ends in themselves. Alternatively, these readings can be used as a basis for a range of interesting tasks.

7. *Textbook materials.* Samples of teaching materials – both good and bad, appropriate and inappropriate – can be exploited as data for awareness-raising activities in a variety of ways.

8. *Lesson plans and outlines.* Apart from being invited to prepare complete lesson plans, student teachers can be asked to perform various tasks based either on "authentic" lesson plans or on lesson plans that have been specially designed to illustrate particular points.

9. *Case studies.* Case studies are another valuable source of data. They can be studies of particular classes, of individual teachers or learners, or of whole courses. Williams (1985) provides two case studies of reading programs that are good examples of the kind of raw material that can be utilized in teacher preparation activities.

10. *Samples of students' written work.*

This list is not intended to be exhaustive, but to provide an indication of the breadth and variety of the data that the teacher educator can use

Rod Ellis

for designing teacher-preparation activities. Any single activity may make use of just one data type or a combination of types.

Different kinds of tasks

The list of tasks that follows takes the form of a number of "operations" which the student teacher can be asked to perform on whatever raw data are provided. An example of the kind of rubric needed for each operation is given to clarify what is involved in each task.

1. *Comparing.* E.g., "Look at the two lesson plans provided and decide which one you prefer and why."
2. *Preparing.* E.g., "Prepare a marking scheme that you could use to correct the attached sample of students' written work."
3. *Evaluating.* E.g., "After watching the video extract, evaluate the effectiveness of the teacher's treatment of oral errors, using the criteria supplied."
4. *Improving.* E.g., "Read the case study of a reading program, paying particular attention to the author's own evaluation. What suggestions can you make for improving the program?"
5. *Adapting.* E.g., "Adapt the following language exercise in order to introduce an information gap."
6. *Listing.* E.g., "Look through the transcript of the lesson provided and make a list of all the different kinds of errors the students make."
7. *Selecting.* E.g., "Now that you have listed all the different kinds of errors in the transcript, decide which errors you would choose to correct if you were the teacher and say why."
8. *Ranking.* E.g., "Look through the language teaching materials attached and then rank them according to how 'communicative' you think they are."
9. *Adding/completing.* E.g., "Read through the article, listing the principles for the teaching of reading. Are there any additional principles you would like to add?"
10. *Rearranging.* E.g., "Look at the video recording of a teacher organizing group work. Make a list of the different steps the teacher follows. What changes to the order of these steps would you recommend?"

Other operations are doubtless possible. Once again, the aim has been to illustrate the range of possibilities. Any single training activity can make use of just a single task or a series of tasks.

A sample teacher preparation activity

Tables 1 and 2 illustrate how data can be combined with operations to devise teacher preparation materials. The aim of the activity is to increase

30

TABLE 1. SAMPLE ACTIVITY SHEET

What is a communicative activity? Below are six criteria that you can use to decide how communicative different classroom activities are. Use these criteria to evaluate the selection of classroom activities attached.

Criteria for evaluating how communicative classroom activities are:

1. *Communicative purpose:* The activity must involve the students in performing a real communicative purpose rather than just practicing language for its own sake. In order for this to occur there must be some kind of "gap" (information or opinion) that the students seek to bridge when they are communicating.

2. *Communicative desire:* The activity must create a desire to communicate in the students. That is, even though speaking is forced on the students, they must feel a real need to communicate.

3. *Content, not form:* When the students are doing the activity, they must be concentrating on *what* they are saying, not *how* they say it. They must have some "message" that they want to communicate.

4. *Variety of language:* The activity must involve the students in using a variety of language, not just one specific language form. The students should feel free to improvise, using whatever resources they choose.

5. *No teacher intervention:* The activity must be designed to be done by the students working by themselves rather than with the teacher. The activity should not involve the teacher correcting or evaluating how the students do the activity, although it could involve some evaluation of the final "product" of the activity when the activity is over. This assessment should be based on whether the students have achieved their communicative purpose, not whether the language they used was correct.

6. *No materials control:* The activity should not be designed to control what language the students should use. The choice about what language to use should rest with the students.

Draw a table like the one below. Put a checkmark if you think the activities meet the criteria. Put an X if you think they do not. In some cases you may not be sure, so put a question mark.

| | Activities | | | | | |
Criteria	1	2	3	4	5	6
1. Communicative purpose						
2. Communicative desire						
3. Content, not form						
4. Variety of language						
5. No teacher intervention						
6. No materials control						

TABLE I. *(cont.)*

When you have finished filling in the table, rank the six teaching activities according to how communicative you think each activity is overall.

1. (most communicative)
2.
3.
4.
5.
6. (least communicative)

Source: Harmer (1983).

the student teacher's understanding of what communicative activities consist of, and in particular to make them aware that a simple dichotomy between "communicative" and "noncommunicative" is not possible. The activity consists of the following:

Data: (1) A set of criteria for evaluating communicative language teaching materials; and (2) a selection of language teaching activities.

Tasks: (1) Evaluating (i.e., using the criteria to evaluate the language teaching activities); and (2) ranking (i.e., ranking the activities according to how communicative the student teachers consider them).

Teacher preparation procedures

What procedures for exploiting the evaluating and ranking activities (Tables 1 and 2) are available to the teacher educator? Here is a list of some of the possibilities:

1. *Lectures.* Lectures can be used to provide straight "input." Alternatively, they can be used as a way of supplying raw material for the student teacher to operate on.
2. *Group/pair discussion.* The student teachers work in groups or pairs using activity sheets.
3. *Workshops.* The student teachers work individually or in groups to prepare something, such as classroom materials, teaching aids, or lesson plans.
4. *Individual work/assignments.*
5. *Demonstrations.* The teacher educator demonstrates a particular technique, using either actual students or the student teachers themselves.

TABLE 2. SELECTED LANGUAGE TEACHING ACTIVITIES

1. *Group work*
Work in groups of three. Study the example and then continue.

Student A to →	Student B to →	Student C (Replies)
Ask Kay to give you her pen.	*Give me your pen, please.*	YES (Here you are.)
Ask Mrs. Wright to give us a sandwich.	*Could we have a sandwich, Mrs. Wright?*	YES (Certainly.)
1. Ask Jerry if he's got a letter for me.		NO
2. We must do some shopping tomorrow. Ask your boss to give you a day off.		NO
3. Ask Adrian to give you his dictionary.		YES
4. If you want more coffee, ask Mrs. Wright.		YES

2. *Communication task*
Practice with your partner:

A: Where are you from?
B: I'm from (country).
A: Which part of (country) are you from?
B: (Town).
A: What's your address?
B: (Address).

3. *Pair work*
Work with your partner and ask each other questions about accommodations in your country. Here are some of the questions:

a. What is the cheapest type of accommodation?
b. Are meals served in all types of accommodation?
c. Does the price of a room always include breakfast?
d. What facilities are provided?
e. Is advance booking advisable?

Rod Ellis

4. *Practice accepting and refusing things*
Copy the table below into your exercise book. Put a checkmark next to each
item if you like it. Put an X if you do not like it.

Item	Like/dislike
1. apples	
2. cabbage	
3. beer	
4. coffee	
5. pork	
6. fish	
7. milk	
8. cakes	

Work with a partner. Offer your partner each item in the table. Your partner
should accept or refuse it and say why. Your partner should then offer you each
item.

5. *Communication task*
Draw your family tree. Use it to talk to your partner about your family. Then
complete your partner's family tree by asking questions. When you have finished,
compare your versions.

Source: Doff, Jones, and Mitchell (1984).

6. *Elicitation.* The educator works with the student teachers and tries
   to draw out opinions on specific points using a question-and-answer
   technique.
7. *Plenary discussion.* There is general discussion of language teaching
   issues with all the trainees together.
8. *Panel discussion.* The teacher educator can use panel discussion in
   several different ways. One way is to invite several student teachers
   to form a panel. The other students then prepare some questions on
   chosen issues to ask the panel. The course leader acts as the chair-
   person of the panel.

A single session may involve just one of these procedures or, as will
often be the case, it may involve a combination of several. For sessions
based on activities, the teacher educator will need to draw up a plan
(on paper or in the head) incorporating appropriate procedures. The
plan in Table 3 has been designed for the sample activity in the previous
section. It is intended to show how selections from the list of procedures
can be used to exploit a particular teacher preparation activity.

TABLE 3. SAMPLE PLAN

1. *In plenary*
   a. Explain aim of activity.
   b. Invite definitions of Harmer's six criteria (with criteria listed on an overhead projector).
   c. Give out activity sheet (Table 1) and ask student teachers to read through definitions of the six criteria.
   d. Deal with any problems regarding definitions as necessary.
   e. Check that they understand instructions for first activity and table.
   f. Individual students complete table for language teaching activity (in Table 1).
   g. Call on individual students to give their responses in (f), together with their reasoning, and deal with disagreements.

2. *In groups*
   a. Divide student teachers into two groups. Instruct Group A to evaluate the language teaching activities (Table 2) starting from activity 2. Group B likewise, starting from Activity 4.
   b. Allow groups up to five minutes to begin discussion, and then move from one group to the other.
   c. Ask both groups to prepare an overhead projector transparency of the results of their discussion.

3. *In plenary*
   a. Invite secretaries of Groups A and B to display and explain results on the overhead projector.
   b. General discussion of results.

4. *Pair work*
   Student teachers work in pairs to prepare an agreed ranking of language teaching activities.

5. *In plenary*
   a. Pairs pass forward their rankings to teacher educator, who enters them on transparency. (While this is being done, pairs evaluate language teaching Activity 5.)
   b. Discussion of rankings from 1 to 5.

6. *Individual assignment*
   Students write an evaluation of Activity 5 in terms of the six criteria and its place in the rank order.

Note: This plan is based on the sample teacher preparation activity.

Summary and conclusion

Since the mid-seventies there have been considerable changes in second and foreign language teaching, accompanied by intensive debate about syllabus design, materials, and classroom practice. In contrast, as Richards points out in Chapter 1 of this book, there has been little discussion of teacher preparation practices (see, though, Holden 1979; British Council 1981; and Jordan 1983). Given the importance of teacher preparation, this is a serious deficiency. This chapter has developed a schema – obviously not the only one possible – for thinking about the content of teacher preparation. To this end, I have suggested that it is useful to distinguish between *experiential* and *awareness-raising* practices. In addition, I have outlined a framework for describing different types of teacher preparation *activities* by listing the various ways in which *data* can be provided, and also the kinds of *tasks* that can be based on the data. Finally, I have described the *procedures* the teacher educator can use. Together these constitute an embryonic taxonomy of teacher preparation materials and practices. Such a taxonomy can serve two principal functions. First, it can act as a checklist that teacher educators can refer to when planning a program. Second, it can be used to introduce would-be teacher educators to the range of options that are open to them. It should be emphasized, however, that the framework is *descriptive*. If we are to develop our understanding of teacher preparation practices further, it will also be necessary to decide upon *evaluative* criteria for making principled selections from the large range of options, both in devising teacher preparation activities and in drawing up teacher preparation plans.

Questions and tasks

Chapter 1 (Richards)

1. Richards draws a distinction between micro and macro approaches to teacher education. Analyze a teacher education program with which you are familiar. What is the balance between micro and macro approaches?

2. Key terms in Richards are *effective teaching* and *classroom management*. What is your understanding of these terms?

3. Summarize Richards by completing the following table:

	Effective teaching	*Noneffective teaching*
Low-inference behaviors		
High-inference behaviors		

4. Having read Richards, what are some of the things you might observe or encourage teachers-in-preparation to observe in the classroom?

5. Research cited by Richards indicates that teachers generally employ a limited repetoire of tasks which essentially define their methodology. Observe a teacher over a number of lessons. To what extent do your observations bear out this claim? Analyze the tasks according to:
  a) response mode demands
  b) interactional mode demands
  c) task complexity demands
  d) what/how/why were decisions made about
    − the order of tasks
    − pacing
    − products
    − learning strategies
    − participation

- materials
- grouping of learners

6. What is the distinction between teacher preparation as training and teacher preparation as education? List those features/characteristics you might find in a program oriented toward training and those you might find in a program oriented toward education.

Chapter 2 (Gebhard, Gaitan, and Oprandy)

7. What are the implications for teacher preparation of the Gebhard et al. claim that "there is little proof that any one way of teaching is better in all settings than another"?

8. How might teachers be encouraged to "reconstruct and revise" their teaching in ways similar to June?

9. What are the advantages and disadvantages of using observation schemes to guide classroom observation?

10. Make a list of the small-scale investigative projects student teachers might carry out to deepen their understanding of their own teaching processes and behaviors.

11. Gebhard et al. state that "when teacher educators describe teaching, rather than make judgments about teaching or the student teachers, there is greater willingness on the part of some student teachers to share their ideas." Do you think that it is the responsibility of educators to judge?

Chapter 3 (Ellis)

12. Consider Ellis's distinction between experiential and awareness-raising activities. Analyze a teacher preparation program you are familiar with. What is the mix between experiential and awareness-raising activities? Do you think the distinction as drawn by Ellis is a useful one?

13. Analyze a teacher preparation program you are familiar with by completing the following table.

Data	% of program	How used
Video transcripts		
Audio transcripts		
Classroom teaching		
Peer teaching		
Microteaching		
Readings		
Textbook		
Lesson plans		
Case studies		
Student samples		
Teacher training procedures		
Lectures		
Group discussions		
Workshops		
Assignments		
Demonstrations		
Elicitation		
Plenary discussion		
Panel discussion		

Part II Investigating teachers and learners in the classroom

The chapters in this section focus on integrating theory and practice in teacher education through investigating the nature of second language classroom interactions. While the chapters differ in focus and perspective, they all provide teachers with procedures and schemes for analyzing and critiquing interactional processes. By outlining ways of investigating classroom action and interaction, and by providing schemes for making sense of classroom processes, they follow logically from the position papers in Part I, which stressed the primacy of the classroom in providing data for teacher education.

In Chapter 4 Day presents and evaluates a number of techniques and procedures for introducing teachers-in-preparation to guided, systematic, and focused classroom observation. Such a program of observation can help student teachers integrate theory and practice as they develop their understanding of language classroom processes.

Nunan also encourages teachers to link theory and practice through an action research cycle of observation, identification of problem or issue, intervention, and evaluation. He argues that classroom practitioners should be involved in curriculum development and innovation, and that this can be achieved through encouraging teachers to adopt an action research orientation to their own classrooms. However, a necessary prerequisite to such research is the development of appropriate skills in classroom observation and analysis. To this end, a four-stage workshop procedure for developing observational and analytical skills is outlined and illustrated with data from a workshop conducted with a group of teachers of English as a second language to adults.

In Chapter 6 Wright also highlights the need for teacher development programs to achieve a balance between theory and practice, suggesting, in fact, that this is a primary goal of all teacher development programs. Unfortunately, this goal is not always achieved, and Wright suggests that an investigation of teacher and learner roles can help to draw both theory and practice together as well as provide a point of reference for participants in teacher development programs. This is because teacher –learner relationships lie at the heart of classroom interaction. Wright describes a workshop procedure that encourages participants to explore teacher and learner roles.

The procedures outlined by Nunan and Wright evolved from inservice

Part II

programs, whereas Day develops his proposals within the context of initial teacher education. Despite the particular context, however, all of these procedures can be adapted to a wide variety of pre- and inservice teacher education programs. Each author also shows that practical classroom decision making is always underpinned by theories of language and learning.

4 Teacher observation in second language teacher education

Richard R. Day

This chapter is concerned with observing second language classrooms within the context of teacher education. The purpose is to describe one component of a teacher education program: observation by the student teacher of experienced teachers. In addition to presenting a number of techniques and instruments and discussing their advantages and disadvantages, I examine the role that observation plays in a teacher education program. The chapter begins with a rationale for including observation of experienced teachers in teacher education. This is followed by an examination of observational techniques and instruments that are appropriate in observing second language classrooms.

Why student teacher observation

In considering approaches to teacher education, it is helpful to make a distinction between what Leinhardt and Smith (1984, as cited in Good and Brophy 1987) call *subject-matter knowledge* and *action-system knowledge*. Subject-matter knowledge refers to the specific information needed by teachers to teach content. Action-system knowledge refers to information dealing with teaching and learning in general, regardless of the subject matter. Included in action-system knowledge are such issues as classroom management and teacher expectations.

One way in which student teachers can begin to acquire action-system knowledge is through guided, systematic, and focused observation of experienced second language teachers. Such a process will aid the student teacher in conceptualizing what goes on in the second language classroom. Having a formal program of observation can assist the student teacher in:

1. developing a terminology for understanding and discussing the teaching process
2. developing an awareness of the principles and decision making that underlie effective teaching
3. distinguishing between effective and ineffective classroom practices
4. identifying techniques and practices student teachers can apply to their own teaching.

A successful program in second language teacher education thus helps student teachers develop an integrated set of theories and belief systems that can provide them with a framework for effective teaching.

Techniques and instruments for observation

There are two broad approaches to observing second language classrooms, qualitative and quantitative. The division of techniques and instruments into these two approaches does not imply that either one is preferable to the other. The purposes of the observation must determine the technique and instrument to be used. Nor does the separation imply that one or the other should be used exclusively. Indeed, a combination of both approaches is important in second language teacher education.

Qualitative approaches

Techniques in qualitative approaches are generally referred to by several terms, including educational ethnography (Good and Brophy 1987) and wide-lens (Acheson and Gall 1987). They are derived from work in the social sciences, particularly anthropology, in which fieldworkers attempt to make a complete record of all the events that occurred in a given situation.

The general goal of a qualitative approach is to provide rich, descriptive data about what happens in the second language classroom. An ethnography of a second language classroom attempts to capture the essence or spirit of what was going on during the observer's presence, and is especially useful when the observer wants to capture a broad picture of a lesson rather than focus on a particular aspect of it. In second language teacher education programs, written ethnographies are useful in introducing student teachers to the complexity of the second language classroom. Student teachers are often not aware of what complex environments their future classrooms are until they attempt to describe what actually happens in one. Written ethnographies are also beneficial to student teachers in helping them see the multiple roles of the second language teacher. Another advantage is that they allow the student teacher to compare and contrast a teacher's use of both subject-matter knowledge and action-system knowledge during a lesson.

The main disadvantage of qualitative approaches lies in their very nature – they are so broad that it takes a highly trained observer to do a competent and reliable observation. An untrained observer may be overwhelmed by the complexity of what goes on and not be able to focus on important events as they unfold in the classroom.

Several representative techniques and instruments that are qualitative in their approach will now be considered.

WRITTEN ETHNOGRAPHY

Written ethnography is the classic technique used in a qualitative approach. The observer, seated in a strategic position which allows the widest possible view of the entire classroom, either attempts a written account of the entire proceedings of the classroom activities for a set period of time or takes extensive and detailed notes from which an account of the activities is reconstructed later.

In attempting such a record, the observer should have on hand a good supply of writing instruments and paper, and a watch for recording the time as the observation progresses. It is generally regarded as helpful for the student teacher to record the time of the beginning and ending of activities and the occurrence of significant events.

The written statements in an ethnography should be as descriptive and objective as possible, and should not be judgmental or evaluative. For example, instead of writing "Students are interested in the lesson," it is more helpful to write, "The students are focusing on the task at hand." An observation such as "As the class ends, six students rush up to the teacher to talk to her, four begin talking to each other in their first language, and six move slowly to the door, attempting to use English" might be more beneficial than something such as "The class ends in confusion with a lot of talking."

A complete ethnographic record often goes beyond observing the teacher, the students, and the interaction between them. It also includes information about the classroom (e.g., size, seating, furnishing, physical equipment), the quality and quantity of visual aids, room temperature, and so on.

Appendix 1 is an example of a record of an advanced class of ESL students in an American university. The observer was enrolled in a teaching practicum course. Note the detail included in the description. A written record such as this helps to sensitize student teachers to the complexity of teaching and to bring to their attention events of which they might not be aware.

The advantages of a written ethnography are those mentioned previously for any qualitative approach. In addition, relative to other observational techniques, it provides more information about the social context of the classroom, which may be useful in interpreting behavior.

However, there are disadvantages in asking student teachers to attempt written ethnographies. There is so much activity in the second language classroom that the student teacher often has a great deal of difficulty in keeping up with the action. The student teacher may tire quickly, and fail to keep an accurate record of events. Further, the anecdotal record or written ethnography may be affected by the biases of the student teacher. It is a difficult task to record events in the classroom reliably and accurately, for what is perceived is heavily influenced by the observer's own experiences. It is difficult to be objective and neutral.

Another disadvantage of a written ethnography is that it does not address specific questions; therefore, the information collected is often inappropriate for addressing specific issues. Further, since it does not focus on a particular set of classroom behaviors, it is difficult to compare the results with other classes.

AUDIO AND VIDEO RECORDINGS

Audio and video recordings are a type of ethnographic observation, which are similar to and different from written ethnographies in fundamental, yet obvious, ways. They are alike in that the focus may be a rather wide lens. All are capable of allowing observation, or attempted observation, of events taking place in the classroom as a whole.

The most obvious difference is the medium by which the recordings or observations are made. In addition, unlike a written ethnography, audio and video recordings permit teachers to see and hear themselves as their students see and hear them. They are the most neutral techniques for observation. Finally, along with their complete objectivity, audio and video recordings have the potential of capturing the essence of the classroom, and can be listened to or viewed over and over, allowing the participants to agree on an interpretation of an event or behavior.

One of the drawbacks to the use of both audio and video recordings, however, is the fact that they are intrusive, with the latter much more so than the former. One way of lessening the impact of equipment in the classroom is for the student teacher to set up the equipment before the students arrive, and allow the students to examine the equipment before class begins. The teacher who is being recorded might attempt to take advantage of the equipment as a focus for part of an activity or lesson.

As the number of students in the classroom to be observed increases, so does the degree of complexity of the observation. It is relatively easy to videotape a group of six or seven students and the teacher; the teacher plus a class of thirty to forty students is another matter. The student teacher will learn by experience what can be best captured on tape with the equipment, and will become more adept at the process over time. Since most observations in teacher education programs are concerned with the teacher, often the most useful results are obtained when the camera is focused on the teacher.

The discussion thus far has treated both the written ethnography and audio/video recordings as focusing on the class as a whole, without regard to any particular issues or behaviors. However, it is possible to modify the procedure to focus on individual behavior or a set of behaviors. For example, rather than attempting to focus on everything that occurs in the classroom, the student teacher might try to record what happens when the teacher gives instructions. Acheson and Gall (1987) refer to this technique as selective verbatim, by which they mean an exact transcription of particular verbal statements.

There are several advantages to this technique. To begin with, the student teacher's attention is focused on the particular behavior being observed. If it is verbal behavior of some sort, then the student teacher, in examining the record later, is able to concentrate on the verbal exchanges – what the teacher said to the student and what the student said in reply. This allows the student teacher the opportunity to evaluate the effectiveness of the behaviors. Another advantage is the neutral, objective nature of the data, even if the observation is written and not recorded in some fashion. This is possible because the student teacher is not attempting to record all that is said during the lesson, but only a selected set of behaviors.

As a written technique, it is easy to use. Observers do not have to be as highly trained as they need to be to do a full-scale ethnography. Finally, the data are often relatively simple to interpret, especially in comparison to the mass of data collected by an unlimited ethnography.

There are two other problems, however, with the use of a limited or selected ethnography. If the teacher is aware that the student teacher plans to record use of *yes/no* questions, for example, the teacher might modify his or her behavior. It is my experience that in practice teachers have simply too much to do to focus or concentrate for any degree of time on their use or nonuse of the target behavior. Finally, the student teacher could choose rather uninteresting or trivial behaviors on which to focus. If this occurs, it will be apparent when the student teacher examines the data that there is very little to be learned about what was recorded.

Quantitative approaches

Techniques or instruments found under a quantitative approach to second language classroom observation generally take the form of a checklist or a form to be filled in or completed. The behavior or behaviors in question are indicated in some fashion, and the observer's role is to record their occurrence and, as appropriate, the time. There are almost

Richard R. Day

as many instruments as there are observers, for they are easily devised and easily employed in the classroom. Often, an instrument is made up or an existing one is modified when the student teacher and the teacher discuss what behaviors the student teacher might observe. These instruments may be divided into frequency counts or classroom observation scales and are designed to examine teacher behavior, student behavior, or the interaction between the teacher and students or among students. In this section, I examine a representative sampling of these instruments and show how they may be used by student teachers observing the second language classroom.

Before discussing these techniques and instruments, some of the general pros and cons associated with quantitative approaches need to be considered. Among the main advantages is, as noted previously, that they are relatively simple to construct or revise and to use. Unlike qualitative approaches, the observer who uses these instruments does not have to be highly trained in their use and interpretation. In addition, depending on the instrument, they may give the actual number of behaviors per unit of time, allowing for comparison among students or across classes.

The chief drawback to their use is that the units of observation may be trivial aspects of the teaching and learning process. Or they may not be crucially involved with or related to the concerns or purpose of the observation. Further, the actual behaviors observed may not explain all of the facts of the focus of the observation or the problem. Finally, aside from the behaviors being recorded by the observer, the teacher will most likely not know what else the students did during the observation period.

A major factor associated with quantitative approaches used in observing the second language classroom involves the concept of *inference*. Instruments may differ as to the degree of inference they require the observer to make, ranging from relatively low-inference items to high-inference items (see Richards, this volume, Chapter 1). A low-inference item is one that is readily recognizable and specific (e.g., "student raises hand"); a high-inference item refers to more covert, less specific behavior (e.g., "teacher asks a known-answer question," where the observer may have to infer if the teacher knows the answer to the question). Depending on the purpose of the observation, either low- or high-inference instruments are used, although low-inference instruments are generally preferred in teacher education observations.

The advantages to the use of low-inference instruments are their ease of use and the confidence that can be placed in the data they generate. The latter factor concerns reliability, a key issue in observing any behavior, especially in research situations.

The disadvantages to the use of low-inference instruments have to do mainly with their nature. Research has not established a causal rela-

48

tionship between student learning and most codable behaviors of teachers. However, such a lack does not decrease the value of coded observations as a tool to help observe events in the classroom.

Seating chart observation records

There are a variety of techniques for observing teacher and student interaction based on the use of seating charts. Acheson and Gall refer to such observation instruments as Seating Chart Observation REcords (SCORE) (1987: 97). The concept is relatively simple: Using a seating chart of the classroom to be observed, the observer records the occurrences of the targeted behavior or behaviors.

The preparation of a SCORE instrument begins with making a seating chart. Since second and foreign language classrooms utilize many different seating arrangements, I recommend that a seating chart be constructed in the class to be observed. Boxes are best used to represent students, for they allow sufficient space to record the data unambiguously. The students' names may or may not be placed in the box. Other indications of student identity can also be used, such as F = female, M = male, or numbers. Figure 1 illustrates one possible way of diagramming a seating chart.

The flow of verbal interaction may be indicated by arrows, with the head of the arrow indicating the direction of the flow or the person to whom the utterance was directed. I have found that the arrows generally can be confined to the box, unless it is desirable to show student–student interaction across boxes. The arrow can be crossed to indicate the number of times the interaction occurred; an arrow crossed four times may be used to show a verbal behavior that occurred five times. An indication of the type of verbal behavior helps in the coding procedure. For example, an arrow with the letter G next to it and placed in a student box could indicate that the student responded to a general solicit by the teacher. The letter S might indicate a spontaneous utterance, and so on.

SCORE instruments have a number of advantages associated with them, including ease of use and interpretation. They can be created for a particular purpose with no difficulty. Acheson and Gall report that a great deal of information about classroom interaction can be consolidated on one page with a SCORE instrument (1987: 97). Another benefit is that SCORE instruments allow examination of individual students without losing sight of the behavior of other students in the classroom. Finally, unlike other low-inference instruments, SCORE instruments allow the observer and the teacher to examine important features of classroom behavior (e.g., at- or off-task behavior). The disadvantages for the use of SCORE instruments are the same as for other low-inference instruments.

Richard R. Day

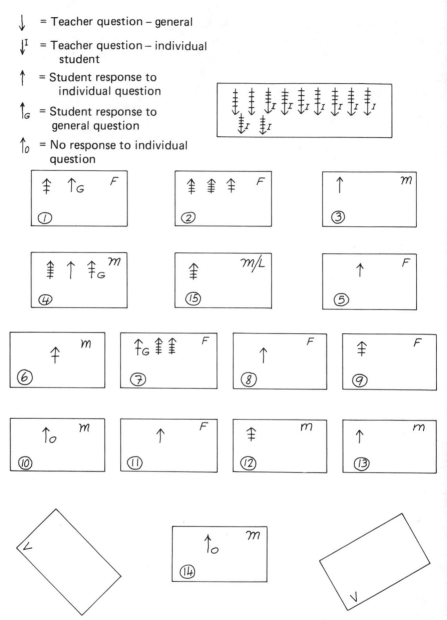

Figure 1 SCORE showing verbal interaction. V = vacant seat; M = male; F = female; L = latecomer.

In working with student teachers, I have found SCORE instruments particularly helpful in three areas: teacher and student talk; at-task; and movement patterns.

Teacher and student talk

Teacher and student talk, referred to by Acheson and Gall (1987: 105) as *verbal flow,* is a technique used to record who is talking to whom and how frequently. Student teachers use it to record teachers' questioning behavior and how they praise students; in addition, a verbal flow can also be used to code student questions and responses.

Figure 1 is an example of a SCORE instrument used to code the verbal flow of an ESL classroom. It was prepared in the classroom by the student teacher and captures the nature of the verbal flow in the classroom. Through it, we learn that the teacher generally called on students individually – 45 times; she used a questioning technique of general soliciting (calling on the class in general) only 10 times. Two male students sitting in the back of the room failed to respond when called on. We can also notice the existence of what Adams and Biddle (1970) label an "action zone." The students seated in front of the teacher in the first three rows generally received more opportunities to talk and took more turns at talking than did other students in the class.

At-task

Coding at-task behavior of students is helpful in that it gives the teacher knowledge about what students are doing in the classroom. For example, in supervising a student teacher, I used a self-designed SCORE instrument for at- and off-task behavior in an advanced ESL listening comprehension class, and recorded such behavior in two-minute intervals. Every two minutes, I quickly observed the entire class individually, and noted what each student was doing, the activity, and other information that had been agreed upon with the student teacher in advance. I learned that one student was sleeping during several of our coding periods. During a subsequent discussion about the observation, the student teacher was amazed to learn this. He was not aware that the student had been off-task, much less asleep, during the lesson. It turned out that this particular student was having difficulty in the class and had exhibited other types of problem behavior. The student teacher used the information obtained from the at- and off-task observation to have a conference with the student in an attempt to determine what the student's problems were.

One of the difficulties in attempting to code at-task behavior is often the high-inferential nature of the categories used. It is a rather low-inferential task to code students who are out of their seats or the room, playing or sleeping. But it is a high-inferential task to decide if students talking during a group-work activity are at- or off-task, unless the observer is close enough to hear the speech. It is also a high-inferential task to determine if a student who is writing something in a notebook during a conversation class is off-task, as the student could possibly be writing down a vocabulary item that came up during the lesson.

Movement patterns

The purpose of the SCORE instrument is to chart the movements of the teacher or students, or both, during a lesson. It is felt that the nature of the teacher's movement may be related in some fashion to classroom management (e.g., discipline or holding student attention). The coding of a teacher's moves during a lesson might also indicate biases toward certain students, much in the same way a verbal flow can. The coding of student moves has the potential of revealing whether they are at-task.

In a second language classroom, movement patterns can be coded to trace what a teacher does during activities that are not teacher-fronted. Such a coding can be a helpful demonstration to the student teacher of the impact that teacher movement may have on the teaching and learning processes. For example, a student teacher who codes a teacher's movements in group-work activities could determine if a group is being slighted by the teacher and, consequently, may not be at-task as frequently as groups that receive the bulk of the teacher's attention.

Other quantitative instruments

In this section, information is presented on the observation of three phenomena in the second language classroom: teacher expectations, classroom management, and motivation. The three instruments used to observe them are quantitative in nature but are not SCORE instruments.

Teacher expectations

Since the publication of Rosenthal and Jacobson's (1968) research on teacher expectations as self-fulfilling prophecies, there has been a great deal of interest and research on the topic of teacher expectations in content areas. Good and Brophy, in a review of the research, observe that teacher expectations can be expected to affect student achievement, attitudes, beliefs, attributions, expectations, motivational patterns, and classroom conduct (1987: 144). While there has been no research to my knowledge on this topic in second language classrooms, there is no reason to think that second language teachers would be different from others. Therefore, teacher expectations is a fruitful topic for student teachers to explore.

Good and Brophy offer a number forms by which teacher expectations may be observed (1987: 162–72). I have used a number of these successfully in my work with student teachers. One of these is displayed in Appendix 2; it addresses the giving of praise by the teacher, a critical aspect of teacher expectations. When used by my student teachers in observing others, they learned that some teachers give no praise at all, while other teachers praise a great deal. Such findings generate insightful discussions about the role of praise in classroom teaching.

In using forms such as Appendix 2, it is important to devise a system for identifying individual students. One easy way is through the use of a seating chart, in which each student is assigned a number. Regardless of the means of student identification, the coding is relatively simple. For example, in the form in Appendix 2, every time the student teacher observes the teacher praising an individual student, he or she codes the behavior category and indicates to which student it was addressed. This type of form can be readily modified to suit particular needs or purposes.

Classroom management

Classroom management is a topic about which student teachers often know little and have a great deal of anxiety. I find that having them observe experienced teachers and code aspects of classroom management is very helpful. Through such observation and subsequent discussion, student teachers realize that classroom management does not just happen or evolve, and that teacher behavior can have a direct influence on student behavior.

Good and Brophy (1987: 256–9) suggest four forms for observing classroom management. In Appendix 3, one form is presented that is used to determine how a teacher handles transitions and group management. Student teachers have found this useful in observing ESL classes that contain a lot of group- and pair-work activities. Such observations often reveal the difficulty even experienced teachers have in providing an orderly transition from group work to a teacher-fronted activity.

Motivation

Among the most widely discussed topics in second language learning is the role of motivation in the successful acquisition of the target language. Appendix 4 presents a form from Good and Brophy (1987) that may be beneficial in observing teacher behaviors believed to be directly related

Richard R. Day

to student motivation. It involves low-inference as well as more moderate-inference categories, and may be modified as needed.

It should again be stressed that research has not established a causal relationship with any of these behaviors and second language acquisition. They are behaviors, however, that influence the atmosphere of the classroom and, as a result, the setting in which students learn the target language. Making student teachers aware of them by observing experienced teachers helps them understand how teachers may indirectly affect the acquisition process.

Conclusion

While there are a number of approaches to helping student teachers understand and appreciate what goes on in the second language classroom in general and the teacher's role in particular, observation of second language classrooms is an exceptionally effective way. However, for observation to have a critical impact on student teachers' professional development, it must be guided and systematic. The careful use of the approaches and techniques presented in this chapter may be of use in achieving this goal.

Appendix 1   Ethnography of an ESL classroom

Ethnographic observation

Advanced Academic Listening and Speaking Class: March 1, 1988
Background: The class is a bi-weekly, university level, advanced, academic language skills class for non-native speakers of English. There are fifteen students from various Asian cultures. In the last class period, the students handed in homework in which they listed topics they would like to work on for group in-class presentations (one of the course objectives). The lesson plan is to have the students decide on their presentation groups and their topics. Today's class is being video-taped by the observer.

BEGIN
12:00   The teacher comes in the room and sets up the desk area. He
        seems a bit nervous, perhaps due to being video-taped. The
        students are sitting down and talking among themselves. The
12:03   teacher silently draws in a seating chart of the class. He takes roll,
        calling students one by one as he fills in the seating chart.
        Meanwhile, two students are getting their discussion question
        sheets ready to give to the other students (this is for the next class,

(Printed by permission of Lester Loschky.)

54

when they will lead a discussion). The teacher says he wants to do some house-keeping. He writes on the blackboard and says, "No more *Science Editor* tape notes." Oohs and aahs come from the students. The teacher smiles. He says, "I wrote 'Yeah' in my lesson plan by this, so you guys did just perfectly," as he points to the piece of paper. He says they will be busy enough with their other homework, such as the workbook, the discussion questions, and

12:06   their in-class presentations. The students listen silently. The teacher asks the students to type their discussion questions and the answers they make for them. He says, "I don't hear any 'Yeahs' for that one." "Yeah!" says one student. "Crazy," says the teacher in mock humor. The class laughs. The teacher asks the two students to pass out their discussion questions to the others. The students begin to pass them out. Both students have to give everyone two different questions. One student has both questions on a single sheet of paper, but the other has his questions on two separate slips of paper. Soon there is confusion because of all the different slips of paper being passed around the class. The teacher

12:10   realizes this too late. He explains that the students shouldn't separate the two questions on different slips of paper. "One person did it the way I wanted. The other person didn't." "Who has both of Yuu Gyeong's questions?" asks the teacher. Only a few students' hands go up. "Who doesn't have both of Yuu Gyeong's questions?" Many hands go up. The teacher reaches over to a pile of extra questions on his desk. "Oh, you handed these to me," he says. The class breaks out in laughter. The teacher hands out the questions to the students who don't have them. The teacher writes

12:13   on the board and says, "I'm sure you will be interested in this topic; it's 'Women's Liberation: The Struggle for Equality.' Since we have a lot of young women in this class, I'm sure you can get a good debate going." The students write down the assignment in their notebooks. The teacher then writes their next reading assignment on the board and briefly explains that it covers outlining a speech. Students write down the assignment in their notebooks silently. The teacher asks if the students have any

12:16   questions. After waiting for a few seconds, there is no response, so he goes on to the next topic. The teacher explains to the students that they are to pair up for their group presentations. He explains that he has paired the students by their responses on their homework about the topics in which they were interested. He asks the students to see if they like the matches he has made, and if not, they can see about pairing with other students. He hands back the students' homework sheets to each student. "Keiichi, it looks like

12:18   you might be interested in working with Yuu Gyeong." The students move into pairs to begin working. As the students get settled into the task, laughs and animated conversation begin to erupt from the groups. The teacher begins to circulate among the students. He heads for the back of the room where four students who hadn't come to the last class or hadn't done their homework are sitting together. He asks the students to discuss which topics they would like to work on and to try to form two groups. Two students immediately form a pair, leaving the other two to work

12:21 together. The teacher then goes to the front of the class where two students appear to be having difficulty. The students are smiling uneasily and questioning the teacher. The two students don't seem to want to work together. The teacher says he thought their pairing would be difficult but tries to help them find a common interest. "Just see if you can agree on one thing," he says. Another student nearby in the left center of the room asks the teacher a question about the grouping procedure. He also seems to be having difficulty with his partner. "You're gonna hafta 'bend' a

12:23 little bit," says the teacher. The student laughs. The teacher circulates to the front right part of class to check on another pair of students. One student, an art major, explains that they are interested in doing a presentation on Picasso. "You're both interested in that?" asks the teacher. The other student replies affirmatively. The teacher goes on to check with the pair sitting behind them. The pair checks to make sure they understand the assignment correctly. The teacher confirms that they understood it. The teacher then circulates to the back of the room

12:26 again to check on the progress of the last four students. The teacher discusses the situation with them. "You're gonna have to compromise," he says. Various students appear to be more interested in working together than others. The pair in the left center of the room seems quite silent. Most of the others are actively discussing their topics. The level of busy noise in the room

12:29 is quite high. The teacher goes back to the pair in the front who were having trouble earlier. They ask him about the types of topics they should choose. The teacher tells them, "You don't want them to fall asleep. It's gotta be interesting." One student in the pair asks if they need to use statistics in the presentation. The teacher replies that if statistics work with the particular presentation, they should use them. The teacher then goes to the blackboard and

12:31 starts writing. He is writing a set of heuristic questions for the students to use in developing their presentation topics. Some students, especially in the middle of the front of the class, are talking and occasionally laughing and seem actively engaged in the task. The pair in the front, to the left, who were earlier having trouble, are discussing their topic. One or two students start copying the heuristic questions from the blackboard. Others

12:35 discuss their topics. The teacher finishes writing on the board. "Excuse me. Can I have your attention. I don't want to disturb your working hard, but here are some questions, some of which you may have already been considering, that I would like you to answer. If you have already found the answers, then you don't have to worry about them, but keep them in mind. So please write them down." The students take notes of the questions. One has already finished. The teacher asks, "Did you already take notes? OK." The teacher then asks, "Do you have any questions about these questions?" The students do not respond. The teacher calls on individual students one by one. None of the students indicate that they have any questions. The teacher says he has one more

12:40 question, but that they don't have to write it down. It is regarding what each student can contribute to their pairs in terms of library research, writing of the presentation and giving the presentation. He says that both students must take the same grade, so they don't want to have one weak member. Most students are silent, though one laughs and makes a comment in a low voice. The teacher smiles and asks a particular student "Do you want to do all of the work?" "No," replies the student, giggling. The teacher tells the

12:42 students that they will have ten more minutes to go through the heuristic questions, and that those who finish early can go on to brainstorming their topics in more detail. He explains that what he means by "brainstorming" is "mind mapping," which the class has briefly covered before. One student asks if they have to write down every answer. The teacher says that they don't need to write down their answers as long as they go through each question. The

12:44 students begin working again busily.

Richard R. Day

Appendix 2 Individual praise

FORM 4.3. Individual Praise

USE: *Whenever the teacher praises an individual student*
PURPOSE: *To see what behaviors the teacher reinforces through praise, and*
to see how the teacher's praise is distributed among the students
Whenever the teacher praises an individual student, code the student's
number and each category of teacher behavior that applies
(consecutively).

BEHAVIOR CATEGORIES	STUDENT NUMBER	CODES
1. Perseverance or effort, worked long or hard	*14*	1. *3*
	23	2. *3,4*
2. Progress (relative to the past) toward achievement	*6*	3. *3*
	18	4. *3*
3. Success (right answer, high score), achievement	*8*	5. *1*
4. Good thinking, good suggestion, good guess or nice try	*8*	6. *1*
	8	7. *1*
5. Imagination, creativity, originality		8. ___
6. Neatness, careful work		9. ___
7. Good or compliant behavior, follows rules, pays attention		10. ___
8. Thoughtfulness, courtesy, offering to share; prosocial behavior		11. ___
		12. ___
9. Other (specify)		13. ___
		14. ___
		15. ___

NOTES:

All answers occurred during social studies discussion.

Was particularly concerned about #8, a low-achieving male

	16. ___
	17. ___
	18. ___
	19. ___
	20. ___
	21. ___
	22. ___
	23. ___
	24. ___
	25. ___

Appendix 3 Transitions and group management

FORM 6.1. Transitions and Group Management

*USE: During organizational and transition periods before, between, and
after lessons and organized activities*
*PURPOSE: To see if teacher manages these periods efficiently and avoids
needless delays and regimentation*
*How does the teacher handle early morning routines, transitions be-
tween activities, and clean-up and preparation time?*

Record any information relevant to the following questions:

1. Does the teacher do things that students could do for themselves?

2. Are there delays caused because everyone must line up or wait his turn?
   Can these be reduced with a more efficient procedure?

3. Does the teacher give clear instructions about what to do next before
   breaking a group and entering a transition? *Students often aren't clear
   about assignment so they question her during transitions and while
   she is starting to teach next group.*

4. Does the teacher circulate during transitions, to handle individual needs?
   Does he take care of these before attempting to begin a new activity?
   *Mostly, problem is poor directions before transition, rather
   than failure to circulate here.*

5. Does the teacher signal the end of a transition and the beginning of a
   structured activity properly, and quickly gain everyone's attention?
   *Good signal but sometimes loses attention by failing to
   start briskly. Sometimes has 2 or 3 false starts.*

Check if applicable:

_____ 1. Transitions come too abruptly for students because teacher
            fails to give advance warning or finish up reminders when
            needed

_____ 2. The teacher insists on unnecessary rituals or formalisms that
            cause delays or disruptions (describe)

___✓___ 3. Teacher is often interrupted by individuals with the same prob-
            lem or request; this could be handled by establishing a general
            rule or procedure (describe) *See #3 above.*

___✓___ 4. Delays occur because frequently used materials are stored in
            hard to reach places *Pencil sharpener too close to
            reading group area, causing frequent distractions.*

_____ 5. Poor traffic patterns result in pushing, bumping, or needless
            noise

_____ 6. Poor seating patterns screen some students from teacher's view
            or cause students needless distraction

_____ 7. Delays occur while teacher prepares equipment or illustrations
            that should have been prepared earlier

Richard R. Day

Appendix 4 Motivational analysis of tasks and activities

FORM 8.4. Motivational Analysis of Tasks and Activities

USE: Whenever particular classroom tasks or activities are observed
PURPOSE: To identify the motivational elements built into the task or
activity
Check each of the motivational elements that was included in the observed task or activity.

A. EXTRINSIC MOTIVATION STRATEGIES

_____ 1. Offers rewards as incentives for good performance
_____ 2. Calls attention to the instrumental value of the knowledge or skills developed in the activity (applications to present or future life outside of school)
_____ 3. Structures individual or group competition for prizes or recognition

B. INTRINSIC MOTIVATIONAL FEATURES OF THE TASK OR ACTIVITY

_____ 1. Opportunities for active response (beyond just watching and listening)
_____ 2. Opportunities to answer divergent questions or work on higher level objectives
_____ 3. Immediate feedback to students' responses (built into the task itself, rather than provided by the teacher as in C.8 below)
_____ 4. Gamelike features (the task is a game or contains gamelike features that make it more like a recreational activity than a typical academic activity)
_____ 5. Task completion involves creating a finished product for display or use
_____ 6. The task involves fantasy or simulation elements that engage students' emotions or allow them to experience events vicariously
_____ 7. The task provides opportunities for students to interact with their peers

---

FORM 8.4. (*Continued*)

C. *TEACHER'S ATTEMPTS TO STIMULATE STUDENTS' MOTIVATION TO LEARN*

_____ 1. Projects intensity (communicating that the material is important and deserves close attention)

_____ 2. Induces task interest or appreciation

_____ 3. Induces curiosity or suspense

_____ 4. Makes abstract content more personal, concrete, or familiar

_____ 5. Induces dissonance or cognitive conflict

_____ 6. Induces students to generate their own motivation to learn

_____ 7. States learning objectives or provides advance organizers

_____ 8. Provides opportunities for students to respond and get feedback (asks questions during group lessons, circulates to monitor performance during seatwork)

_____ 9. Models task-related thinking and problem solving ("thinks out loud" when working through examples)

_____ 10. Includes instruction or modeling designed to increase students' metacognitive awareness of their learning efforts in response to the task (includes information about mental preparation for learning, about the organization or structure built into the content, about how students can impose their own organizational structures on the content to help them remember it, or about how to monitor one's own comprehension and respond to confusion or mistakes)

NOTES:

(From T. L. Good and J. E. Brophy, *Looking in Classrooms,* 4th ed., pp. 350–1. Copyright © 1987 by Harper & Row, Publishers, Inc. Reprinted by permission of the publisher.)

5 Action research in the language classroom

David Nunan

This chapter takes as its point of departure the notion that classroom teachers should be involved in curriculum research and development as these relate to their own classrooms and that a primary goal for inservice teacher education is to give teachers ways of exploring their own classrooms. However, such involvement presupposes certain skills and knowledge in classroom observation and research. In particular, teachers need to be able to conceptualise their practice in theoretical terms, they need to be aware of issues amenable to action research, and they need to have skills in data collection and analysis. These skills can be developed through action research projects wherein professional development programs can feed into a constant cycle of intervention, monitoring, and modification to classroom practice.

In this chapter I shall describe a program designed to develop skills in classroom observation and action research. The program is illustrated with data from workshops conducted with senior teachers of English to speakers of other languages from within the Australian Adult Immigrant Education Program (AMEP). Given the heterogeneous nature of the AMEP, a centralised, imposed curriculum is unsuitable. A consequence of this is that classroom practitioners need to play a central role in curriculum development, including monitoring and evaluation. To this end, it is crucial that teachers develop a range of skills in planning, monitoring, and evaluating their own professional activities.

Background

It will be helpful first to draw a distinction between assessment, evaluation, and action research. *Assessment* refers to the set of processes through which we make judgments about a learner's level of skills and knowledge. *Evaluation* refers to the wider process of collecting and interpreting data in order to make judgments about a particular program or programs. The data we draw on during the evaluation process will usually include learner assessment data, but it will include other information as well. Obtaining information about what students have or have not learned, however, is only a first step. A necessary second step is to determine why particular results were or were not obtained. A third step is to decide what, if anything, we intend to do about these results.

It is important that teachers be involved in program planning and evaluation as well as the more customary role of program implementation. This is particularly true of educational systems such as the AMEP, in which curriculum development happens at the local level. But it is also important in centralised systems where, in Schwab's (1983) terms, 'the curriculum is created in Moscow and telegraphed to the provinces'. In centralised and decentralised systems alike, the teacher provides the interface between the syllabus and the student. The teacher is therefore admirably placed inside the 'black box', as Long (1980) calls it, and is potentially well placed to provide insights into classroom learning and teaching. One of the problems with teachers as researchers, however, is that they often lack appropriate training in the collection and interpretation of classroom data (see, for example, Pica and Doughty 1985).

One way of encouraging teachers to develop research skills is to get them to adopt an *action research* orientation to their classroom. A set of procedures for conducting such research is set out in Kemmis and McTaggart (1982). Their concept of action research is captured in the following statement:

The linking of the terms 'action' and 'research' highlights the essential feature of the method: trying out ideas in practice as a means of improvement and as a means of increasing knowledge about the curriculum, teaching and learning. The result is improvement in what happens in the classroom and school, and better articulation and justification of the educational rationale of what goes on. Action research provides a way of working which links theory and practice into the one whole: ideas-in-action. (p. 5)

Kemmis and McTaggart's statement is an important one. It highlights the fact that action research is not simply research grafted onto practice. Rather, it represents a particular attitude on the part of the practitioner, an attitude in which the practitioner is engaged in critical reflection on ideas, the informed application and experimentation of ideas in practice, and the critical evaluation of the outcomes of such application.

Cohen and Manion (1980) draw a distinction between applied research and action research. They suggest that applied research is more rigorous and does not claim to contribute directly to the solution of problems. Action research, on the other hand, is less interested in obtaining generalisable scientific knowledge than knowledge for a particular situation or purpose. Action research is *situational,* or context-based, *collaborative, participatory,* and *self-evaluative.* They go on to suggest that action research can be utilized towards five general ends:

1. as a means of remedying problems diagnosed in specific situations, or of improving in some way a given set of circumstances;
2. as a means of inservice training, providing teachers with new skills and methods and heightening self-awareness;
3. as a means of injecting additional or innovative approaches to teaching and learning into a system which normally inhibits innovation and change;
4. as a means of improving the normally poor communications between the practising teacher and academic researcher;
5. (although lacking the rigour of true scientific research) as a means of providing an alternative to the more subjective, impressionistic approach to problem solving in the classroom.

(Cohen and Manion 1980: 211)

I am particularly concerned here with the second of these outcomes, that is, with the potential of action research to contribute to professional development, particularly in encouraging self-directed teachers, who are capable, through action research, of furthering their own professional self-development.

The notion of the self-directed teacher as classroom researcher is consonant with several other trends in teacher development. For instance, Bartlett (this volume, Chapter 13) and Lange (this volume, Chapter 16) both argue a case for the reflective teacher. Such a teacher is one who "knows the art and craft of teaching... The *craft* of teaching relates to the teacher's specific knowledge of the subject matter, knowledge on teaching that subject matter, and knowledge on teaching in general. The *art* of teaching involves the combination of knowledge and experience in the many decisions that teachers make as they interact with learners" (Lange, pp. 247–8).

Lange also develops a model for teacher education which is experiential and problem oriented. Action research is a tool which is particularly amenable to such an experiential, problem-oriented approach.

Curriculum development and professional practice within the AMEP

The AMEP is a large, federally funded English language program, which has annual student enrolments of 130,000. These are taught by 1,500 teachers in 300 language centres throughout Australia. Until the early 1980s, the AMEP had a centralised curriculum, with a fixed syllabus incorporated into a set of teaching materials. With a growing diversity of learners, particularly in the wake of large-scale refugee intakes from

Southeast Asia, it was realised that such a centralised curriculum was unable to accommodate the diversity of learner types. A decision was therefore made to abandon the centralised curriculum for a localised or school-based curriculum model based on a learner-centred philosophy. The idea was for teachers to become the principal agents of curriculum development, as it is the teachers who are best placed to diagnose and cater for learners' needs. With teachers as the principal agents of curriculum development, such development itself becomes largely a matter of appropriate teacher development.

The learner-centred curriculum model created a whole new set of professional development needs. A smorgasbord approach (i.e., one in which a list of self-contained options is proposed at the beginning of the semester from which teachers self-select) was recognised as inadequate, and individual state professional development units, along with the National Curriculum Resource Centre (now the National Centre for English Language Teaching and Research), moved to develop comprehensive and integrated training programs, which would provide teachers with skills in curriculum development and classroom research and evaluation.

The action research inservice program

Preliminary to the program, participants were asked to video- or audiotape their classrooms over several days, and then to select and transcribe a 10- to 15-minute segment in which there was a 'critical incident', or in which a problem occurred, or in which they were trying something new. In other words, it was not sufficient for participants simply to transcribe 10 minutes of inactivity or routine activity. Teachers found that the very act of selecting a particular incident or event revealed something of their own attitudes towards and beliefs about language learning and teaching.

The aims of the inservice program were (1) to introduce participants to techniques and procedures for investigating classroom processes; (2) to provide participants with the opportunity of applying techniques to their own teaching; (3) to assist participants in identifying and examining their own attitudes and beliefs about language and learning; (4) to provide participants with the opportunity of identifying areas for further investigation within their own classroom.

There are five stages to the program, each with its own subsidiary steps:

1. Observing classrooms part 1: theory and practice
2. Observing classrooms part 2: methods and techniques
3. Issues for investigation

4. Investigating your own classroom
5. Developing an action research proposal.

STAGE I   OBSERVING CLASSROOMS PART I : THEORY
AND PRACTICE

Stage 1 is designed as a general introduction to classroom observation. Participants are encouraged to identify those aspects of the classroom which interest them, and to reveal the preconceptions and beliefs they bring with them to classroom observation. The procedure for this stage is adapted from Ramani (1987). The resources include a set of handouts and a videotape of an ESL (English as a second language) lesson.

This preliminary introductory stage is an important one. As Wright (this volume, Chapter 6) points out:

> A primary goal of all teacher-development programs is to link theory and practice... Often, however, we may fail to achieve this higher-order goal. Perhaps the overall approach to the program is top-down, replete with content in the form of raw, unprocessed theory. Perhaps there is an overemphasis on teaching techniques at the expense of the broader issues of methodology. More often than not, the cause may lie in the lack of appeal to the participants' apprehension of the relationship between theory and practice derived from their own experience. (p. 82)

(See also Ramani 1987 and Bowers 1987a for lucid discussions on the relationship between theory and practice.)

Step 1: Previewing Activity. Participants are introduced to the workshop and are told about the lesson they are about to observe. They are asked to write down the three aspects of the lesson they will be looking at/for during the lesson. These are summarised on the board by the coordinator. Participants usually nominate such aspects as teacher talk, elicitation techniques, wait-time, error correction, variation and pacing of activities, and exploitation of unexpected or unplanned occurrences in the classroom. Some of the issues discussed in the prereading usually make their appearance in the aspects the teachers wish to observe, and this reinforces the notion that observation is not value free but will reflect the beliefs and attitudes we have internalised through various means.

One group of teachers came up with the following list:

Wait-time	Materials
Repair techniques	Student–teacher interaction
Fun	Scope of student response
Questioning	Amount of direction

Class organisation	Digressions, good and bad
Lesson objectives	Variety of activities
Student/teacher talk time	Student–student interaction
Control and initiative	Lesson cohesion
Who asks questions	Ideological aspects of lesson content
Context for language	Teacher language
How language is practised	Eliciting techniques
Methods used	Evaluation possibilities

Step 2: Viewing the lesson. Participants then view the lesson and make notes while they are doing so. The lesson which I use for this stage is a teacher-centred lesson with little group work.

Step 3: Individual and small-group task. Working individually, participants write down the three aspects of the lesson they considered most satisfactory and why, and the three things they found unsatisfactory and why. With this step, teachers are making evaluative judgments of the lesson they have observed. They then work in small groups to share their responses and come up with group reactions. This involves negotiation and discussion to reach a consensus and forces teachers to reveal their own preconceptions, value judgments, and theoretical perspectives.

One group of AMEP teachers, who had been divided into six small groups, came up with the following reactions to the teacher-dominated lesson they had observed:

GROUP 1

Liked	*Disliked*
Interesting presentation – authentic material	Overcontrolled lesson
Simple lexis	Too much instructional language
Animated – good voice range	Very little eliciting
	Answered own questions
	No change of pace

GROUP 2

Liked	*Disliked*
Preparation	Limited student interaction
Authentic material	Didn't capitalize on opportunities for communication as they arose
Friendly, relaxed manner	
Teacher's language well controlled, natural	No wait-time
	Objectives unclear

GROUP 3

Liked	Disliked
Students were interested	Objective to practice Wh-questions not met
Good use of authentic material	No wait-time
Objective of listening for gist was met	No opportunity for digression; one student eager to talk was not followed up
	Introduced too much and didn't give time for digestion; pace too fast
	Too much teacher talk

GROUP 4

Liked	Disliked
Lesson cohesive and well planned	Pace too fast to complete any task
Authentic materials involving 4 macroskills	No encouragement for students to listen to each other
Interesting context	Lack of student interaction

GROUP 5

Liked	Disliked
Authentic materials	Teacher talk dominant
Listening comprehension seemed to occur	No cohesion – students' responses not taken up
Good preparation and sense of order	Set agenda of questions
	Information dominant

GROUP 6

Liked	Disliked
Authentic, appropriate materials	Teacher dominant, students passive
Clear production of tape	Lack of student interaction
	Not enough wait-time
	Not enough student practice
	Information given not elicited
	Aim/purpose unclear
	Feedback from only a few students

Step 4: Feedback. The aspects are listed on the board in two columns, labeled *liked* and *disliked*. Participants, working in their small groups, then identify which of the statements made by other groups they agree with and why, and which they disagree with and why. Once again, this

is an evaluative process, often involving considerable discussion and negotiation. Each group then reports back to the whole group.

Step 5: Whole-group discussion. There is a general discussion of the outcomes of Step 4. The coordinator focuses on the extent to which the issues and areas nominated in Step 1 are reflected in Step 3. It is also important to focus on conflicting opinions from different groups and to stimulate discussion on the assumptions and belief systems underlying these various opinions. In the list here, for instance, most groups liked the use of authentic materials. This led to an animated discussion on why authentic materials were considered good.

STAGE 2 OBSERVING CLASSROOMS PART 2: METHODS AND TECHNIQUES

The aim of Stage 2 is to sensitise participants to the issues, problems, and questions which might be amenable to action research, and to train them in the use of various observational techniques and instruments. A selection of some of the observation instruments used in the workshop can be found in the Appendix to this chapter.

Step 1: Previewing activity. Participants are given copies of some observation schedules, and are taken through these. The schedules relate to lesson analysis, classroom management, task analysis, and classroom interaction. Each handout is discussed, and queries or problems are clarified.

Step 2: Small groups. Participants are asked to nominate which aspect of the lesson they would like to work on: lesson analysis, classroom management, task analysis, or classroom interaction. They form small groups accordingly and view a videotaped lesson which focuses on group work. They then complete the tasks on their handout. Group 4 (on classroom interaction) is the only one required to complete their schedule in real time (i.e., while actually viewing the lesson). The other groups complete their tasks at the conclusion of the viewing period.

Step 3: Feedback. Each group reports back on the results of Step 2, and the techniques and instruments which they used to analyse the lesson are discussed. The utility of the instruments and modifications which might be made to them are discussed.

One of the problems in using real data is that teachers can become absorbed with the shortcomings of the teacher and lesson on which the observation is based. While it is only natural for teachers to be critical,

David Nunan

it is important that this part of the workshop not degenerate into simply a critical analysis of the lesson. The important thing is for the participants to reflect on the nature of classroom observation, and the strengths and weaknesses of the chosen instruments.

Another potential problem is the tendency for some teachers to view any lesson which has been videotaped as exemplary. The facilitator must therefore point out very clearly from the beginning that no assumptions about the "right" way to teach are being made, and that this is not the point of the exercise. In fact, it would defeat the purpose of the workshop if model lessons which had been carefully worked out and rehearsed were used.

STAGE 3   ISSUES FOR INVESTIGATION

Based on their experiences during Stages 1 and 2, participants explore some of the issues which are amenable to investigation. It is convenient to classify these as relating either to the teacher or the learners. Tables 1 and 2 give some idea of the issues teachers might explore. Nunan (1989) contains an extended discussion of ways in which these issues might be turned into problems for investigation.

STAGE 4   INVESTIGATING YOUR OWN CLASSROOM

The focus now turns to the participants themselves. This stage is based on the lesson transcript which participants have prepared prior to the training program.

Step 1: Preliminary. Participants select a partner with whom to work. While this stage can be done on an individual basis, participants get much more out of it if they work with someone else. A degree of trust is required for this step, and this is something the coordinator needs to attend to at Stages 1 and 2.

Participants are asked to select some area or aspect of teaching which interests them and to analyse the interaction, noting in particular issues relating to the aspect they have selected. As they work they make notes, which form the basis of a short oral report back to the whole group.

Step 2: Classroom analysis. Participants analyse their lesson extract using whatever tools they like and provide data on type of student, aim of lesson, area investigated, what analysis revealed about current practices and beliefs, what it revealed about the roles of teacher and learners, whether it revealed anything unexpected or surprising (and what it was), whether there was a problem, and what issue or question it revealed which might be followed up.

TABLE I. ISSUES AND SAMPLE INVESTIGATIVE QUESTIONS FOR TEACHERS

Issue	Investigative questions
Planning	What are the bases on which I select my goals and objectives?
	What are the major factors I take into consideration when selecting content?
Implementation	What is the relationship between the lesson plans I draw up before class and what actually happens in class?
	To what extent does my teaching reflect a systematic procedure of specifying objectives, selecting content and learning tasks, and evaluating the effectiveness of instruction?
	To what extent is it ad hoc?
	What events in the classroom cause me to deviate from my planned lessons?
Classroom management	Some of my learners are disruptive. Is there anything in my behaviour towards them which might account for this?
	What effect will modified behaviour on my part have on them?
	What aspects of learner behaviour do I respond to?
	How efficient/effective am I at setting up group work?
Talk	How much talking do I do in class? Is this too little, or too much?
	What happens when I vary the amount of talking I do?
	How clear and/or useful are the explanations I give to students?
	What sort of questions do I ask?
	How and when do I correct errors? With what effect?
	What typical patterns of interaction are there between myself and my learners?

Source: Nunan (1989).

Step 3: Feedback. Each participant then summarises the results of his or her analysis for the whole group. This step needs to be carried out briskly, particularly if there are more than fifteen participants. If there are more than twenty participants, this activity will have to be conducted in subgroups of eight to ten. It also needs to be carried out sensitively, as the self-disclosures can be embarrassing. Teachers tend to be their own harshest critics, as the following comments demonstrate. These comments were provided by participants in response to the question: What did you discover about your own teaching as a result of your self-analysis?

David Nunan

TABLE 2. ASPECTS OF LEARNER BEHAVIOUR WHICH MIGHT BE INVESTIGATED IN THE CLASSROOM

Issue	Sample investigative question
Learner language: developmental features	In my teaching, I generally provide an application task to follow up a formal presentation. Which language items do learners actually use in the application task? Do learners learn closed class items (e.g., pronouns/demonstratives) when these are presented as paradigms, or when they are taught separately over a period of time?
Learner language: interaction	In what ways do turn taking and topic management vary with the size and composition of learner groups? Are learners more effective at conversational management when such techniques as holding the floor and bringing in another speaker are consciously taught?
Tasks	Which tasks stimulate the most interaction? Which tasks work best with mixed-ability groups?
Strategies	Is there a conflict between the classroom activities I favour and those my learners prefer? Do my best learners share certain strategy preferences which distinguish them from less efficient learners?

Source: Nunan (1989).

Teacher talk
I praise, but it is rather automatic.
There was a lot of teacher talk.
I give too many instructions.
I need to give clearer instructions.
There was excessive teacher instruction.
There was too much teacher talk.
Need more comprehension checking.
Need to do more eliciting.
I had tried to avoid the comprehension question list, but ended up asking just as many questions of my own.
Instructions were unclear.
Some explanations were nonsensical.
I gave no praise.
Instructions and explanations were inadequate.

Explanations to class were confusing.
There were excessive teacher digressions.

Teacher behaviour
I was trying to respond to contrary notions during the lesson (e.g., intervention versus nonintervention).
I glossed over difficult topics too quickly.
I realised later there could be strategies to make problems simpler.
I am overdirective.
There was too much teacher domination.
I dominated too much.
I took centre stage, was condescending.
Need for more positive reinforcement.
Need to exploit opportunities as they arise.
I spent more time on particular activities than I had thought.
I found that I dominated when I thought I hadn't.
I am not so different from other teachers.

Lesson preparation/structuring
Objectives were not clear.
I need to give more thought to timing (wait-time) and not worry too much about silences.
I need to develop a more analytical approach to my teaching.
Need to complete lessons as planned.
The lesson was not sufficiently well prepared.
I had planned an activity to stimulate conversation, but set up these activities in a way which prevented this.
I need to search for solutions to problems more thoroughly.

Content
There is a need for cultural input.
Student interest in the topic was lower than I had thought it would be.
There was not enough cultural information provided for the task to be completed successfully.

Student behaviour
Students need to help each other more.
There should be more use of the students' first language in the classroom.
Students need to be made aware of lesson objectives.
Need to encourage self-monitoring and self-correction.

Other
There are umpteen aspects of my teaching which need improving.
Context is important.

STAGE 5   DEVELOPING AN ACTION RESEARCH PROPOSAL

This final stage is designed to introduce participants to the concept of action research as a professional development tool.

Step 1: Whole-group discussion. The coordinator introduces participants to the concept, explaining in some detail the nature and purpose of action research, and outlining a procedure for conducting an action research project. Participants are also provided with a sample set of questions and issues for investigation. The group then works through the things they discovered about their own teaching (Stage 3, Step 3) and formulates research questions.

Step 2: Nominating areas for investigation. Participants, working individually, then nominate those issues they wish to investigate as a result of taking part in the workshop. One group of participants came up with the following:

Methodology
Task analysis and the different demands that tasks create
What materials/methods students do/do not respond to
The learning and teaching of vocabulary

Classroom management and interaction
The occurrence of digressions within a lesson by teachers and students and the extent to which these lead to useful learning outcomes or simply distract, confuse, and mislead students
The management of classroom interactions
Effective and ineffective giving of instructions
How to increase student talking time (Do students think this is valuable? Does it enhance learning?)

Professional development and self-evaluation
How do teachers perceive peer analysis? In what ways is it helpful, threatening, inhibiting?
How teacher development and action research can improve cohesion / sense of progression from the students' perspective
Peer teaching/learning for teachers
Promoting personal responsibility for professional development
Using classroom analysis with new teachers to assist them in developing their own practices more effectively

Applying skills
Encouraging and monitoring students' use of English outside the classroom
Encouraging the use of English outside the classroom

Affective factors
Student attitude towards games and drama activities
Student perceptions of language learning

Evaluation and assessment
Evaluating effectiveness of teaching
Methods of postlearning arrangement assessment
How to develop classroom tests for end-of-course assessment

Acquisition
Whether plateaus in language learning really exist

Step 3: Whole-group feedback. The participants each give a short oral presentation, outlining the aspect or area of their own classroom which they intend to investigate. At this point, the major task for the workshop leader is to help participants formulate or reformulate their areas for investigation into a question that is realistic and feasible given the time and expertise available. The tendency at this point is for teachers to nominate issues too large in scope for the average practitioner.

Conclusion

Encouraging teachers to become their own classroom researchers can have a beneficial effect in all areas of the curriculum. In particular, it has great potential for professional self-development and renewal. In his handbook on tasks, procedures, and methods of research for teachers, Walker takes this view:

As teaching has become increasingly professionalized and the management of educational organizations more systematized, so 'research' has increasingly become something that teachers are expected to include in their repertoire of skills. By 'research' I do not mean detailed knowledge of the literature or high levels of proficiency in the skills conventionally required by testing and survey research. For one thing, to become expert in either of these areas demands more time, more training and more experience than most teachers are able to accumulate. What is required of teachers, of schools and of school systems is a range of other research skills, usually in relation to an immediate issue in one's own institution. (Walker 1985: 3–4)

According to Walker, skills will be needed for:

reviewing a range of curriculum proposals and judging their likely impact in practice;
evaluating practice, performance, and policy in teaching and administration;
providing evidence and analysis of the school's program for management purposes;

David Nunan

interpreting and assessing information coming to the school from a variety of sources, including examination boards, assessment and performance units, and the academic world.

Similarly, Hook suggests that a knowledge of and expertise in classroom observation will provide teachers with:

1. the ability to monitor and describe both their own and their pupils' activities and behaviours;
2. an understanding of instructional methods and materials and their application;
3. an awareness of the relationship between classroom behaviours and pupil growth;
4. the ability to modify or change their behaviours on the basis of their understanding of classroom settings.

(Hook 1981: 23)

I believe that the procedures outlined in the body of this paper marry happily with the observations of Walker and Hook.

In setting out those procedures, there has been little opportunity for critical appraisal, and there are certainly problematical aspects of the sort of training program I have outlined. Following Walker (1985), I would suggest that the following questions brook large:

1. Does one begin by immersing teachers in research projects, providing instruction in research methods only when this is requested or seems necessary, or does one begin by providing instruction in research methods followed by gradual practice in actual cases?
2. To what extent should research projects be collaborative or individual exercises?
3. Should projects focus on the particularities of specific situations, or be situated in relation to generalised, propositional knowledge (i.e., should the concern be with cases or samples)?
4. Should one prioritize short-term needs or long-term values?
5. How does one identify the appropriate audiences for the research?

Whatever the solutions or resolutions to these dilemmas, I am at one with Stenhouse (1975) in this assertion:

The uniqueness of each classroom setting implies that any proposal – even at school level – needs to be tested and verified and adapted by each teacher in his own classroom. The ideal is that the curricular specification should feed a teacher's personal research and development programme through which he is increasing his understanding of his own work and hence bettering his teaching... It is not enough that teachers' work should be studied: they need to study it themselves. (Stenhouse 1975: 143)

Appendix: Worksheets, checklists, and schedules for lesson observation and analysis

Analysing the lesson

Complete the following

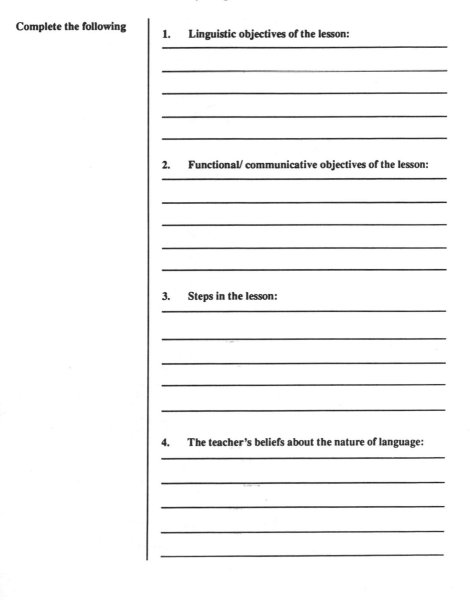

1.   Linguistic objectives of the lesson:
_____

_____

_____

_____

_____

2.   Functional/ communicative objectives of the lesson:
_____

_____

_____

_____

3.   Steps in the lesson:
_____

_____

_____

_____

4.   The teacher's beliefs about the nature of language:
_____

_____

_____

_____

David Nunan

5. **The teacher's beliefs about the nature of learning:**

_____

_____

_____

_____

_____

6. **Learner groupings (what percentage of the lesson was devoted to the following organisational patterns?):**

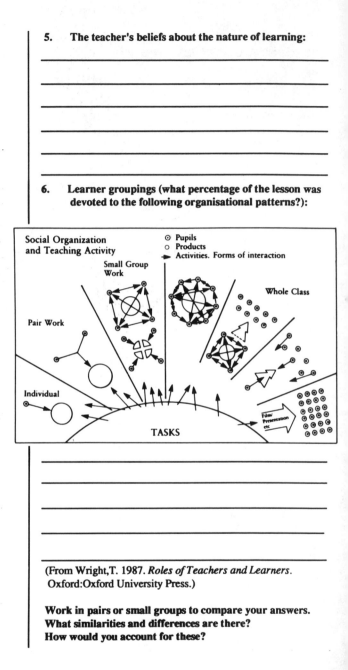

_____

_____

_____

_____

(From Wright,T. 1987. *Roles of Teachers and Learners.*
Oxford:Oxford University Press.)

**Work in pairs or small groups to compare your answers.
What similarities and differences are there?
How would you account for these?**

Classroom management

1. Rate the lesson according to the following key:

Key:
1   Does not at all reflect what went on
2   Only marginally reflects what went on
3   Neutral
4   Describes rather well what went on
5   Is a totally accurate reflection of what went on

1.	There were no cultural misunderstandings	1	2	3	4	5
2.	The class understood what was wanted at all times	1	2	3	4	5
3.	All instructions were clear	1	2	3	4	5
4.	Every student was involved at some point	1	2	3	4	5
5.	All students were interested in the lesson	1	2	3	4	5
6.	The teacher carried out comprehension checks	1	2	3	4	5
7.	Materials and learning activities were appropriate	1	2	3	4	5
8.	Student groupings and sub-groupings were appropriate	1	2	3	4	5
9.	Class atmosphere was positive	1	2	3	4	5
10.	The pacing of the lesson was appropriate	1	2	3	4	5
11.	There was enough variety in the lesson	1	2	3	4	5
12.	The teacher did not talk too much	1	2	3	4	5
13.	Error correction and feedback was appropriate	1	2	3	4	5
14.	There was genuine communication	1	2	3	4	5
15.	There was teacher skill in organising group work	1	2	3	4	5
16.	There was opportunity for controlled practice	1	2	3	4	5
17.	Students were enthusiastic	1	2	3	4	5
18.	General classroom management was good	1	2	3	4	5

Adapted from an RSA checklist

(Adapted from Nunan, D. 1988. *The Learner-Centred Curriculum*. Cambridge: Cambridge University Press.)

2   Work in pairs or small groups to compare your answers.
What similarities and differences are there? How would you account for these?

David Nunan

Task analysis

1. To what extent are the following statements an accurate reflection of the lesson?

    Key:

1	not at all
2	slightly
3	very
4	completely

The teacher used realia and authentic materials.	1	2	3	4
Learners rehearsed, in class, skills they will need in real communicative situations outside class.	1	2	3	4
The objectives of the lesson were clear to the learners.	1	2	3	4
There were opportunities for controlled practice of specific language points.	1	2	3	4
The activities were challenging but not threatening.	1	2	3	4
Learners were required to do something (e.g. solve a problem, come to a conclusion, complete a task).	1	2	3	4
Learners were required to cooperate.	1	2	3	4
Learners were required to share information (i.e. there was an information gap component to the lesson).	1	2	3	4
There was an evaluation component to the lesson which would allow learners to judge the degree to which they had succeeded or failed.	1	2	3	4
The activities would have been suitable for a mixed ability class.	1	2	3	4

(Adapted from Nunan, D. 1988. *Syllabus Design*. Oxford: Oxford University Press.

Work in pairs or small groups to compare your answers.
What similarities and differences are there?
How would you account for these?

Working with a partner, select the five most important characteristics of a lesson from the above list.
(Or, alternatively, provide your own characteristics).
For those characteristics which are not reflected in the lesson, suggest ways in which it might be modified to reflect these characteristics.
Suggest a follow-up task.

Classroom interaction

Watch the lesson again, and place a tally mark against
the following events each time they occur.

	Tallies	Total
1 Teacher asks a display question (i.e. a question to which she knows the answer).		
2 Teacher asks a referential question (i.e. a question to which she does not know the answer).		
3 Teacher explains a grammatical point.		
4 Teacher explains meaning of a vocabulary item.		
5 Teacher explains functional point.		
6 Teacher explains point relating to the content (theme/ topic) of the lesson.		
7 Teacher gives instructions/ directions.		
8 Teacher praises.		
9 Teacher criticises.		
10 Learner asks a question.		
11 Learner answers question.		
12 Learner talks to another learner.		
13 Period of silence or confusion		

**In small groups,
discuss the following**

1. Compare your tallies. What similarities and differences
   are there?
   How would you account for these?

2. What insights into the lesson, if any, did this activity provide?

3. Do you think there would be any value in audio recording
   and rating a segment from one of your own lessons?

6 Understanding classroom role relationships

Tony Wright

Themes and tasks in teacher development programs

A primary goal of all teacher development programs is to link theory and practice. There are a variety of means for achieving this. Often, however, we may fail to achieve this higher-order goal. Perhaps the overall approach to the program is top-down, replete with content in the form of raw, unprocessed theory. Perhaps there is an overemphasis on teaching techniques at the expense of the broader issues of methodology. More often than not, the cause may lie in the lack of appeal to the participants' apprehension of the relationship between theory and practice derived from their own experience. (See Widdowson 1984 for a controversial view on some of these issues.)

This chapter reports on one solution to the problem: Link both pre-service and inservice programs to a common central theme – teacher and learner roles. There are several reasons for making a focus on teacher and learner roles a central issue in teacher education.

(1) The importance of teacher and learner roles in an understanding of language teaching has recently been highlighted in several important studies. Richards and Rodgers (1986), for example, in an analysis of language teaching approaches and methods, discuss the role relationships implicit in different approaches to language teaching. The connections forged between views of language, views of learning, and the central teacher and learner relationships are a valuable contribution to establishing a broader view of the language teaching and learning process. Figure 1 illustrates the centrality of teacher and learner roles to any teacher development program.

Teaching can be seen as mediating between language and the learner within the formal context of the classroom. There are theories of language and theories of learning, but a theory of teaching can be drawn only from classroom experience, or at least can be informed only by that experience. Thus the relevance of language or learning theory can be seen only from the teacher's and the learners' viewpoints. A further implication is that teacher and learner roles must always be seen in relation to the three poles of the teaching and learning process outlined in Figure 1.

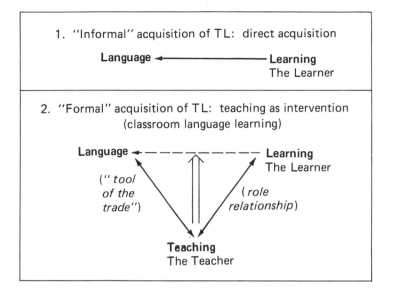

1. "Informal" acquisition of TL: direct acquisition

Language ◄─────────────── Learning
                           The Learner

2. "Formal" acquisition of TL: teaching as intervention
   (classroom language learning)

Language ◄── ── ── ── ── ── Learning
                           The Learner
("*tool*
of the   (*role*
trade")   *relationship*)

            Teaching
            The Teacher

Figure 1   Language learning: formal and informal

At the critical level of methodology, Riley (1984) puts the role relationship at the top of the agenda by focusing on learner-centered approaches to teaching as a counterpoint to more "traditional" approaches. His collection of research and position papers contains some notable additions to our understanding of this central theme (see for example Gremmo and Abe 1984). Finally, Brumfit (1984) hints at the potential of a wide diversity of teacher and learner behaviors in his discussion of fluency and accuracy. A key theme is the need for variety of learning tasks for different linguistic and communicative focuses and the concomitant need for a flexibility of teacher and learner roles. None of these valuable and provocative sources can ever be more than a blueprint for practice, however. They are templates to be set against experience – experience that can be gained only in the classroom. A consideration of teacher and learner roles therefore generates a wide range of important pedagogical and methodological issues.

(2) The teacher-learner role relationship lies at the very heart of the classroom process. Learning a language is a social activity above all, and in a classroom setting, it is subject to a unique set of social conventions. These derive in part from the deeper and less accessible social and psychological dimensions of the teacher-learner relationship. The language classroom is a social setting with its own conventions, norms, and behaviors (see Breen 1985). It is an essentially human institution,

with all the positive and problematical characteristics of such an institution. At a more accessible level are other influences on the role relationship, such as the learning tasks mediated, the nature of the language data being worked upon, and the physical organization of that setting. At the surface we are able to observe in-role and out-of-role teacher and learner behavior in any classroom through the interaction of participants, content, and tasks. All these layers are interconnected and mutually supporting.

These issues can thus be approached from different standpoints, depending on the interests of participants and overall program goals. An investigation of roles raises and addresses issues related to both classroom behavior and underlying value systems and attitudes held by individuals and groups. It also touches on issues that arise from a consideration of expectations of learning content and the ways in which teaching and learning take place. Naturally, decisions have to be made as to the emphasis placed on such issues in a teacher preparation program. These questions assist the program designer in first planning and later reacting to the outcomes of action during the program. Their existence also helps avoid the temptation to transmit models of behavior and to indulge in cure-alls. Further, risks of using blanket terminologies (e.g., teacher as "facilitator" or "guide") without reference to actual activities or behaviors can also be avoided by constant reference to the issues raised by the teacher-learner relationship.

(3) An understanding and awareness of the intricacies of the social and psychological processes of the classroom is central to effective teacher development, for this focus captures not only the reality of the classroom but also has direct personal relevance to participants on teacher development programs. Questions raised by an exploration of teacher and learner roles have an implicit appeal to the concerns of new entrants to the profession. They may be asking themselves, "What do I actually do when I teach?" and "What have I got to offer learners?" Experienced practitioners may have such questions as "Should I change my ways? Am I succeeding at present? What do new ideas mean for my daily work?" and "What is the basis for what I am doing in the classroom at present?" An understanding of roles also mediates between theory and practice, because it focuses on the people most intimately involved in the translating of theory into practice, who are able to test and modify theory through practice, and who are in the enviable position of being able to derive theory from practice – teachers. Investigating roles of teachers and learners thus has both theoretical and, most importantly, personal relevance.

The procedures outlined in the remainder of this chapter are based on these three characteristics of the teacher-learner role relationship.

Some tasks and procedures for raising issues of teacher and learner roles

From attitudes and values to the classroom and back

Participants in inservice programs do not usually attend such programs to have their value structures rearranged or attitudes changed. Rather, participants would most probably prefer that these remained intact; it may well be presumptuous as well as unrealistic on the part of the program leaders to insist that fundamental changes at this level be accomplished. However, effective participation in a program may necessitate teachers coming to terms with their deeper levels of thought and action. A particularly effective method of approaching the question of attitudes and values is through observation of teaching wherever this is possible, and reflection on that experience. The procedure that follows was designed to let teachers match their own perceptions of teacher and learner behavior with what they observe in a classroom (particularly when what they might observe is in some way different or alien to them) and then later to reflect on the observation.

STAGE I

The participants first undertake awareness activities aimed at orienting them to salient features of classroom activity and at the same time penetrating the deeper, more personal layers of experience and value. Reactions to views about teacher and learner behavior are the basis of these activities. The choice of initial input is important. Video recordings of classroom activity may seem an obvious choice for input media, but I rarely use them, as they preempt so many issues and sometimes deflect the attention away from the sorts of "remembering work" that may raise the values and attitudes to the surface. Rather than stimulate participants to reveal personal views, video recordings have a tendency to impose their own schemata.

Rather, the use of written descriptions of lessons, which let readers "read in" detail and provide their own visual representations (see Day, this volume, Chapter 4, for an example), or questionnaires such as the following prove a productive way of starting the process. The very open-endedness of either written descriptions or questionnaires is likely to provoke more remembered material from participants.

Identifying beliefs and attitudes about language learning

Quickly respond to the statements that follow by checking them if you agree with them, putting an X if you disagree with them, or leaving them blank if you cannot make up your mind.

1. Teachers usually stand up at the front of the class when teaching.
2. Learners are usually arranged at desks in rows.
3. Teachers decide on how fast the learners should work on learning tasks.
4. Teachers set questions for the learners to answer.
5. Learners make mistakes which teachers correct.
6. Classrooms are noisy, busy places.
7. Learners compete with each other to give answers to teachers' questions.
8. The textbook usually guides the lesson.

Now do the following:
a. Compare your responses with a colleague's.
b. With your colleague, add three more statements that you think typify the classroom situation in which you are normally accustomed to working.
c. For statements that you were unable to decide upon a response to, note your difficulties. Discuss them with your colleague.

Now look at the following statements. These statements describe classroom behavior that could be positively or negatively valued. Put + by the ones you think should be encouraged and put − by the ones you would discourage.

1. Learners stand up when they answer questions.
2. Teachers praise correct answers from learners.
3. Teachers always provide model answers to learning exercises.
4. Teachers follow lesson plans.
5. Learners collaborate on answers to questions or exercises the teacher sets.
6. Learners suggest how exercises might be done.
7. Learners respect teachers' experience and knowledge.
8. Teachers investigate the processes of their own classroom.
9. Learners reveal personal details about themselves in class.
10. Teachers discipline learners.

Again, compare your answers with a colleague.

Now form a small group, say, five persons, and try to write up to five more statements that accurately reveal personal attitudes regarding teacher and learner behavior in classrooms.

STAGE 2

A class discussion follows the group work. During this discussion, the session leader collects the "typical classroom" statements participants have produced and elicits the features from the original list that have been checked. (Alternatively, participants can write their own material on flip charts.) Further items that may come up during this phase are added if participants agree that they are typical of their own situation.

The new statements about valued and unvalued classroom behavior are then collected, and participants are asked to compare the lists and to find common themes. These are recorded by the participants as they emerge, with assistance from the session leader if necessary.

STAGE 3

Participants are now invited to consider the following questions:

— Is there a link between what we value and our behavior in the role of teacher?
— Would we expect to see similar behavior in classrooms other than our own?
— What factors might influence teachers and learners to behave differently in different classrooms?

The questions are linked to the themes drawn from the previous activity. The group's findings are discussed and noted.

STAGE 4

This stage involves preparation for observation and is motivated by these questions:

— What sorts of behavior or features of the lesson shall I watch for and listen to?
— What will these tell me about classroom role relationships?
— In what ways does the classroom I observe differ from mine and in what ways is it similar to my own?

The group members, either individually or in pairs, now generate a set of questions or themes to guide their observations. See Nunan (this volume, Chapter 5) for examples of teacher and learner behaviors the participants can focus on during an observation.

STAGE 5

The participants now observe an actual lesson and attempt to focus on the questions they have generated. Afterward they are encouraged to compare their impression of the lesson with that of the teacher. See Day (Chapter 4) and Nunan (Chapter 5) for guidance on how to complete classroom observations.

STAGE 6

Stage 6, postobservation, is a crucial stage in the sequence of activities. Decisions about how to deal with the feedback can affect the next stage of the program if the program is continuing. The initial stage of the feedback attempts to see how far participants were able to answer their own questions and what might have prevented them from doing so. This can lead to a discussion on the very purpose of observation itself. Participants could at this stage be asked to consider how useful such procedures would be in their own situation if new ideas were being tried out and how far teachers could monitor their own work when using a new idea in their own classrooms. This is especially valuable if the next phase of a program involves work on new teaching techniques or materials that embody new methodological principles. One of the main aims of such retrospective work is to keep open the links to the prospective work, and to seek to clarify links between one's expectations and the realities that might confront the teacher or observer. Further, there needs to be a way of making this plain – hence the use of the stored material from the first session outlining themes and ideas that participants have established. These may now be used as the basis for discussing the potential effects of change, guided by such questions as "What aspect of classroom behavior is most sensitive to the effects of an altered teacher role?" and "Will altered teacher roles affect...?" (Here any of the earlier themes can be entered and as many as seems fit be dealt with, while others are saved for later work.)

It is at these critical junctures that participants may come to an awareness of how different classroom roles may on the one hand be seen as behavior, and on the other as reflecting deeper beliefs, attitudes, and values regarding the classroom process. It is crucial that the session leader not be judgmental at these junctures – it is a paradox that the "trainer" may be expected to be so. While it may be easier said than done, and often the session leader may be forced to give his or her own views, it is often more productive to act reflexively, constantly challenging the participants to believe in the importance and relevance of their own views. One way of avoiding judgmental behavior is for the session leader to change roles and become the observer while the group holds its own evaluation. This is naturally a more risky venture, but it is well worth trying if the group is amenable to the idea. After all, many of the participants we deal with happily adopt a learner role congruent with norms from their own sociocultural and classroom backgrounds; one way of demonstrating alternative possibilities is to adopt a variety of roles as program tutor or leader. This course of action might, however, lead to disappointed expectations among participants, so it needs to be introduced judiciously and constantly monitored and evaluated. It can prove to be a rich source of issues and themes when working on the deeper levels of teacher and learner roles.

Exploring the implications of new teaching materials and ideas

Working on the "tools of the trade" (e.g., teaching techniques and materials) in a vacuum is always going to present teacher educators and participants with problems. Without access to live classes or opportunities to actually practice with new ideas and materials, participants in inservice programs may resent an abstract approach, lacking as it inevitably does the opportunity for live feedback and evaluation. Yet the embodiment of any new teaching approach is either the material or the techniques that carry it to the classroom. In this section, I focus on the more problematical experience of introducing new ideas and techniques to participants when they may have been removed from their normal classroom environment for "refresher courses."

Underlying any set of teaching materials or techniques is a series of assumptions regarding the nature of language and learning. Further, there may be explicit statements about the ways in which teacher and learners should work on the materials in the classroom. (See, for example, Candlin and Edelhoff's *Challenges: Teacher's Handbook, 1982.*) More often than not, however, the actual classroom processes and the roles that these activate are implicit, whether in rubrics, teachers' notes, or in the nature of the exercises themselves. These hidden agendas are the substance of any effort to bring teachers to an understanding of the materials or techniques. They can be approached in two ways: (1) by examining and uncovering the views of language and seeing what these mean for teachers' and learners' roles or (2) by examining the vehicles – the tasks, activities, and exercises – that the learners and teachers are called to work on, again uncovering the implications for potential classroom practice. In practical terms, the process may be of limited value, the feedback from live trials being a missing link. From the point of view of teachers' awareness, however, the process is extremely valuable, equipping them with the means of being critical, both of current practice and of future developments. This awareness also appeals to the deeper levels of awareness referred to in the previous section, touching on attitudes toward language, knowledge, and the learning process. With any teacher development program that features teacher and learner roles as a central focus, these deeper levels of awareness are a constantly unfolding phenomenon and are always borne in mind as a point of reference.

STAGE I

Let us assume that new materials which are founded on new interpretations of grammar are the focus of the course or program. The first phase of the work may involve a series of awareness-raising tasks focused on the participants' views on the nature of language and language learning.

Task 1
Comment on these views regarding the nature of grammar and the teaching and learning of grammar. Do you agree with any of them? Which ones? Are

there any that you cannot agree with? Would you add anything further to
any of them?

1. Students learn grammar through constant correction and repetition of
   forms and structures.
2. It's a waste of time actually teaching grammar; students learn it anyway.
3. It doesn't matter if we make mistakes – the message is much more
   important than the form.
4. It is pointless trying to teach grammar in isolation from the other major
   areas of language. In fact, the areas are so strongly interconnected that we
   should adopt an integrated approach to language teaching.
5. Students expect and want us to "do grammar" in our classes. Why should
   we disappoint them?
6. Now that we know that the communicative approach is the best way to
   do things, we can drop all the old grammar-based material.
7. There isn't a grammar of English that has descriptions to cover every
   aspect of language.

Participants are invited first to do the task on their own, and then to
compare their views with those of a colleague. They are then asked to
move directly to the next task.

Task 2
Comment on these errors made by learners. For instance, can you classify
them? Is there a pattern in the errors? Any other comments?

1. *He makes me to do it.
2. *He made me sit down and told me about it.
3. *Nowadays all children are to go to school.
4. *This instrument is called thermometer.
5. *There are a few mosquitoes, so we suffer from malaria.
6. *If I tell him he would come.
7. *He ran too fast to catch the bus.
8. *In the South West there is so much forest.
9. *In the past we had traveled on foot.
10. *I am thinking you are wrong.

Are these the sorts of error that your students make? What links can you see
between the treatment of error and your role as a language teacher? How
closely does the treatment of error relate to the teacher's general attitude to
and views on the nature of language? Are students' errors a reasonable basis
from which to begin teaching?

When participants have completed these two tasks, they are asked to
consider Barnes's (1976) characterizations of "transmission and interpretation teachers" in the light of their relationship with participants'
views on grammar and on learner error. (See Wright 1987: 62 for a
summary and discussion.) The consideration of these two poles of teachers' attitudes to knowledge and the behavior associated with the attitudes
allows participants the opportunity to see how their own attitudes to-

ward grammar relate to their attitudes toward error and the status and acquisition of knowledge in general. Questions that teachers might ask of teaching materials are now generated. For example, "Does the material allow for different interpretations, or is only one outcome or answer possible?" "Is the teacher always the final arbiter of right and wrong with the materials, or can learners impose their own definitions of right and wrong?"

STAGE 2

Participants are now presented with some new teaching material to work on. They are invited first to attempt the language learning task for themselves and then to discuss its implications in line with the questions they have generated and the questions that accompany the material. The session leader can at this stage act as an observer while the participants are doing the tasks, noting different working styles and acting as a guide where necessary. An example of the material that might be used by the group follows:

Task: How Shall I Say It?
A department head wanted to call a staff meeting, so he sat down to write a memo to the staff members. He was fairly new to the job and was anxious to give as good an impression to his staff as he could. However, he was faced with a seemingly infinite range of choices as to how to phrase his memo.

Some of the ideas that came to him appear below. Which one did he finally choose and why did he reject the others?

1. Staff meeting. 2 p.m. Tomorrow.
2. Can we have a staff meeting at 2 p.m. tomorrow?
3. How about a staff meeting at 2 p.m. tomorrow?
4. Let's all meet at 2 p.m. tomorrow.
5. When the staff meets at 2 p.m. tomorrow we will discuss the following.
6. Could the staff get together for a meeting at 2 p.m. tomorrow?
7. I hope no staff member will forget the staff meeting at 2 p.m. tomorrow.
8. Is it all right if we have a staff meeting at 2 p.m. tomorrow?
9. We'll have a staff meeting at 2 p.m. tomorrow.
10. I think we ought to have a staff meeting at 2 p.m. tomorrow.
11. There will be a staff meeting at 2 p.m. tomorrow.
12. At 2 p.m. tomorrow staff should meet in the teachers' room.

What features of grammar does this exercise exploit? Is there a correct answer?
What sorts of activity would the teacher have to undertake in a class where the learners were working on an exercise like this?
Do you find this type of exercise unusual? How would your learners react to this type of task?

Having worked through these tasks, participants should now be in a position to draw up a list of criteria with which to evaluate any new teaching technique or teaching materials that they may be asked or wish to work with in their own classes. The combination of awareness-raising and experiential processes outlined earlier generates a vast amount of material, and the session leader is faced with the daunting task of assisting the participants in making sense of it all. By constantly referring back to the teachers' own experience and knowledge of their own classrooms, the session leader should be able to elicit themes that characterize the norms of the classrooms where they work. At the same time, one has to be aware of the possibility of discussion becoming too abstract or diffuse (or even too theoretical). Too often teacher educators assume teachers to be in a state of pretheoretical or atheoretical ignorance before they embark on such programs; yet participants have most likely built up theories over years of actual experience in the classroom. The role of teacher educators might better be to make these theories explicit during the course.

One advantage of the procedures outlined here is that the tasks may be attempted in any order, depending on the focus of the program as a whole. Thus one could begin with Barnes's conceptualization of "transmission and interpretation teachers" (a deeper-level task, probing values and attitudes) and move on to the materials, ending with a discussion of the nature of the view of language being presented. A more risky but nonetheless exciting alternative is to allow participants to work through the materials in any order that they wish to and with whatever organization of the group they prefer. These choices depend on the underlying philosophy of the program itself; if the program is to introduce participants to a process syllabus, for example, the latter course would seem most natural. Even if the aspirations of the program are no more than "refreshment," the organizational issues hinted at earlier must be confronted. Designers of programs, session leaders, and tutors all transmit their roles through the ways in which they organize their programs. This in itself could become a central issue in a teacher development program, where appropriate.

Introducing teacher and learner roles

I shall here briefly describe a procedure worked out with a colleague, Roy Taylor, for introducing preservice trainees[1] to major themes in language teaching, including teacher and learner roles. Through a series of four lessons in a language unknown to the participants, we introduce such broad themes as views of language, views of learning, classroom

---

1 The course referred to is a 4-year bachelor of education (honors) undergraduate course for overseas students in teaching English as a second language. The sequence outlined takes place in the first four weeks of the course.

organization, selection of language items for teaching and learning, and teacher and learner roles, showing how the themes interrelate and how they are interdependent – that by altering one element, the others change, too.

STAGE 1

Stage 1 consists of lessons in a foreign language. In each of the four sessions, the group is taught the foreign language for forty minutes, the teacher choosing a different "method" each time. The "methods" include an adaptation of the Direct Method, a Grammar-Translation lesson, Community Language Learning, and what we call an "immersion" lesson in which the group is cast adrift with a written text in the foreign language, dictionaries, and grammars, and asked to try to translate the text into English.

STAGE 2

The lesson is followed up with a short evaluation session that focuses mainly on how the group enjoyed the lesson, whether they feel they learned anything, how similar it was to previous learning experiences (of language and other subject areas), and what they think were the positive and negative features of the lesson.

STAGE 3

A follow-up session outlining the main theoretical bases of each lesson is held, concentrating on learning theories and linking these with views of language. Teacher and learner roles are introduced to link in with these themes. All the more "abstract" ideas are linked to actual procedures and examples in the lessons. Short readings relevant to the theoretical basis of each lesson are also discussed, both in these sessions and as take-home assignments.

STAGE 4

The trainee group is divided into smaller working groups at the end of the sequence of four sessions and is asked to draw up a summary of the main features of the language lessons they have participated in. (A sample of some students' summaries is included in the Appendix.)

The course in TESOL principles and methods then proceeds to explore the themes laid down during the language learning sequence in more detail and depth, with longer sessions on learning and factors affecting learning, such as motivation and sociocultural factors. Teacher and learner roles are not only a focal point of reference but a unifying feature, for they are a channel to the actual classroom situation in which teaching and learning take place. The depth of the training group's work is naturally limited by their near total lack of experience as teachers. Nevertheless, as learners they have a great deal to offer to the debate. Our experience after three years of running this course is that groups are better able to see the relevance and implications of teaching techniques and teaching materials (which are introduced in the second phase of the program) when these are placed in a broader framework.

Implications for further work

The rationale and procedures set out in the preceding sections are aimed at demonstrating some of the possibilities that a focus on teacher and learner roles can bring about in teacher development programs. As I stated earlier, they are illustrations of ongoing work in what is a comparatively new field. Thus there are doubts and questions. These may be summarized as follows:

1. What sorts of task are most suitable for raising teacher-learner role issues in teacher development programs? Are awareness-raising exercises potentially too threatening to participants, particularly when they engage value and belief systems? A great deal of sensitivity to participants' feelings and cultural backgrounds is predicated. This is particularly the case when dealing with language issues with nonnative speaker participants. (It may be of interest to note that all the activities described have been used with nonnative speakers of English from a wide variety of cultural backgrounds.)
2. What sorts of task sequence are desirable? Do we begin at the deeper levels of values, attitudes, and beliefs and work outward? Do we begin by examining abstractions like teaching material? Or start with on-the-spot classroom observations? My experience to date suggests that the former and the latter are suitable, but that examining abstractions is best informed by remembering or observational work. As I have already suggested, there are exciting possibilities for participants to devise their own routes through banks of tasks once work has begun, starting at whatever level they feel is appropriate.
3. When should these issues be introduced to a teacher development program? At the outset? Or when the agendas have been laid down? One observation I have made is that once participants confront the deeper issues, they are intuitively attracted to them and, because they perceive the personal relevance of the issues, pursue them relentlessly to the near exclusion of other issues. Program designers need to work out plans with this in mind if they are to use teacher and learner roles as a theme. Alternatively, one may argue that, despite its in-

herent risks and drawbacks, the more open-ended approach advocated in this chapter, with issues as the primary content of the programs, renders redundant an instrumental approach concentrating on techniques and "new ideas" in a linear, instrumental fashion.

4. The "trainer role" paradox is inevitably a critical issue in programs that focus on teacher and learner roles. One is forced to reconsider one's own role in the light of participating in values- and attitude-related activities. Yet participants have expectations. To what extent does one disappoint and challenge these expectations? How does the "trainer as model teacher" scenario stand up under such scrutiny?

A natural development of the issues I have been discussing is the potential for action research as an element of teacher development programs. (See Hopkins 1985 for an excellent introductory guide to this area, and Nunan, this volume, Chapter 5.) Teacher educators contentedly implant new ideas in teachers in inservice programs and sincerely wish them well when they return to their classrooms. However, they often fail to provide them with the means to monitor and explore their classrooms once they return. Seen in the light of curriculum renewal and reform, these proposals are not without significance. Not only do teachers require understanding of new ideas, they also need the means to examine the effects of these ideas. Through action research, a unity of purpose of curriculum design, syllabus design and development, teacher development, and the means of evaluation is forged. An extension of the types of reflective activity I have outlined is action research – reflection lays the foundation. The next challenge for all participants in curriculum implementation, from teacher development program designers to teachers – some may say to classroom language learners – is to begin to explore this area.

Appendix: Group reactions to four different methods of instruction

Content	Method 1	Method 2
Language items	Teacher selects vocabulary.	Teacher selects grammar/ vocabulary.
Language skills	Listening and speaking.	Writing and reading.
Teacher's role	Trainer (very strict).	Teacher (strict).
Learner's role	Mechanical.	Depressing.
Classroom organization	Teacher in front of class.	Teacher in front of class.
Learning theory	Inductive: "Audiolingual," "Direct."	Deductive: "Grammar Translation."
Advantages	Learners are less pressured, thus encouraged to learn in a relaxed way.	Learners can generate sentences because rules are given.
Disadvantages	Time consuming because people learn at different speeds.	Neglect of spoken form.
Like	Easier to remember.	A faster system to remember.
Dislike	Learners were forced.	Learners are very much pressured.

Method 3	Method 4
Students select items.	Teacher selects items (texts).
Speaking, listening, and writing (a little).	Reading.
Helper (tutor/counselor).	Advisor (assistant).
Not very active as a whole.	Active (have to translate, write, etc.).
Students in a circle with teacher outside of circle.	Teacher in front of class.
Affective: "Community Language Learning" (CLL).	Deductive: "Immersion" (total immersion).
More engagement and involvement for the learner. Facts are not united.	Helps cultivate independence.
The students who do not get involved will not fully benefit from CLL.	Materials selected are irrelevant to learners.
The students are under no pressure to talk.	—
Difficult to memorize if learners do not participate in class and do not listen carefully.	In the end, if learners are fast, frustration occurs.

Questions and tasks

Chapter 4 (Day)

1. Select a teacher preparation program you are familiar with. What is the balance between subject-matter knowledge and action-systems knowledge?

2. Make an ethnographic record of a videotaped lesson or part of a lesson along the lines suggested by Day. What does it reveal about the lesson that was not immediately apparent from a casual viewing? How long did it take you to compile the ethnography? (Express this as a percentage of actual lesson time.) What are the difficulties likely to confront student teachers in doing an ethnography? How might these be overcome?

3. Analyze a lesson or lesson segment using one of the following:
— seating chart
— verbal-flow diagram
— at-task chart
— movement-pattern diagram
What insights did this provide? What would be the likely advantages/difficulties for student teachers in undertaking this exercise?

4. What is the sense in which Day uses the term *classroom management*? Is this similar to or different from the sense in which Richards (Chapter 1) uses the term?

Chapter 5 (Nunan)

5. How is the term *action research* defined by Nunan? What are its key characteristics? Why should teachers be encouraged to adopt an action research orientation to their classrooms? What problems are likely to be created by this?

6. How might the program described by Nunan be integrated into a program you are familiar with? What changes/adaptations/modifications would you make?

7. Analyze a lesson or part of a lesson using one or more of the instruments set out in the Appendix to Nunan. What insights are revealed that are not immediately apparent from a casual or unstructured observation of the lesson?

Chapter 6 (Wright)

8. Wright stresses the importance of studying teacher and learner role relationships, arguing that awareness of these relationships is central to effective teacher development. List and prioritize the reasons he advances for this argument.

9. What are the dangers of getting preservice and inservice trainees to confront their own attitudes and value structures? How does Wright suggest that issues relating to values and attitudes be raised?

10. Select some teaching materials and develop a series of tasks, along the lines suggested by Wright, that teachers-in-preparation might undertake, which might reveal assumptions in the materials about the nature of language and language learning.

11. How potentially useful is the technique of teaching student teachers a foreign language as a way of introducing major themes in language teaching? Evaluate the procedure outlined by Wright. What changes, modifications, or adaptations, if any, would you make?

General

12. Using data from Chapters 3–6, summarize the benefits to teachers-in-preparation of direct classroom observation and analysis.

13. In what ways do Chapters 3–6 address the problem of relating theory and practice?

14. What similarities and differences are there in the programs described by Nunan and Wright?

Part III The practicum

In many teacher education programs, the practicum or practice teaching experience is the central component. It is through the process of teaching a class of foreign language learners and receiving feedback that the student teacher has a chance to apply knowledge and skills gained elsewhere or to develop strategies for handling the different dimensions of a language lesson. Although a number of other chapters in the book deal with processes that relate to the practicum, the three chapters in this section are devoted specifically to this subject.

Freeman in Chapter 7 examines the interaction between the teacher educator and the student teacher. The language teacher educator is presented as one who can intervene in, confirm, and/or redirect the student teacher's learning process throughout the practice teaching experience. Freeman outlines various types of intervention, which are distinguished by the educator-trainee relationship on which they are based and/or the purposes they are meant to achieve. Freeman proposes that to be maximally effective, the form of intervention and the relationship it establishes should match the aspects of teaching that intervention is intended to teach the student teacher. The chapter concludes with a paradigm for how and why to intervene in the student teacher's practice teaching.

In Chapter 8 Gebhard describes an ethnographic study in practice teaching based on seven inexperienced ESL (English as a second language) student teachers. He describes the interaction that takes place during the practicum and explores the behavior changes that take place as a result of such interaction. The research indicates that five of the seven teachers changed in four main areas: setting up and carrying out a lesson, use of classroom space, selection of content, and treatment of students' language errors. The implications of the study for teacher educators and researchers are also discussed.

In the last chapter of this section, Pennington explores five metaphors for teaching: teaching as magic, teaching as art, teaching as profession, teaching as craft, and teaching as science. She opts for the view of teaching as profession, which requires the development of both skills and judgment. The practicum provides an arena where knowledge and skills can be developed. In particular, it can help the student teacher develop self-knowledge and knowledge of the students. Techniques for developing such knowledge are provided.

Part III

The authors of these chapters share a common concern with the concept of professionalism. Underlying each chapter is a view of the teacher as autonomous professional, and each author approaches the practicum with the educational implications of professionalism in mind. Of particular significance is the establishment of appropriate relationships between teacher educator and student teachers.

7 Intervening in practice teaching

Donald Freeman

Teaching is first and foremost a "helping profession," which depends on the relationship created between the teacher and the learner. It is crucial, therefore, to determine which forms of help, or teaching, are most effective within that relationship. Such a determination depends on a number of variables: the purpose of the help (its objective), the particular context in which the help is being offered, and the interactions that make up the process of offering and receiving it. This chapter examines a specific teaching–helping relationship, that of language teacher educator and student teacher, within the context of practice teaching. The purpose of this relationship is for the student teachers to develop, practice, and refine their competence as language teachers.

A particular orientation to teacher preparation in language teaching underlies this stated purpose. It assumes that the goal is for student teachers to develop the independent capacity to make informed teaching decisions and to assess the impact of those decisions on both their own and their students' learning (Freeman, 1989) – in the words of Orem (1981), "to know what they do, how and why." This orientation relies on two broad educational strategies, *teacher training* and *teacher development* (Freeman 1982; in press), which when in balance lead to achievement of this goal. (See Richards, this volume, Chapter 1.)

The key issue is balance: between the strategies themselves, and also between the strategy and the content to be taught by that strategy. A "training" strategy, when it is used exclusively, can lead to an overemphasis on teaching skills and behaviors at the expense of developing the student teacher's independent resources and capacity to take charge of what he or she is doing. It does not follow however that "training" has an exclusively negative impact; rather, there are aspects of teaching that are most effectively and efficiently conveyed, or taught, in this manner.

The "development" strategy, in contrast, emphasizes the processes of reasoning that underlie what the student teacher does in the classroom; the teachers' relation to what they know and how they know it (Shulman 1987) is the central focus. This is clearly appropriate and effective for complex and idiosyncratic aspects of teaching, although it may be less so for discrete teaching skills or behaviors. The appropriate balance depends, then, on the subject matter: the aspects of teaching to be learned

Donald Freeman

or taught. Thus the teacher educator–student teacher relationship must be seen within this broad framework; its purpose, interactions, and outcomes – both intended and actual – must be viewed according to the aspects of teaching they address.

In this chapter I propose a general view of the teacher educator–student teacher relationship and discuss three types of intervention that can take place within it in order to achieve particular purposes. These purposes are based on what the educator is trying to teach the student teacher about teaching and reflect the former's perceptions of the practice teaching segment as well as teaching overall. However, the way in which those perceptions are conveyed – the process of intervening – is itself teaching, and is as important as what the educator intends to convey. There is, therefore, a peculiar duality: in intervening, the educator *teaches* the student teacher *teaching*. The student teacher, in turn, learns from both the *content* and the *process* of the intervention (Freeman 1987).

Thus an examination of the relationship between the content and the process of such interventions seems important. Before doing so, however, it may be useful to define the scope of the following discussion by clarifying a few key terms.

A glossary of key terms

By *student teacher* I mean anyone engaged in learning to teach, whether through a formal educational setting, such as a course or practicum; on-the-job orientation; training; or an inservice program. The term *student teacher* need not imply someone with little or no previous teaching experience. He or she may be new to teaching generally, to language teaching specifically, or may be experienced in either or both. The level and type of the student teacher's experience helps determine the type of intervention the educator chooses.

By *teacher educator* I refer to the individual who oversees and in some way facilitates the student teacher's learning process. I purposefully do not use the term *teacher trainer,* as I want to maintain a distinction between the processes of teacher training and teacher development as outlined earlier, which coexist within the superordinate framework of teacher education (Freeman, 1989). Insofar as *teacher trainer* can refer to the person who oversees practice teaching, it would be accurate. If it connotes *how* that function is exercised, it limits, in effect, the educator to one strategy of intervention and thus confuses the discussion.

By *practice teaching* I mean any portion of teaching, from micro-teaching to teaching an individual lesson to a sustained practicum, over which the student teacher has direct and individual control. Thus a master teacher—student teacher arrangement (that is, one in which master teacher and student teacher co-teach a class) may qualify as practice teaching in this definition; it depends entirely on whether the student teacher is responsible and therefore accountable for the teaching that takes place. Practice teaching can occur as part of a formal teacher education program or it can be part of an on-the-job orientation or development effort, as long as there is someone who fulfills the function of teacher educator in that context.

Finally, by *intervention* I refer to the way in which the teacher educator expresses specific *perceptions* and *input* about the practice teaching to the student teacher. This includes both the *process* (how the teacher educator intervenes) and the *content* (what input he or she introduces). *Perceptions* refer to what the teacher educator sees in the practice teaching, and *input* refers to what the teacher educator may decide to include in the intervention based on what he or she has seen. The term *intervention* has an unfortunate clinical ring to it, which is not my intention; I have not, however, found a more suitable word.

The relationship

Intervention in practice teaching is based on the view that the student teacher can be helped to teach more effectively through the input and perceptions of the teacher educator. There is a basic assumption that one person can teach another to teach; otherwise student teachers would simply be left to figure it out on their own. This contrasts with the "self-help" view, according to which student teachers learn to describe, diagnose, and thus alter their own practice. In this view (Fanselow 1987b) the educator supplies the system of description and trains the student teachers in its use, but leaves the conclusions up to them. While these two views need not be completely opposed, they do differ significantly in their definition of the role of the educator.

Central to the interventionist view is the notion of what it means to foster change in other people by helping them do or learn something. Gibb, in a brief article titled "Is Help Helpful?", asserts:

Helping is a central social process ... Help, however, is not always helpful. The recipient ... may not see it as useful. The offering may not lead to greater satisfaction or to better performance. Even less often does the helping process ... lead to continuous growth on the part of the participants. (1964: 25)

Gibb goes on to outline typical reactions that the recipient of the proffered help may have, noting:

Donald Freeman

TABLE I. THE HELPING RELATIONSHIP

Orientations that help	Orientations that hinder
1. Reciprocal trust (confidence, warmth, acceptance)	1. Distrust (fear, punitiveness, defensiveness)
2. Cooperative learning (inquiry, exploration, quest)	2. Teaching (training, giving advice, indoctrinating)
3. Mutual growth (becoming, actualizing, fulfilling)	3. Evaluating (fixing, correcting, providing a remedy)
4. Reciprocal openness (spontaneity, candor, honesty)	4. Strategy (planning for, maneuvering, manipulation)
5. Shared problem solving (defining problems, producing alternative solutions, testing)	5. Modeling (demonstrating, giving information, guiding)
6. Autonomy (freedom, interdependence, equality)	6. Coaching (molding, steering, controlling)
7. Experimentation (play, innovation, provisional try)	7. Patterning (standard, static, fixed)

Source: Gibb (1964: 25).

In certain cases the recipient . . . becomes more helpless and dependent, less able to make his own decisions and initiate his own actions . . . less willing to take risks, more concerned about propriety and conformity. We have also seen . . . recipients become more creative, less dependent upon helpers, more willing to risk decisions, . . . less concerned about conformity, and more effective at working independently and interdependently.

What then distinguishes the help that spawns independence from that which tends to perpetuate dependence by the recipient? Gibb summarizes, in Table 1, seven distinguishing characteristics. Taken at face value, these characteristics suggest an educating process predicated almost entirely on the needs of the student teacher; it is hard to envision how the requirements of the content would fit. In Gibb's view, the student teachers would determine, in conjunction with the teacher educator, what they needed to address or improve in their teaching; there would be little place for the teacher educator to tell or show the student teachers what they ought to do, even if that were necessary. What happens, for example, if the student teacher is presenting misinformation about the language? Prescriptions based on the educator's perceptions in the practice teaching or on an understanding of teaching could, in this view, create dependence and resentment in the student teacher.

The problem is, however, that teaching does include aspects that are unequivocal. If the student teacher presents inaccurate information about the language, for example, the teacher educator will most likely feel the need to correct it. Teaching also includes aspects that are commonly agreed upon, although not necessarily absolute. If, for example, the student teacher consistently ridicules students' contributions while simultaneously encouraging their active participation in the lesson, it may help to point out that such ridicule will most likely frustrate the students.

The danger comes in assuming that teaching is uniquely a matter of objective principles about language and learning, and that all aspects can – or should – be laid out by the teacher educator for the student teacher. Such a doctrinaire approach can lead to formulaic teaching and to prescriptive intervention by the educator in everything the student teacher does. Idiosyncratic aspects of the student's teaching are stymied as the relationship becomes a matter of the student teacher replicating the educator's views and practices in the classroom.

This can become a form of "learned helplessness" (Abramson, Seligman, and Teasdale 1978), where the student teacher comes to depend on the teacher educator's standards and criteria in a "Did I do it right?" relationship. Given the goal of fostering independent teachers who know what they are doing and why, such a relationship is not productive. There may be instances, depending on the aspects of teaching to be taught and the level of the student teachers' previous experience, where such intervention is temporarily appropriate. For instance, Copeland (1980) reports a preference among a group of beginning teachers in preservice training for directive supervision.

The intervention creates a relationship that links the student teacher, the teacher educator, and the content through a specific process. But the form of intervention must vary according to what the student teacher needs to learn. Each intervention must integrate content (i.e., what aspect of teaching is to be taught) and process (i.e., how that content is presented). The following three synopses each describe a form of intervention designed to achieve a particular purpose in the learning of teaching.

The directive option

In the directive form of intervention, adapted from "the supervisory approach" (Freeman 1982), the teacher educator comments on the student teacher's teaching, making concrete proposals for change. The educator establishes the purpose of the intervention, determines the points to be raised with the student teacher based on the observation, and makes a brief statement on each point to which the student teacher may or may not respond. Discussion often ensues from the intervention, but the roles are very clear: The teacher educator "directs" and the student teacher "does."

For example, after observing a vocabulary lesson in which the teacher has modeled new vocabulary from a picture, the teacher educator may feel the student teacher needs to use the students' prior knowledge in structuring the lesson. Having established this as the purpose of the intervention, the educator may propose that the student teacher elicit known vocabulary from the students before introducing new items, in order to see what they already know. A discussion may follow on what to do with the elicited vocabulary, during which the educator may make suggestions or give further direction.

The purpose of directive intervention is to improve the student teacher's performance according to educator's criteria. This form of intervention rests explicitly on the teacher educator's view of what constitutes good and effective teaching (Freeman 1983; Gebhard, this volume, Chapter 10), which is to some extent inherent in all supervision. It is the student teacher's job to implement the changes proposed by the educator to achieve that end.

In one sense, this directive process is the most common form of intervention to teach teaching. It seems to grow out of that almost natural urge to tell another person how to do something. Whether it is effective or not depends in large measure on the content of the intervention.

Telling the student teacher how to elicit known vocabulary deals with a technical skill in teaching. It is something that one can tell another how to do and allows for concrete evaluation. There are other positive effects: It may lead to attitudinal changes in the students, who may come to feel more engaged in the lesson, and it may help student teachers to realize that students bring a lot of knowledge to the learning situation.

Consider, however, if directive intervention were used explicitly to redirect the student teacher's attitude. The educator might have observed impatience and a lack of tolerance on the student teacher's part, and may have intervened by saying, "I'd like you to be a little more patient with your students." In this instance, the directive process does not suit its content, the issue of attitude. By invoking subjective criteria for patience, the educator has not framed the content of the intervention in a concrete or accessible manner. The student teacher is being asked to change personality traits rather than actions.

This does not imply that complex and subjective aspects of teaching, such as attitude, cannot be addressed through this form of intervention. However, it is incumbent on the educator to present them in accessible ways so that the student teacher knows exactly what to do. In this case, the educator might say, "I noticed that you seemed to cut students off as they were answering. I'd like you to try this: When you feel you need to come in, count to five silently before you do so." Although this intervention is directive, it is concrete; it leaves the student teacher knowing precisely what steps to take. However, it may be harder to assess whether that external change leads to the internal shift in attitude sought by the educator. Thus, while it is possible to address such aspects of teaching through this form of intervention, other forms may be more effective.

The alternatives option

Another intervention involves the use of alternatives. The educator chooses a point from the practice teaching and raises it with the student teacher. The educator then proposes a limited number of alternative ways to handle that point in the lesson. The student teacher rejects or selects from among the alternatives. Discussion follows about the student teacher's criteria for the choices he or she has made.

The purpose of this intervention is to develop the student teacher's awareness of the choices involved in deciding what and how to teach and, more importantly, to develop the ability to establish and articulate the criteria that inform those decisions. Thus the student teacher's actual choice of alternatives is less important than the *reason* for choosing the alternative. The educator limits the number of alternatives so that they can be easily remembered and discussed. Having only two alternatives implies a right or wrong answer, so three or four are preferable. Likewise the alternatives need to be sufficiently distinct that each provokes discussion, yet must not be so absurd as to be easily dismissed.

The educator avoids showing a preference for any of the alternatives. If the purpose is to direct a specific change in the student teacher's classroom practice, then the whole exchange can easily become loaded and potentially manipulative. In such a case, it is preferable to address what needs to be changed through directive intervention, so that both parties know where they stand.

Because the alternative options form is based on the student teacher's activity and not on the educator's criteria for how to improve that activity, it lends itself to addressing the less technical aspects of teaching. To return to the attitudinal example cited earlier, with this option the educator might say:

> "I noticed that you seemed to interrupt as students were answering; one thing you could do would be to set a time limit for the student to answer – you could even bring an egg timer; another thing would be to ask the same question to three students at the same time and let the fastest one answer; or you could ask other students to help the student having problems..."

The student teacher's response to each alternative is the heart of the intervention. In the responses, and in the subsequent querying by the educator (Ed), criteria for the student teacher's (ST) actions and decisions begin to emerge:

ST: I don't like the timer idea...
Ed: Why not?

ST: Well, for one thing, it puts too much pressure on the student. And for another, it's pretty hokey.

Ed: What about the other alternatives?

ST: The second one might help a bit; I'm not sure. The reason I usually cut a student off is because he's taking so long to answer that I'm afraid the others will get bored.

Ed: So how would this help?

ST: It would give the others something to do...

Ed: Wouldn't the third alternative do the same thing, asking the question to three people at the same time?

ST: Yeah, but that would create a lot of competition in the class.

Ed: Why don't you want to have competition?...

In this discussion, the student teacher has begun to articulate the issue: that of keeping the whole class engaged while one student is answering. At the same time, the student teacher is establishing a criterion for teaching: to avoid creating pressure or competition in the classroom. The educator has played the role of devil's advocate, provoking the student teacher through specific alternatives to begin examining the reasons for what he or she is doing.

The intervention could proceed in a variety of ways while preserving the same focus (i.e., what the student teacher did in interrupting students) and the same purpose (i.e., having the student teacher clarify the reasoning behind that decision). For instance, after the discussion might continue thus:

ST: I don't like any of those alternatives.

Ed: Why not?

ST: Because they're all pretty artificial...

Ed: How are they artificial?

ST: Oh come on! Using an egg timer...Or turning the class into a shouting match over who gets the answer first.

Ed: Why is that bad?

ST: Well because...

Thus the discussion turns to the student teacher's reasons. The student teacher might also try, consciously or not, to avoid choosing an alternative. Or there could be an attempt at role reversal in which the student teacher would try to draw the educator into stating a preference by asking for direction:

ST: Which one would you do?

Ed: I'm not sure. It would depend on what I was after.

ST: I don't understand.

Ed: Well, I might use the timer if I wanted to inject some pressure into the process.

ST: Pressure wouldn't work too well with my students – they'd all freeze up.
Ed: Have you tried it?
ST: Yeah, when we played a game last week...

It is worth noting here that while moving temporarily out of the querying role, the educator was able to work toward the same purpose of having the student teacher identify reasons for the actions he or she took.

At the core of this form of intervention is self-discipline on the part of the educator. He or she needs to resist the temptation to become what Curran (1976) refers to as an "answer person," supplying solutions to problems or expounding reasons for classroom decisions. Such a stance is out of place in addressing the student teacher's reasoning process and can become counterproductive by creating a dependency, albeit temporary, of the student teacher on the educator. Such power may be seductive for the educator, but it does not lead to independent thought and action on the part of the student teacher.

Thus if the educator intends to address aspects of technical practice observed in teaching, he or she can do so through directive intervention. If, however, the educator wants to address complex issues of pedagogical reasoning, he or she needs to use a process of intervention in which the student teacher takes on more responsibility. The alternatives option offers a structure for that shift in that the intervention remains focused on specific aspects of the practice teaching, while delving into the pedagogical reasoning and decisions on which that teaching is based.

The educator retains control, however, by directing the student teacher to specific issues in order to facilitate development of certain criteria. Thus this form of intervention does not afford the student teacher complete jurisdiction over what he or she does. It does not achieve the fullness of the helping relationship described by Gibb, which brings us to a third form of intervention.

The nondirective option

In *On Becoming a Person*, Carl Rogers makes the statement in regard to psychotherapy that "no approach which relies on knowledge, upon training, upon the acceptance of something which is taught, is of any use in changing a person" (1961: 32). Rogers goes on to outline a process that he refers to as client-centered therapy (see also Rogers 1951), through which the client discovers or comes to recognize the meaning and rationale of his or her own behavior. Curran, a student of Rogers, describes this as the capacity for "self-agency" (1978): arriving at the solutions that one can find only for oneself.

What is crucial, then, in this form of interaction is how to structure the role of the other, be it Rogers's therapist or Curran's language teacher. To cast the issue in the terms used here: What form of intervention can preserve the student teacher's capacity for "self-agency" and at the same time give the educator a productive role in the process? The critical element lies in the relationship of the student teacher and the educator, which must:

1. allow the student teacher to sort through the practice teaching experience without interference or direction from the educator, to find individual solutions; and
2. allow the educator to participate in this process and to contribute from knowledge and experience without directing the student teacher to specific conclusions or courses of action.

The purpose of this intervention (called a nondirective approach in Freeman 1982), then, is to provide the student teacher with a forum to clarify perceptions of what he or she is doing in teaching and for the educator to fully understand, although not necessarily to accept or agree with, those perceptions. Further, it allows the student teacher to identify a course of action based on his or her own perceptions and what the educator offers, and to decide whether and how to act. The balance to be struck is between "understanding" (with the educator recognizing the student teacher's "world") and "standing" (with the educator "standing" in relation to what he or she has understood) (Curran 1976, 1978).

Stevick (1980: 106) describes this process of "understanding" as "hold[ing] back from asking questions, telling about [one's] own experience, and from making suggestions." It is, Stevick acknowledges, an "unnatural" way of interacting, but the understander does so because of "faith in the other person's ability to come up with what he needs. Questions, suggestions, or the understander's own experiences," Stevick continues, "would only lay on . . . expectations and pull [the other person] into the understander's world."

How does this nondirective intervention work in practice? Returning to the student teacher who cut students off, the educator using a nondirective intervention might initiate the discussion with this observation: "I noticed that at times students didn't get to complete their answers to your questions – that sometimes you moved on without having them finish their responses." The discussion might continue:

ST: Huh, I didn't think I did that. I always waited . . . Well, actually with Juan I did kind of cut him off because he takes forever to get anything out.
Ed: You got kind of impatient waiting . . .

112

ST: Not impatient, no . . . so much as worried that other students were getting bored. I figure if it bugs me, it must get to them. I mean, they have to be with him all day long. But I suppose they could be used to it by now.

Ed: So it's hard to know what effect Juan is having on the others, but it gets to you.

ST: Yeah, sometimes; it depends on how I am. Maybe today I was more nervous because you were there and I wasn't sure we were going to get to the last activity which I really wanted you to see . . .

Ed: You mean to the role play?

ST: Yeah, I wanted to get through that . . .

Ed: Sounds like you were invested in that activity and maybe your mind was ahead on it, and Juan seemed to be slowing things down.

ST: I guess I kind of felt that way . . .

This stage might continue, or it might wind down as the student teacher identifies some of the things that went on in the lesson and why. The educator signals involvement and "understanding" of what the student teacher is saying by responding with summarizing comments. When it seems appropriate, the educator "stands" to contribute from his or her experience and perceptions, yet does not propose solutions or direct courses of action. That choice remains up to the student teacher. It is worth noting the explicitness of the transition: It is almost like putting in the clutch before shifting gears in an automobile.

Ed: You know this situation we've been talking about – the tension between what is going on at the moment versus what you have planned. A couple of thoughts come to mind . . . I am really aware of it in the morning when I'm getting my kids ready for nursery school and the little one wants to tie her own shoes, and all I can think about is what I have to do. I find it helps if I can see it from her point of view – that she really wants to do it herself. Seeing it that way doesn't make my issue go away, but it helps to balance things and can release some of the pressure I feel. Sometimes, too, I just put her in the car and let her tie her shoes as we drive.

In "standing," the educator is careful not to choose an example from the language classroom or even from teaching. Rather, to reinforce a neutral stance vis-à-vis the student teacher's experience, the educator selects an example from another realm, yet one that captures the essential issue in the teaching situation in the student teacher's view. This allows the student teacher to make whatever connections he or she chooses, to pursue the point or to drop it – in short, to "come up with what he needs."

This form of intervention addresses the full complexity of teaching.

While it may start from a focus initiated by the educator, the course it takes is determined for the most part by the student teacher and by their interaction. The student teacher works from an individual view of teaching, to articulate that view with reference to the practice teaching segment, to address the problems in it, and to discover independent solutions. The role of the educator is to support, yet not direct, in that process. While the educator draws on the wealth of personal experience and understanding of teaching, he or she is careful to keep the perspective that it is the student teacher who is learning to teach. Thus on the surface, this nondirective form of intervention comes closest to Gibb's criteria for effective and helpful help.

Intervention: from training to development

Teaching someone something as complex and multifaceted as language teaching cannot be limited to one form of relationship between the educator and the student teacher; it requires, in a sense, a true harmony of ends and means. The content itself – language teaching – requires examination of its parts: specific skills and aspects of knowledge. One must likewise consider the whole: What is effective language teaching? Most importantly, one has to examine the reasoning and decision making that bind the parts and the whole together in the activity of teaching a particular lesson (Freeman 1989).

Access to the content may be achieved in different ways. The student teachers can be "told" the parts, but each person must arrive at the whole independently in order for it to be meaningful. Each student teacher must come to realize that the connections between the parts and the whole depend on individual reasoning, the clarity of which allows one to adjust the parts so that they fit more effectively into one's view of the whole.

To intervene in this process the teacher educator must place what the student teacher is doing in practice teaching within his or her view of the whole of teaching. This view can come from two sources: in the directive or alternatives options, it comes from the educator's view of effective teaching; in the nondirective option, it represents a melding of the student teacher's and the educator's views. The teacher educator then intervenes to create change in the student teacher's reasoning or decision-making process. The change may be finite and immediately assessable – that is, trainable – as in the directive option, or it may be internal and open-ended – that is, developmental – as with the other two options.

Table 2 summarizes the interrelation between the options, viewed along a continuum from training to development. It describes the central

TABLE 2. TRAINING/DEVELOPMENT: A MODEL FOR EDUCATING TEACHERS

	Training ⟶ development continuum			
	Directive option	Alternatives option	Nondirective option	
Central issue	"What do I teach?"	"How do I teach?"	"Why do I teach what I teach?" "Why do I teach as I do?"	
Stance: observer–teacher relationship	Observer is authority; teacher is implementer	Observer is foil, "devil's advocate"; teacher is chooser of alternatives	Observer is "understander," outside perspective, "seed planter"; teacher is chooser, implementer, authority	
Contents of observer's response	Discrete points that can reach mastery through specific courses of action	Possible alternatives illustrating a choice; variety of mastery possible	Open-ended discussion, based on a "questing"/"understanding" relationship	
Techniques	Brief statements with a 15-second limit (see Stevick 1980) "Standing" responses (see Curran 1976)	Alternative possible solutions (see Freeman 1982)	Open-ended questioning, "questing," "understanding," "seed planting" (see Curran 1976; Freeman 1982)	

issues each addresses and the relationship, content, and principal techniques of each intervention.

Concluding thoughts

The purpose of intervention is change: change that moves the student teacher toward, or in relation to, a view of the whole of language teaching. When the educator intervenes "to help the student teacher do a better job," *better* implies a view of "good" versus "bad" teaching (Freeman 1983; Gebhard, this volume, Chapter 10). As Gibb observed, certain forms of change tend to perpetuate the student teacher's dependence on the educator's view of teaching, because assessment is based on the latter. Other forms point toward increasing interdependence and a shared assessment of change. In any case, change implies a view of language teaching on which the change is based and toward which it moves.

Thus the issue is not who intervenes with whom. Although the relationship between educator and student teacher may generate friction, it would be a mistake to assume that by removing one of the protagonists the intervention becomes more objective and thus less problematical. No intervention is value-free. Even when one intervenes through reflection or self-observation to change one's own teaching, one does so based on what one sees as "good" teaching.

Descriptive systems such as FOCUS (Fanselow 1987a), COLT (Allen, Fröhlich, and Spada 1984), or TALOS (Ullman and Geva 1982) or indeed clinical supervision (Cogan 1973; Acheson and Gall 1980) are based on the assumption that by seeing what is happening in the classroom, the student teacher can control and alter it. (See also this volume, p. 19, for more information on such systems.) In each system, the categories of that perception represent a defined view of teaching, which values certain aspects while downplaying others. Further, when self-applied, the systems are only as useful or accurate as the perceptiveness of the person who applies them (see Gebhard, Chapter 8). As with any inclusive system, the changes the student teacher makes through it are describable only within it. Otherwise the change is either not significant or calls into question the comprehensiveness of that system.

Therefore the student teacher–teacher educator relationship must not be seen as something to be systematically controlled or eliminated; rather it is the key that must be exploited. Two perceptions create a dialogue. The student teacher and the educator talk about teaching using the practice teaching segment as an immediate source of reference and vocabulary for their discussions. In this dialogue, their roles are different. The educator's job is to help the student teacher move toward an understanding of effective teaching and independence in teaching. While the educator's knowledge and experience aid in defining the former, they can interfere with the student teacher achieving the latter.

The final arbiter in the dialogue must thus be the student teacher: how the particular intervention affects how he or she teaches. The effects are not always immediately evident, however. The teacher educator needs the capacity to see beyond what was intended through the intervention to what actually happened. This is, after all, a learning process, and as such it depends on what is happening within and for the learner.

8 Interaction in a teaching practicum

Jerry G. Gebhard

This chapter presents a study of a preservice master of arts teacher education practicum for inexperienced English as a second language (ESL) student teachers. The seven student teachers in this practicum were required to teach in an ESL program set up by the department for people in New York City who want to study ESL (beginning through advanced) at a very low cost.

One purpose of this chapter is to describe how the interaction in this practicum provided opportunities for student teachers to change their teaching behavior. The initial research questions included:

1. Are there changes in the teaching behavior of student teachers while they are participating in a practicum for inexperienced ESL teachers?
2. If there are changes in teaching behavior, what opportunities are made available through the interaction that can possibly account for these changes?
3. If there are no apparent changes, how does the interaction seem to block student teachers from change?

In economy of space, the focus here is on questions 1 and 2: in other words, on the kinds of interaction that seem to provide opportunity for change to occur. How interaction seems to block student teachers from change is of equal importance (see Gebhard 1985 for a description of how interaction set up opportunities for as well as blocked June, a student teacher in the practicum described in this chapter, from changing her teaching behavior).

It is important to realize that the focus of this research was not on the student teachers, as in a case study approach, but on the patterns of interaction between the participants in the practicum (student teachers, teacher educator, ESL students). It is by focusing on the interaction between people, and not on the people themselves, that insight can be gained into how opportunities are provided (or blocked) for student teachers to change their teaching behaviors.

A second purpose of this chapter is to show how researchers in the field of teacher education can break away from skills-based views of teaching so as to gain fresh insight into the professional development of teachers. As Lanier and Little (1986) point out, researchers in teacher education have widely accepted the conclusions of researchers, such as Berliner, Brophy, Gage, and Good, on teaching effectiveness, and, as Zumwalt (1982) clearly points out, teacher educators have taken research findings on effective teaching and directly translated them into skills to be mastered by student teachers in their teacher education programs. In turn, researchers have focused on whether or not student teachers in teacher education programs can master these teaching skills.

Although this line of research informs teacher educators about the effects of skills training on teachers, as Joyce and Showers (1981) and Peck and Tucker (1973) make clear, it does not, as Zimpher and Ashburn (1985: 16) point out, "contribute to our knowledge of the professional development of teachers." Such studies, in other words, do not allow teacher educators to understand the experiences teacher educators and student teachers go through together in their programs and the consequences these experiences have on the student teachers' development as teachers during and after the programs. This chapter is designed to further knowledge about the developmental change process through focus on the interaction between participants, a focus that is greatly needed.

Procedures

In the behavioral sciences, we have been slow to absorb that every problem worthy of extended intellectual effort demands a special set of methods. A new problem cannot be assumed to be resonant to a research design guided by a paradigm developed for research on a previous problem. (Birdwhistell, cited in McDermott 1980: 2)

In agreement with this view, the procedures I used were designed especially for this study.

Data were collected through participant observation. I accomplished this by joining the practicum as a student teacher and interacting with the other seven student teachers in completing the course requirements: team teaching an ESL class three mornings per week for twelve weeks, attending weekly three-hour seminars, being supervised, and doing assigned readings, investigative projects on teaching, and observation tasks, among other activities.

Acting as a participant-observer was modeled after a method that some ethnographers use to gain access to cultural behavior. For example, Philips (1982) enrolled in law school in order to understand how law students acquire the language of lawyers. K. M. Bailey (1980) joined a French class in order to study what it means to be a foreign language student.

The research process included gaining the trust of the other prac-

Jerry G. Gebhard

ticum participants. Central to this process was this insight by Berreman:

Every ethnographer when he reaches the field is faced immediately with accounting for himself before the people he proposes to learn to know. Only when this has been accomplished can he proceed to his task of seeking to understand the way of life of those people. (1962: 5)

Thus, the participants in the practicum were informed as to the purpose of the research and that the findings were not to be used to evaluate them as individuals, but rather to describe the activities and interactions among them. More importantly, my aim was to consistently behave in ways that reflected this statement by not judging them or their teaching, thus allowing trust to grow between the practicum participants and myself.

As trust grew it was possible to audiotape their classroom teaching, seminar meetings, informal discussions over coffee, and other activities, thus providing what Mehan (1979) calls a "retrievable data base" through which ongoing and later analysis could be done. Trust also afforded access to student teachers' lesson plans, journal notes on their classroom teaching – including stated problems and insights – and written feedback from the teacher educator.

Analysis was done on an ongoing basis, and focused on making sense out of journal notes on observations and discussions, as well as the audio recordings and corresponding transcripts. One analytical focus was on the changes student teachers made in their teaching behavior. This analysis was made easier through the use of Fanselow's (1977a, 1987b) FOCUS (Foci on Communication Used in Settings), an observational category system designed to describe the multiple aspects of communication. Analysis of the kinds of activities and interaction within them was likewise done through studying research journal notes, tape recordings, and transcripts. Finally, an analysis was done of the changes in teaching behavior in relation to the interaction in the practicum. The aim was to discover patterns of interaction that provided opportunities for student teachers to change the way they teach.

In doing this analysis, discussions with Ray McDermott and John Fanselow, my consultants, and reading the work of ethnographers, such as Frake (1980); ethnomethodologists, such as Garfinkel (1967) and Wieder (1974); conversational analysts in Atkinson and Heritage (1986) and Schenkein (1978); and interaction analysts, such as McDermott and Roth (1978), McDermott, Gospodinoff, and Aron (1978), and Scheflen (1973), proved valuable. They offer an important insight: that interaction determines how people behave. To better understand how this

120

happens, the focus of inquiry needs to be on the interaction going on between participants in a social event.

Findings

Changes in teaching behavior

There is strong evidence that five of the seven student teachers changed aspects of their teaching behavior while participating in the sixteen-week practicum. Table 1 outlines four areas in which teaching behavior changed. Although some student teachers seemed to change more dramatically than others, the changes in Table 1 are common to the five student teachers.

As Table 1 shows, student teachers began their practicum teaching through teacher lecture and questioning. The pattern of interaction between the teacher and students was much like the pattern described in Bellack et al. (1966) and Hoetker and Ahlbrand (1972). The student teacher structured the lesson, solicited responses from students, and reacted to these responses. Although some teacher lecture and questioning continued, by the second half of the practicum the student teachers, to various degrees, were setting up and carrying out their activities in a variety of ways. They were having students do group problem-solving tasks, group discussions, pair work, and individual seat work. In addition, the patterns of interaction subsequently changed. Students solicited information from the student teacher and from each other, and reacted to each others' ideas.

The use of classroom space also changed. The student teachers began by using very little of the available space. Students sat in rows and the teacher stood in the front of the classroom. Some student teachers had students write on the blackboard, but for the most part students did not move around much. During the second half of the practicum student seating changed to serve the activity (e.g., back-to-back while practicing telephone conversations, in small-group circles, in whole-class semicircles, or standing up and walking around the classroom). At least two student teachers had students spaced around the room, while doing silent reading. At least one student teacher expanded the class to the hallway. Another student teacher made use of a kitchen located in the building by having students teach each other how to prepare foods native to their countries. Likewise, the student teacher in at least two classrooms taught from the back of the room, and another student teacher left the room completely while students carried on an activity.

Student teachers also expanded the content of their teaching. At the

121

TABLE 1. CHANGES IN TEACHING BEHAVIOR OF STUDENT TEACHERS

Teaching area	Behavior at start of practicum	Behavior during second half of practicum
Setting up and carrying out lesson	Primarily teacher-centered lecture or teacher questioning (teacher solicit, student response, teacher react).	Whole-class discussion (mostly teacher-directed); small-group discussions (without teacher); pair work (interviewing, functions of language practice); individual seat work (silent reading, writing tasks); teacher-centered lecture less (more student solicits and reactions).
Use of classroom space	Students sit in rows; teacher stands in front; some arrangement of chairs into groups.	Reorganization of chairs (back-to-back, circles); use of tables; students stand at blackboard and walk around room; teacher moves around room; use of space outside classroom (hallway, kitchen).
Selection of content	Primarily a focus on the study of language itself (e.g., vocabulary, grammar, pronunciation); some focus on functions (agreeing, introductions, asking for information, etc.)	Some study of language continues; "real-life" content (e.g., talking about family based on photos students bring in) and the "study of other things" (e.g., putting together a jigsaw puzzle, writing a "Dear Abby" letter, sharing recipes, watching a film).
Treatment of students' language errors	No treatment, or treatment limited to two basic strategies: (1) repeat sentence with correction using emphatic stress at point of correction; (2) write correction on board and lecture.	Some adaptation to original error treatment strategies; additional strategies used: stopping student at point of error and doing mini-drill; telling student to write down error and correction; having students work in groups to correct list of sentences with errors; having students take home their own sentences with errors and finding out the corrections.

start of the practicum, the lessons focused for the most part on language itself: vocabulary items, grammar, and pronunciation. Some lessons began with the intent to teach a point of grammar or a list of vocabulary. Other lessons began with a "real-life" topic, such as "My favorite foods," and after a brief time on this topic, turned to the study of relevant vocabulary (e.g., food) or to a point of grammar. For example, one student teacher had students write down two lists, one on "What I like about New York City" and another on "What I don't like about New York City." She had students copy their lists onto the board, after which she went over the sentences, corrected them, and gave explanations about grammar and punctuation.

However, at the start of the practicum at least two student teachers had students work with the functions of language, such as "asking for information," "introducing oneself," and "requesting a favor." Students first studied the language needed to express these functions and then practiced the language with the student teacher or with each other.

Although language itself remained the content of many lessons throughout the practicum, at least four student teachers greatly expanded their use of "real-life" content without shifting most of the lesson to grammar or some other technical aspect of language. For example, students brought pictures into one class and spent the full period talking about family members. In another class students read "Dear Abby" and then wrote their own letters to Abby. In another class students read about Halloween, and then gave short lectures on Halloween and similar holidays in their native countries. In one class students discussed news items about crime after reading short newspaper articles.

Student teachers also changed the way they treated students' language errors. At the start of the practicum two student teachers did not treat student errors at all. Instead they focused on the content of their lessons (e.g., grammar or functions). The other student teachers did treat errors, although their strategies seemed to be limited to two basic patterns (see Table 1).

By the second half of the practicum all the student teachers were treating student errors, and all but one seemed to have developed a number of strategies for treating errors. Student teachers used a variety of strategies, including (1) stopping the student at the point of error, doing short drills, and then continuing with the lesson; (2) collecting errors, writing the sentences with the errors on the board, and having students either correct the sentences in groups or go to the board to correct them; (3) collecting errors and designing exercises for future classes; (4) writing the sentence with the error in it on a piece of paper, along with the corrections; (5) approaching an individual student and whispering the correction in his or her ear.

Opportunities for change

Student teachers seem to have opportunities to change their teaching behavior when:

1. interaction is arranged so that student teachers can process aspects of their teaching through multiple activities;
2. interaction affords student teachers chances to talk about their teaching;
3. student teachers are given a break from their usual teaching setting and a chance to teach in a new setting.

CHANGE THROUGH MULTIPLE ACTIVITIES

The practicum included many kinds of activities. Student teachers were required to team-teach an ESL class, observe their own teaching (through video and audio recordings) and other student teachers' teaching (through classroom visits, through an observation room, and through video), do investigative projects of their own teaching behavior, read about teaching, discuss teaching in a seminar and during supervisory sessions, and write about teaching and observation experiences in a journal. (See Gebhard 1986, and Gebhard, Gaitan, and Oprandy, this volume, Chapter 2, for further discussion of change through multiple activities.)

One finding is that multiple activities, as opposed to any single activity, provided opportunities for student teachers to process and change their teaching behavior. In order to illustrate how this happens, I will trace the changes that June, one of the student teachers, made in her treatment of student errors as a result of the activities in which she participated.

June was one of the student teachers who did not treat student errors at the beginning of the practicum. She had stated to her teaching partner (myself) that as a result of reading Dulay, Burt, and Krashen's (1982) book *Language Two* for another course, she believed that error treatment does not help students master the second language and can even interfere with their acquisition process.

However, June was required to observe her peers teaching, and they were treating student errors. The topic of error treatment also came up during supervision of her teaching: The teacher educator on a number of occasions advised her to collect student errors and give students feedback on their language errors. Likewise, June was required to read an article on error treatment by Fanselow (1977b), which outlines different strategies for error treatment. The topic of error treatment also came up in seminar meetings, including what kinds of errors can be treated, how they can be treated, and when treatment is possible.

Thus, although June was not treating student errors in her class, she had opportunities to consider error treatment. I believe that it is through these multiple activities that June made a decision to treat student errors. She started correcting errors toward the end of the first seven weeks of the practicum, and by the end of the practicum she had developed several strategies for treating student errors.

In summary, when student teachers teach a class they are confronted with putting their knowledge into practice. They behave in ways they believe are appropriate, and they often gain a sense of how the lesson went. However, if an activity is available that allows them to further consider their teaching experience, such as a discussion with a supervisor who observed their lessons, they have the chance to process their experience one step further, possibly even to the point of making decisions about how they would teach the same lesson differently next time. The more activities that are made available to the student teachers, the more steps they can make toward an understanding of themselves as teachers and their teaching behaviors. For example, if in addition to teaching a class and receiving verbal and written feedback from a supervisor, student teachers have the chance to observe their teaching on video, discuss the teaching experience with peers, read about lessons or teaching behaviors similar to (or different from) the ones they attempted to implement in their classrooms, or write about the experiences in a journal, the student teachers will have far more opportunity to gain an understanding of themselves as teachers, the consequences of their teaching behavior, and changes they might make in their teaching.

Meredith (1984) makes clear that change is a consequence of discovery and rediscovery through multiple experiences. He states that each activity "may be a small and insignificant event in its own right, and we probably overestimate the importance of any one event while underestimating the importance of all of them taken together" (p. 48). For example, the reduction of smoking in America is not the result of any single event, but a consequence of the Surgeon General's report on smoking and lung cancer, magazine and newspaper articles, news specials on TV, warning labels on cigarette packages, political activism by nonsmokers, and more.

CHANGE AND CHANCES TO TALK ABOUT REAL TEACHING ISSUES

Student teachers had many chances to talk about their teaching experiences with each other and with the teacher educator through seminar meetings, supervisory conferences, observation-room discussions, and journal correspondence. Discussions also took place over the phone, in the cafeteria, at the local pizza shop, or simply in the hallway. A major outcome of this investigation is that such discussions did not occur in a vacuum – that very specific behaviors were used to provide student teachers with the opportunities to talk about teaching.

Such settings were important because they provided opportunities for student teachers to discuss their classroom observations and teaching experiences, allowing them to work through real teaching problems and issues. Talk also afforded student teachers chances to raise "cognitive questions" (Smith 1975; Curran 1978) – questions the student teachers did not know they had until they had the opportunity to ask them. Student teachers also gained new insights through the responses they got to their questions. When these responses were in the form of alternative ways to teach, the student teachers were also given the means through which to make decisions about how to change their teaching behavior.

For an illustration of how opportunities for student teachers to talk about teaching helped them to work through their individual teaching issues or problems, raise questions, learn about teaching possibilities, and ultimately to change their teaching behavior, let us return to the developmental change process June went through in her approach to error treatment. As discussed earlier, June did not treat student errors during the first part of her teaching experience. However, her peers were treating errors, and they would talk about the problems they were having and possible ways to treat student errors. During these discussions June had the opportunity to listen to what others said about error treatment and at the same time to consider her own beliefs and raise questions about whether or not to treat student errors. Evidence that she did this is found in the questions she raised during two seminar meetings. During one seminar she asked, "Shall I correct students now or not?" and "Error correction is really like cutting off communication, isn't it?" In another seminar she asked, "Isn't error correction really like changing the subject?"

June received several responses to her questions, all dealing with how to treat errors without cutting off communication. One student teacher suggested she collect sentences with errors in them as the students work in small groups, later write them on the board, and have students correct them. Another student teacher suggested she tape-record the class, go home and listen to the students' use of language, and design a lesson based on common errors. The teacher educator suggested that she write down sentences with errors on pieces of paper and give them to individual students to correct for homework.

As a possible consequence of these and other interactions June worked through the issue of whether or not to treat student errors, and at some point she made a decision to treat errors. Likewise, the questions she raised about teaching changed, reflecting the changes she had made in her approach to the treatment of student errors. Instead of asking questions related to whether or not to treat student errors, June began to ask questions such as, "How do you get students to care about the corrections?" The teacher educator responded thus:

"A way to show a student that you care about her development in English is to go up to her before class or after class and write down a correct way and an incorrect way and say, 'Which one is correct?' Just to show that you personally care about, you know, her development, that this is something that you have been thinking of and you wanted to ask about again just to make sure she is paying attention to it."

The teacher educator's clearly stated expectations helped maximize the benefits that student teachers reaped from talking about teaching. Student teachers were told at the beginning of the practicum and were consistently reminded that they were expected to focus their discussion on their teaching and that the point of the practicum was to provide them with chances to explore their teaching behavior and its consequences by trying out and analyzing alternative ways to teach.

In order to provide opportunities for student teachers to focus on their own teaching behavior and its consequences (rather than on abstractions about teaching), the teacher educator designed activities that directed the student teachers' attention to their own and each others' teaching. For example, student teachers were required to audio- and videotape their classes, and these tapes were used as the focus for seminar (and sometimes supervisory) discussion. Student teachers were also asked to make short transcriptions of sections from these tapes at home or in the seminar, and the student teachers practiced coding the interaction using FOCUS (see the Appendix for an overview of FOCUS categories). Likewise, student teachers talked about their lesson plans, findings from observations of other classes, and their investigative projects of their teaching on self-selected areas of interest (see Gebhard, Gaitan, and Oprandy, this volume, Chapter 2, for a detailed discussion of these activities).

Finally, the teacher educator's behavior during interaction with the student teachers constructed an atmosphere conducive to open talk about teaching. The following scene illustrates how the teacher educator (Mark) set up opportunities for student teachers to do most of the talking. (*Note:* Each period inside a parenthesis stands for one second of silence.)

June: I'm tired (..) Uhm, I've really enjoyed it. Very much fun.
Mark: Mm-hmm. (..)

June: Of course, you know, anxiety about the, you not knowing what to do and (..)

Mark: Yeah.

June: And stuff like that.

Mark: So despite the initial anxiety, still you were (.)

June: Yeah. I really had fun. It was very – it was fun (...)

Brent: Taking the two classes, I've experienced both extremes. At the end of the first class I was totally overcome with a sense of despair, you know. It was almost crushing, you know. Helplessness. Uncertainty. Frustration. At the end of today's class I was walking on air.

Mark: Mm-hmm. Mm-hmm.

Brent: I have a feeling that, you know, the sense of elation that I walked out with today is probably a little false, but it was satisfying.

Mark: Yeah, yeah. Nice to know that it wasn't going to be all like it was the first day. (..) Yeah. (...)

Anne: Yes. I wasn't nervous or anything.

The teacher educator, Mark, constructed an atmosphere conducive to talk. He did not judge the student teachers' feelings about their experiences. He did not, for example, tell the student teachers that one kind of feeling is more valid than another. Rather, he paraphrased back to them what he understood them to be saying and showed that he was listening to them through his use of such language as "Mm-hmm" and "Yeah." Furthermore, Mark did not interrupt them. Instead he used silence as a way to provide (1) time for them to process their ideas and feelings (as Rowe 1986 has also recommended) without the threat of having to talk constantly, and (2) chances for them to talk when they have something to say.

CHANGE THROUGH A BREAK FROM ESTABLISHED PATTERNS

One of the most striking observations was how teaching behavior dramatically changed after student teachers were given the chance to make a complete break from one teaching context and to begin afresh in another. For example, after six weeks of interaction with an advanced class June was assigned to a low-intermediate class. Although she had begun to treat student errors in the advanced class, after she changed classes, she began treating errors much more frequently.

June's change can be understood from at least two perspectives. First, she was provided with a new context to work in, one in which she believed the type of interaction with the students needed to be different (e.g., more error treatment was needed for a low-intermediate class than for an advanced class). Second, June was also set free from established patterns of interaction between herself and the advanced class, which included student expectations of her behaviors. For example, since June did not treat students' errors frequently in the advanced class, the ESL students learned not to expect her to do so, and thus did not provide chances for her to do so. However, since there were no such expectations in the new low-intermediate class, June's change to fairly frequent error treatment was easier.

So what?

One purpose of my research was to describe the interaction in an ESL teaching practicum in relation to how this interaction provided opportunities for student teachers to change their teaching behaviors. A second purpose was to break away from an "effective teaching" model of research and to explore the actual processes going on in a teaching practicum. So what? What have I discovered that can be useful to both teacher educators and to researchers in teacher education?

Implications of this study for teacher educators

These findings show how interaction in a teaching practicum can be arranged so that student teachers have opportunities to change their teaching behavior. Teacher educators can arrange the teacher education experience, at whatever level, so that (1) the student teachers are afforded chances to process their teaching through multiple activities, (2) the interaction affords them chances to talk about their teaching experiences and plans, and (3) the student teachers are given a chance to break away from one context in which they have been working and work in another.

Although these particular interactional arrangements seem to have a powerful influence on the changes that five student teachers made in their teaching, I am not presenting my findings at this point as prescriptions for teacher educators to follow. Rather, I encourage teacher educators to use the interactional arrangements presented in this chapter as suggestions in their own exploration of ways to help student teachers change their teaching, and in so doing, to help student teachers see teaching differently.

A less obvious implication of the findings for teacher educators is that the entire process of arranging interaction so that student teachers have opportunities to change also addresses a much larger issue: how teacher educators can empower student teachers to be able to make their own decisions about what and how to teach, as Freire (1970) has advocated. As Fanselow (1987b) and Jarvis (1972) point out, to assure that student teachers are being prepared to enter the real world of teaching, teacher educators need to shift responsibility for decision making to classroom

Jerry G. Gebhard

teachers. By providing student teachers with opportunities through the interaction to change their teaching behaviors, teacher educators are also providing student teachers with opportunities to raise their own questions and to make decisions (e.g., "Should I treat students' errors?" "How can I get students to pay attention to their errors and the corrections?").

Implications of this study for researchers

If teacher educators believe that the purpose of research in teacher education is to understand the processes going on in teacher education programs and how these processes affect the participants in the programs, they cannot deny the relevance of this study. In addition, if researchers are interested in more than *what* is going on in teacher education programs and want to focus on how participants in the programs arrange interaction to accomplish teacher education, the focus needs to widen and include not only what participants are doing but also how they are doing it. This means that the interaction between people is of utmost importance. Within such an interactional focus questions include:

How does the interaction provide student-teachers with opportunities to change? to make their own decisions? to solve teaching problems?
How does the interaction block student-teachers from change? from making decisions? from solving teaching problems?

It is hoped that this chapter has provided some insights into those factors that facilitate, and those that block, professional development and change.

Appendix

FOCUS: FIVE CHARACTERISTICS OF COMMUNICATION
(Major Categories)

Move		Message		
What is being done?		**How is it being done?**		
Who or what is communicating to whom or what?	What is the purpose of the communication?	What mediums are used to communicate?	How are the mediums used to take in or communicate content?	What areas of content are communicated?
Source/Target	**Move Type**	**Medium**	**Use**	**Content**
			attend	
	structuring	linguistic		life
teacher			--------------	
			characterize	
	soliciting	nonlinguistic		procedure
			present	
student			relate	
	responding	paralinguistic		study
			reproduce	
other			--------------	
	reacting	silence		unspecified
			set	

Bold letters are abbreviations for the categories.

9 A professional development focus for the language teaching practicum

Martha C. Pennington

Whether implicitly or explicitly, every teacher preparation program embodies a philosophy of teaching that connects performance goals to training methods and course content. In the ideal case, each program requirement is covered by an explicit rationale that relates course content to specific outcomes for program graduates. Such a rationale incorporates (1) an articulated philosophy or theory of teaching and (2) statements relating that philosophy or theory to one or more specializations for which preparation is offered in the program. Accordingly, the question of how to prepare language teachers resolves itself ultimately into the question of what the nature of language teaching is. The answer to this question requires, first, defining a general theory or philosophy of teaching and, second, determining how this general theory relates to the particular case of teaching a second language (Richards, this volume, Chapter 1).

This chapter provides background discussion and practical techniques for the preparation of language teachers based on a philosophy of teaching as profession. The discussion of professionalism is set in a context of other views of teaching, and the notion of teaching as profession is shown to provide a conceptual bridge between a context-free, empiricist view of teaching and a more context-dependent, individualistic view. A distinguishing characteristic of the notion of teaching as profession is the centrality of career growth as an ongoing goal. This chapter explores the implementation of this conception of professionalism in language teacher preparation programs through a series of specific activities for the practicum component.[1]

Implications of teaching philosophy for teacher preparation

Different conceptions of teaching have different implications for teacher preparation. For some people, teaching is a kind of mystical experience

1 The activities described in this chapter were designed for a prepracticum course taught by the author from 1982 to 1985 at the University of California at Santa Barbara in the TESL Certificate Program. Susan Jasper, an instructor in the TESL Certificate Program of the University of California at Santa Barbara, provided valuable input in the development of some of the exercises.

that is hard to explain or describe. Stevick (1980: 295), for example, speaks of teaching as "the mystery-behind-mystery," the "simple, daily miracle." From this perspective, individual acts of teaching are essentially irreplicable and noncomparable, and the inherent characteristics of individual teachers are the strongest predictor of classroom outcomes. Under this abstract view of teaching, in which the teaching act cannot be analyzed and described in rational, consistent terms, teacher development or evaluation cannot be justified:

From this perspective, teachers are born, spontaneously as it were, when they stand in front of a class and begin to teach. Hence, the only relevant experience for prospective teachers is actual teaching. (Pennington 1989: 9)

In a less radical conception, teaching viewed as a kind of "artistic" performance depends in large measure on the characteristics of the particular teacher and so cannot be reliably predicted from teacher preparation: "Under the conception of teaching as art, teaching techniques and their application may be novel, unconventional, or unpredictable" (Darling-Hammond, Wise, and Pease 1983: 291). However, teacher preparation can be of value for helping refine natural abilities and for synthesizing elements of the teaching "craft" into an individual teaching style.

In a research-oriented approach to language teaching, some educators (e.g., Long 1980; Long and Crookes 1986) are attempting to provide an empirical basis for teacher preparation, through extensive observation, description, and analysis of teaching. According to this empiricist approach, individual acts of teaching represent patterned, systematic variation. Thus, it should be possible to discover on the basis of classroom research a set of observable and replicable component skills of teaching that can be learned and later evaluated in terms of specific behavioral objectives. An empiricist approach to teaching therefore leads to a search for principles of effective instruction, and microskills directly related to these, which all teachers can master. A more holistic approach (Larsen-Freeman 1983; Britten 1985a), on the other hand, leads teacher educators to assist individuals in developing themselves to the fullest extent possible, so that they may ultimately create their own reality, or teaching style. Such a high-inference, *macro* approach to teacher preparation (Richards, this volume, Chapter 1) assumes the need for an extended period of classroom practice in order to learn how to apply teaching techniques in real settings, whereas a focus on low-inference aspects of teaching might operate on the assumption that classroom skills can be developed under idealized conditions outside of an actual classroom.

A strictly empiricist or craft-oriented perspective downplays the individual and the context-dependent, high-inference aspects of teaching, while a highly individualistic view of teaching may underestimate the need for mastery of certain areas of knowledge and skills in preparation for teaching. The concept of profession can be seen to bridge these other conceptions of teaching, allowing for both an individual and a collective, replicable aspect of teaching. Within the framework of teaching as profession, teacher preparation aims at the development of competency standards for the field and for the attainment of a certain level of competency for all individuals, while underscoring the importance of individualized professional growth throughout the teaching career (Darling-Hammond et al. 1983: 291). Professional teacher preparation programs will have as goals the development of an extensive repertoire of classroom skills and the judgment to apply these skills as needed. In this way, teacher preparation moves beyond "training" in the narrow sense to enabling "an individual to function in any situation, rather than training for a specific situation ... preparing people to make choices" (Larsen-Freeman 1983: 265). Thus, the philosophy of teaching as profession offers a rationale for including both holistic and competency-based elements in the teacher preparation curriculum (Britten 1985a; and in this volume: Richards, Chapter 1; Ellis, Chapter 3; and Freeman, Chapter 7).

In addition, a teacher preparation program oriented to developing teachers as professionals will have as central goals (1) to engender an attitude favorable to continued growth and change, and (2) to provide the skills necessary for analyzing teaching performance, for evaluating new ideas, and for implementing those ideas deemed worthy of putting into practice as part of the individual's career growth. Specific suggestions for implementing these goals, which incorporate investigative skills (Gebhard, Gaitan, and Oprandy, this volume, Chapter 2) awareness-raising, and experiential practices (Ellis, this volume, Chapter 3), in a second language teacher preparation program are described in the next section.

The role of education and training in professional preparation

If teacher preparation aims to perpetuate second language teaching as a profession, then training in the narrowest sense will not be adequate, and some broader educational goals must be recognized. For successful language teaching, both education and practical training are needed in the "tools" of the teaching profession: in methods, materials, curriculum, and evaluation. Part of this education involves theory, so that the teacher will have a basis for thoroughly analyzing and evaluating the practical aspects of methods, materials, and curriculum. The effectiveness of both the purely educational and the practical training aspects of the teacher preparation program can be increased by not maintaining the strict separation of these two components that is typical in most programs.

Typically, candidates do not have actual chances to teach until the end of their program. In many cases, they have little or no practical experience of any kind – for example, in the form of simulations, role plays, case studies – before the formal teaching practicum in the final semester. A prepracticum or two-phase practicum program in which students gain simulated and actual teaching experience in the middle of their graduate program may enhance integration of theory and practice.

For the lifelong professional, an important goal is flexibility in teaching approach. This is partly a matter of attitude, an understanding that no one teaching approach is appropriate for every situation. It is also a matter of education and training, so that the teacher develops a wide-ranging repertoire of knowledge and skills that can be called upon to meet the demands of a given student population or classroom situation. For long-term professional development, education can provide the confidence and the knowledge to continue to reach and to grow, while a practicum or prepracticum course can, for example, provide experience in accepting feedback and implementing suggestions offered as feedback by another professional – a colleague or supervisor. Education provides the background for helping the teacher to understand what type of feedback is appropriate in different situations; training can teach the candidate how to give that feedback, both to students and to colleagues, in a way that will be the most beneficial. Education also aims to build tolerance in future teachers and teacher supervisors, reminding them that there are many different perspectives on teaching, all of which may be equally valid. Practical training experiences can also assist in the development of attitudes that are open to differing perspectives and to modification through experience.

Establishing an attitudinal base

Since every teacher and learner is different, teaching is most effective when it is based on two kinds of knowledge: knowledge of the students and knowledge of oneself. Exercises to develop self-knowledge and to better understand one's attitudes toward students supply a basis for analysis of practicum experiences and for continued growth beyond the practicum (see Wright, this volume, Chapter 6). Exercises to uncover the attitudes that the prospective teacher holds about learning and about teaching can capitalize on the candidate's prior experience as a student and use this experience as a starting point for examining beliefs about what constitutes ideal classroom conditions. A series of five exercises to make practicum candidates more aware of their beliefs about language teaching and learning are displayed in Figures 1–5. Figure 1 presents an exercise that asks the candidate to analyze prior experience as a language

YOUR EXPERIENCE AS A LANGUAGE LEARNER

Directions: Check the appropriate boxes in the left-hand column for the language learning activities listed across the top of the chart. After you have finished, notice which boxes you have checked most and consider what this says about your language learning experience. Then complete the following statements:

In general, my language learning experience has been...
My most enjoyable activity has been...

My least enjoyable activity has been...
My most valuable activity has been...
My least valuable activity has been...

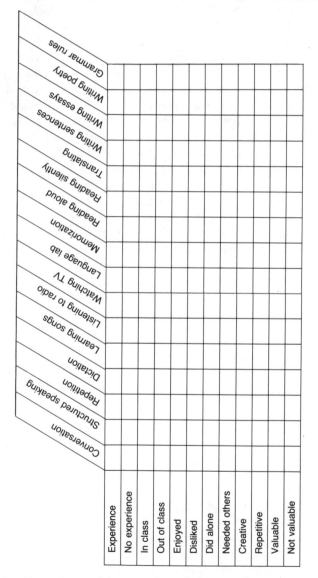

Figure 1   Exercise on language learning experience

ESSENTIAL CONDITIONS FOR A CLASS

Five rules for classroom behavior are identified by Seelye (1984: 291) based on a study by Margaret LeCompte of teachers' "management-type behavior":

1. Do what the teacher says.
2. Live up to teacher expectations for proper behavior.
3. Stick to the schedule.
4. Keep busy.
5. Keep quiet and don't move too much.

These rules represent the expectations that many North American teachers have about appropriate classroom behavior. Which of these rules do you think are absolutely necessary? Are there any circumstances in which such rules could or should be broken? Discuss your responses with others in your group.

Now make lists of classroom characteristics that form the essential conditions for a class in the categories of the behavioral and psychological conditions of the students and the physical environment of the classroom. Include only those features that are absolutely essential conditions for teaching and learning to take place. Then compare your lists to those of others in your group.

Behavioral	*Psychological*	*Physical environment*

Now compare and contrast the lists you developed in your group to the list above that is based on LeCompte's research. Finally, complete the sentences below.

Sentences to complete

The three most essential conditions for a class are . . .
From this exercise, I have learned . . .

Figure 2   Exercise for identifying beliefs about classroom conditions

Martha C. Pennington

THE IDEAL STUDENT

It does not take most teachers long to make a judgment as to whether
individual students are "good," "poor," or somewhere in between. As
teachers, we tend to focus our evaluation on oral and written performance
and other aspects of classroom behavior. When our positive expectations
are met, we classify a student as "good." Problems arise when students,
for a variety of reasons, often cultural ones, do not share our expectations
and are therefore doomed not to meet them.

It may be useful to try to define the "ideal" student and to consider what
causes us to rate a student as a "good" student or a "poor" student.
Consider the questions below to help you complete the sentences at the
end of the exercise.

a. What kind of student do you think is the easiest for you to succeed
   with and why?
   How would you define being successful with a student?
   Do you expect success with all of your students? Why or why not?

b. What kind of student do you like?
   Do you expect most or all of your students to be of this type?
   Are you most successful with this type of student? Why or why not?

c. What kind of student do you think is the hardest for you to succeed
   with and why?
   How would you define being unsuccessful with a student?
   What do you think are the major causes of lack of success with
   individual students?

d. Is there any kind of student that you do not like or that you do not feel
   comfortable with?
   Is there anything that really "turns you off" in a student's behavior?

Sentences to complete

What makes a "good" student is . . .
What makes a "poor" student is . . .
For me, the definition of the "ideal" student is . . .

Figure 3   Exercise to uncover attitudes toward students

learner. Figure 2 is an exercise to make candidates examine their assumptions about the teaching and learning processes and how these are
affected by the general atmosphere of the class and the classroom environment. The exercise illustrated in Figure 3 aids in determining attitudes toward different types of students, and that in Figure 4 helps to
bring attitudes toward teaching to conscious awareness. The exercises
in Figure 5, which ask candidates to examine the contrast between real
teaching situations and their ideal teaching situation, can be used as the
final activity in this series of exercises.

EFFECTIVE TEACHING: WHO GETS THE APPLE?

Answer these questions based on your own experience as a student.

a. What kind of teacher has been most successful with you? How do you define "successful" in this context? To what do you attribute this success?

b. What kind of teacher do you like? Have the teachers you like been the same ones that have been most successful with you?

c. What kind of teacher has been most unsuccessful with you? How do you define "unsuccessful" in this context? To what do you attribute this lack of success?

d. Is there any kind of teacher that you do not like or that you do not feel comfortable with?

Now, brainstorm to make a list of behavioral or personality traits that you think are related to being a "good" teacher. Then compare your answers with those of others in your group. You may also wish to make a contrasting list of characteristics of a "poor" teacher.

Good	Poor

Try to examine yourself in light of the characteristics of "good" teachers which most of the members of your group agreed upon. Put a plus next to those characteristics that you feel reasonably match characteristics of yourself, and put a minus next to those that you do not feel describe you as a person or as a teacher. Now, go back to your group to see if you wish to change anything on your original list of characteristics related to being a good teacher.

Sentences to complete

The most important characteristics of a "good" teacher are . . .
A characteristic of a "good" teacher which I may not at the present time share is . . .

Figure 4   Exercise to uncover attitudes about teaching

Martha C. Pennington

COMPARISON OF REAL AND IDEAL TEACHING SITUATIONS

Think of a real teaching situation with which you are familiar. This can be a classroom in which you have been or are a student or a teacher. What is the teaching situation that you are thinking of?

For each of the points a–f, describe this actual teaching situation in column 1. Then, using the same points a–f, describe what you think would be the ideal teaching situation.

	(1) Actual teaching situation	(2) Ideal teaching situation
a. Characteristics of the school		
b. Characteristics of the administration		
c. Characteristics of the teachers		
d. Characteristics of the students		
e. Success and failure rates of the teachers		
f. Success and failure rates of the students		

Figure 5a   Exercise to compare characteristics of ideal and actual teaching situations

COMPARISON OF REAL AND IDEAL TEACHING SITUATIONS (cont'd)

After you have completed columns 1 and 2 for points a–f, compare your lists with those of others in your group. Then try to summarize the main differences between the actual and the ideal teaching situations that you and others have described, and give reasons for these differences in columns 3 and 4 below. When you have finished filling in columns 3 and 4, complete the sentences at the end of the exercise.

	(3) Main differences between 1 and 2	*(4) Reasons for column 3*
a. Characteristics of the school		
b. Characteristics of the administration		
c. Characteristics of the teachers		
d. Characteristics of the students		
e. Success and failure rates of the teachers		
f. Success and failure rates of the students		

Sentences to complete

The main differences between the ideal and the real teaching situations are...

The primary reasons for these differences are...

Figure 5b   Exercise to explore reasons for differences between ideal and actual teaching situations

Martha C. Pennington

These exercises are intended to be facilitated by an experienced teacher educator skilled in group process who can ensure that each one is carried out in an appropriate format and time frame, and that its implications will be fully apparent to the candidates. The success of the exercises is related to the amount of time spent in completing them. If sections are skipped or covered in a superficial way, the exercise as a whole will not have the impact that it can have if each section is given the same thoughtful consideration. Except for the first exercise, which does not explicitly refer to members of a larger group, the exercises generally involve an introspective part and a group-comparison part, followed by a personal summation in the form of sentences to complete. In all cases, a followup whole-class discussion guided by the teacher educator is important to the success of the exercises. Such guided discussion establishes patterns of interaction in the group and a shared frame of reference for feedback in later stages of the practicum when candidates discuss their own teaching experiences. It also gives the teacher educator important information about the needs and preferences of individual candidates, which is essential if the practicum is to affect their behavior positively and significantly.

Each exercise provides a certain degree of structure to guide introspection and the class discussions growing out of the introspective activities. There is no right or wrong response to any question, nor is a uniform outcome expected among candidates. The teacher educator should allow each candidate to have an individual response to the exercises, and should not insist on a preordained agenda. Any thoughtful response should be accepted as valid. The point of the exercises is to put candidates in touch with their own experiences and attitudes that will be shaping their future teaching and to increase their awareness and acceptance of other behavior and responses in the same contexts, thus opening them up to potential modification by experience. Taken as a set of related activities, the exercises are thus oriented toward long-range developmental goals, rather than toward any immediate response or outcome. In what follows, some general guidelines are offered for the implementation of each exercise.

Your Experience as a Language Learner (Figure 1). The exercise is designed to guide individual candidates in recalling their own experiences as language learners and to provide a basis for comparison across the experiences of different individuals. By filling out the chart, candidates can summarize a great deal of experience in a form that allows easy comparison. Through the choice of categories in the exercise and the visual display in columns, they are led as individuals and as a group to think about the relationship between (a) the positive and negative values they place on certain language learning activities and (b) certain characteristics of the activities, such as whether they involved other people, or took place inside or outside of class. Sometimes the exercise results in a realization that learning experiences that took place outside of class were the most valuable and enjoyable. Other times, participants recall their own positive experience with highly structured learning activities, such as dictation or use of a language lab. Participants are usually surprised by the amount of variation in responses within a group of prospective teachers.

Essential Conditions for a Class (Figure 2). Most candidates will be led by this exercise to see that the five "classroom rules" listed are unnecessarily negative or overly restrictive, and so are in general neither absolutely essential conditions for a class nor necessarily desirable for effective teaching and learning. Some groups start from scratch in developing their own essential classroom conditions, using the three categories provided in the exercise. Here the facilitator plays an important role in helping the group to probe the intent of each of the five rules and the necessity of each proposed essential condition in the listing activity. For example, practicum candidates who start out requiring under *Physical environment* "realia" of various sorts, such as blackboards and pencils, may eventually concede that these are not entirely necessary for some kind of organized learning to take place. Some groups may want to try to rework the five statements into a more positively oriented set of guidelines for classroom behavior. It is not uncommon in either case for groups to end up retaining some aspect of the five statements in their ultimate responses to the exercise, maintaining the need for a basic level of respect and discipline in a classroom as a precondition for teaching and learning.

The Ideal Student (Figure 3). Although human beings are generally selective in their attraction to and their association with other human beings, a teacher must operate from an egalitarian perspective. This exercise is a starting point for reinforcing this perspective by raising the candidates' level of awareness of their own biases about individual students and student behaviors. This goal is accomplished by examining the relationship between individual perceptions of student characteristics, student success, and teaching effectiveness. Through a follow-up discussion in the larger group, the exercise also reveals differences among individual candidates that account for the differences in response to questions a–d. The exercise thus increases self-knowledge while reinforcing the validity of individual differences in perception and behavior.

Effective Teaching: Who Gets the Apple? (Figure 4). It is common for practicum courses to include a class session in which candidates discuss the attributes of "good" and "poor" teachers. This exercise provides a structure for this type of discussion, which builds on the previous exercise and then follows up with a group discussion and an introspective activity that explicitly relates the exercise to the candidate's own attributes. In asking them to consider their own attributes in light of both positive and negative values about teachers, candidates begin to evolve personal standards and goals for their future teaching in the practicum and beyond.

Comparison of Real and Ideal Teaching Situations (Figure 5). The sequence of activities in this exercise is designed to help candidates accomplish several purposes: (a) to increase awareness of experience through identification of certain characteristics of teaching situations with which candidates are familiar; (b) to uncover perceptions of short-comings in existing teaching situations; (c) to realize the constraints under which educational institutions operate; and (d) to establish a view of the kind of teaching situation candidates would like to achieve and what is needed to move toward that ideal. The exercise is particularly valuable if it is done after the exercises in Figures 1–4, as a way of extending and summarizing the insights gained from those exercises.

Developing analytical skills

A case can be made for including a research component in the teacher preparation program to refine certain skills that underlie continuing professional growth. Research experience helps to build a foundation for analyzing the published research on teaching, and so enhances opportunities for continuing education through reading in professional journals. The prospective teacher benefits in a direct way from learning how to conduct research on the behavior of students and teachers in classrooms (Long and Crookes 1986; Gebhard et al., this volume, Chapter 2). In the practicum as well as in other courses, future teachers can learn how to conduct detailed observations of teaching and learning behavior, analyze the data gathered, and put the analysis into practice. Overview and critical assessment of theory and research help future teachers to develop the judgment necessary for putting information into perspective (i.e., for judging its value) and for putting that information into practice (assuming it is judged worthy of putting into practice). Practical training can also be offered for developing judgment, exposing candidates to case studies and other kinds of problem-solving activities. Practice in evaluating information and performance, both of others and of self, should be a key aspect of the teacher preparation program, the main goal of which is ongoing career growth.

To aid in learning how to assess student performance, candidates can be given samples of student productions to evaluate. These may be samples of written work or taped speech samples taken from a variety of student populations. The samples can be analyzed to discover the

---

STUDENT CASE

You are a teacher in a large second language program whose administration includes a director of courses or department chair, several student advisors, and a clerical assistant. In speaking informally with you, a student from your class suddenly states that she is very much dissatisfied with her situation in the United States, so much so that she wishes to return immediately to her home country.

Questions:

1. What is the immediate problem?
2. What might the direct and indirect causes of the immediate problem be?
3. What other potential or actual problems do you see?
4. What else do you need to know (e.g., about the student or about the situation relating to the problem)?
5. How do you obtain the information that you need?
6. What should you say or do (a) when meeting with the student and (b) after meeting with the student?
7. What other people (if any) need to become involved?
8. What are some things to watch out for or to be particularly sensitive to?

Figure 6   Problem-solving activity based on student case

main error types and to try to characterize the learning stages of the students. Based on this analysis, the candidate may then be asked to decide on a proficiency grouping for the students and to make pedagogical recommendations for each of them. Assuming that the students might all be in the same class, the candidate then decides on the main teaching points for a lesson and develops these into a lesson plan. Such an exercise works well as a group activity within the practicum or as an individual project or take-home examination for a practicum course, a methods and materials course, or as a section of a master's exam. This exercise is an example of a kind of problem-solving activity that teachers are involved in quite typically in second language classrooms. Figure 6 provides another example of a problem-solving activity, this one based on a case study.

Student Case (Figure 6). This exercise can be carried out in stages, as a sequence of activities that begins with an individual or small-group analysis of the case and then moves to a whole-class discussion. Given sufficient time, it can easily evolve into an extended discussion on several

145

topics related to the case study, such as: (a) the difficulty of determining the source of student problems; (b) the appropriate role of the teacher in relation to students; (c) the extent to which teachers should become involved in students' personal problems; and (d) the question of when it is appropriate to disclose information about individual students to others with special authority or expertise. These topics generally relate to the larger topic of professional ethics in teaching. The exercise in Figure 6 can therefore form the starting point for a unit in which candidates seek to draft an ethics statement or code, as a way of examining personal values and of trying to codify the philosophy of teaching inherent in a given field.

The exercise in Figure 6 or any other that involves analysis of situations and behaviors can be followed up by a role play – in this instance, a role play of a conference between teacher and student. Role plays for putting teaching ideas into practice, and particularly those emphasizing decision making and communication, are a valuable use of time in the teaching practicum or teaching methods course. The role plays can be videotaped and later analyzed for effectiveness of communication. Many kinds of analytical and simulational activities can be based on videotaped segments of actual classes or commercially available enactments of classes. A sequence of activities beginning with a video viewing and culminating in a role play between teacher and teacher supervisor is illustrated in Figure 7.

Video Viewing and Role Play. Part One of this exercise (Figure 7a) is intended to develop awareness of the differing perspectives that individuals may have on the same teaching event and to shape the communication that will take place in the subsequent role plays. The role plays of Part Three illustrate some of the difficulties involved in effectively giving and receiving feedback on performance and in reaching compromise solutions that are agreeable to more than one person. The viewings should be followed in Part Two (Figure 7b) by general discussion, in which the teacher educator helps the candidates to extend their lists of points. In Part Three (Figure 7c) candidates can be put into groups of four, in which pairs alternate in the two roles as the other two candidates act as observers. The first pair in each group can select the roles that they prefer, and the second pair can perform the role play with a different combination of roles. Feedback can be offered within the group directly after each role play or can be reserved until both pairs have completed their turns. A whole-class follow-up discussion can focus on problems that the pairs faced in completing the task of Part Three.

The sequence of activities can be done more than once, using a different video each time. The video(s) to be used in this exercise should be selected carefully, as the choice of video – especially the first time the exercise is done – affects the outcome of the role plays. Starting out

---

VIDEO VIEWING AND ROLE PLAY

You will view a short videotape segment (10 min.) of a class three times. Each time you will take notes on the video in the spaces provided, according to the instructions. After the observations, you will participate in a follow-up activity and discussion. These activities will supply background for a series of supervisory role plays.

Part One: Observation

First Viewing [Objective Observer]: Watch the videotape the first time as an objective observer: e.g., as a researcher interested only in correctly recording as much data as possible. Record as many specific details about what happens in the lesson segment as you can, focusing on the behavior of both the students and the teacher.

Second Viewing [Complimentary Observer]: Watch the videotape the second time as a complimentary observer: e.g., as a beginning teacher who is very impressed with the person's teaching. Look for things to compliment and list as many positive aspects of the lesson segment as you can find in the behavior of the students or the teacher.

Third Viewing [Critical Observer]: Watch the videotape the third time as a critical observer: e.g., as a supervisor who feels that the teacher is not performing up to par and that definite improvement is needed. Imagine that you are looking for "evidence" to document poor performance. Look for things to criticize and list as many negative aspects of the lesson segment as you can find in the behavior of the students or the teacher.

Figure 7a   Video viewing activity

with a videotaped segment of a poorly taught class or one taught by someone known to the students can undermine the exercise. It is therefore recommended that the exercise be carried out first using a videotaped segment of a class taught by someone unknown to any of the candidates and previously evaluated by the trainer or other supervisor as a good

---

VIDEO VIEWING AND ROLE PLAY (cont'd)

Part Two: Preparation for role plays

As a whole-class activity, compare your list of behaviors in each of the three categories of observation with those of your classmates. Add any observations, compliments, or criticisms that you would like to your original lists. Then summarize your observations in the categories below in preparation for the role plays in Part Three.

Basic Structure of Segment Observed

Main Features of Behavior of Students

Main Features of Behavior of Teacher

Main Aspects to Compliment

Main Aspects to Criticize

Questions to Ask

Figure 7b   Activity to prepare for role plays following video viewing

class.[2] Later, if the candidates' own lessons have been videotaped, they can complete Parts One and Two individually outside of class based on the videotapes of lessons by their practicum classmates, then hold actual postobservation conferences in which each member of a pair seeks to

2 Permission should be obtained in advance from the teacher who has been videotaped for the use of the videotape in the exercise.

VIDEO VIEWING AND ROLE PLAY (cont'd)

Part Three: Role plays

As a follow-up to the video that you just observed, two or more role plays will take place. You will take the role of either the person just observed or the teacher's new supervisor. Both positive and negative roles are provided so that you may try out different combinations of these. Assume that you are having a conference soon after the observation has taken place, as part of the normal teaching evaluation process. The aim of the meeting is to review performance in the class observed and to reach agreement on two potential areas for professional growth/improvement and to develop concrete action steps that both parties can agree on to accomplish the goals.

Teacher: Positive role
You have basic confidence in yourself and your teaching, yet you realize that there is always room for growth and improvement. In the conference, your primary objective is to establish a good working relationship with your new supervisor. Secondarily, you would like to get some constructive advice about your classes from the supervisor, whom you know to have considerable experience and expertise in language teaching.

Teacher: Negative role
You lack basic confidence in yourself and your teaching, and you are not comfortable accepting feedback on your teaching unless it is 100% positive. Because of negative experiences with a previous supervisor, you feel threatened by this conference. Your primary objective is to convince your new supervisor that you are doing a good job and that no one needs to worry about you. Secondarily, you want to establish the fact that you have job security and do not have to listen to any advice.

Supervisor: Positive role
You are a confident and supportive person, with positive attitudes about teachers and teaching. You strongly believe that a "carrot" rather than a "stick" is more effective in changing behavior. Your primary objective is to establish a good working relationship with the teacher. Secondarily, you would like to discuss areas of common ground based on your observation of the teacher's class.

Supervisor: Negative role
You lack confidence in your abilities as both teacher and supervisor. As a consequence, you tend to take a defensive, condescending stance toward those you supervise. Your primary objective is to establish that you are an experienced expert, and know how the teacher can improve teaching performance. Secondarily, you want to establish that you have control over the teacher's job.

Goals (To . . .)	*Action Steps (By . . .)*
1.	
2.	
.	
.	
.	

Figure 7c   Follow-up role plays

interact with the other in a positive, cooperative fashion. The conferences can be accomplished outside of class, with follow-up discussion in the next class period, or during class time, with immediate follow-up on the usefulness of the feedback and the success of the interaction within pairs.

A long class period is desirable for this type of activity, since immediate follow-up is most effective. In general, class periods of two to three hours can be put to good use in a practicum or prepracticum course. This and other types of video-based activities can be more effective than live experiences for certain purposes (Pennington 1985), since the video can be viewed many different times, to reconstruct a scene over and over again. If desired, certain parts can be focused on to make a point relevant to a particular teaching objective, such as facilitating small-group discussions or eliciting responses from individual students. Video-based exercises such as those illustrated in Figure 7 can offer training for real-world observations that candidates will conduct in actual classrooms. Feedback sessions following lessons at the practicum site or lesson demonstrations for peers can be videotaped, and then candidates can discuss the effectiveness of the feedback. In this way, practicum candidates will be preparing for a future as professionals, both as second language teachers and as colleagues or supervisors of other teachers.

Conclusion

As we seek to move second language teaching away from the status of "magic" or "art" and toward the status of profession, an important goal will be public recognition of the existence of the field of second language teaching as such. Part of the professionalization of language teaching involves the codification of the knowledge of the field into explicit goals for teacher preparation and effective methods for achieving these goals. For continuing career growth and individualized development, primary goals are:

- a knowledge of the theoretical base of the field in language learning and classroom research;
- informed knowledge of self and students;
- attitudes of flexibility and openness to change;
- decision-making and communication skills;
- the analytical skills necessary for assessing different teaching situations and the changing conditions in a classroom;
- awareness of alternative teaching approaches and the ability to put these into practice;
- the confidence and the skills to alter one's teaching approach as needed;
- practical experience with different teaching approaches.

Methods that involve the future teacher in practical experiences – both simulations and real-life teaching experiences – and in analysis of these, and which are grounded in educational experiences that include theory and research, constitute a logical preparatory base for the lifelong second language professional. Such methods, which apply the combined insights and skills of these practical and intellectual strands in a practicum component, are a fundamental part of a coherent language-teacher education curriculum directed at the long-term development of its graduates.

Questions and tasks

Chapter 7 (Freeman)

1. To what extent does the relationship between teacher educator and student teacher parallel that between teacher and learner?

2. Freeman implied that the central goal of teacher education is "fostering independent teachers who know what they are doing and why." Do you agree that this is a central goal of teacher education? To what extent does the chapter illuminate ways in which this goal might be achieved?

3. Evaluate Freeman's options for intervention by completing the following table.

Teacher education options	Strengths	Weaknesses
Directive		
Alternative		
Nondirective		

4. As a teacher educator, how would you deal with the following situations if they occurred during practice teaching?
  a) The practice teacher explains a point of grammar incorrectly.
  b) The student teacher fails to deal with four students at the back of the class who constantly disrupt others.
  c) The student teacher persists in drilling a grammar point that is clearly beyond the processing capacities of the learners.
  d) The student teacher does not provide enough wait-time for most pupils to answer questions.
  e) The student teacher talks for 80% of the lesson.
How would you characterize your responses in terms of Freeman's three options?

Chapter 8 (Gebhard)

5. What evidence is there in Gebhard that student teachers do change their teaching behavior as a result of teaching practice?

6. Are the behavior changes described by Gebhard high inference or low inference?

7. What created opportunities for change in teaching behavior?

8. To what extent does the Gebhard chapter reinforce the chapter by Gebhard et al. in Part I?

9. What are the implications of Gebhard's chapter for the organization and management of practicum components in professional development programs?

Chapter 9 (Pennington)

10. What is your understanding of Pennington's concept of "professionalism"? In what ways is her concept shared by Freeman and Gebhard?

11. Design a program that incorporates some of the activities suggested by Pennington along with those of Ellis, Nunan, and Wright.

12. How realistic is the view that teachers should also be researchers? What particular skills and knowledge would they need to fulfill this role? Carry out a survey of practicing language teachers to determine:
  a) how many read journals on a regular basis
  b) which journals they read
  c) what type of articles they look for.

13. Examine a teacher preparation program you are familiar with. Which of Pennington's eight goals (see her Conclusion) are reflected in the program?

Part IV Supervision

The chapters in this section complement the discussion of the teaching practicum in Part III by examining in further depth approaches and options available in supervising student teachers. Despite the extensive use of practice teaching experiences in teacher education programs, the supervision provided within such programs is often left almost to chance. Supervision may be left to a cooperating teacher who has had no training or orientation to the supervision process, or it may be handled in ways that fail to provide the student teacher with the most helpful kind of feedback. These and other related issues are taken up by the contributors in this section.

Gebhard suggests that many second-language teacher educators continually limit themselves when it comes to supervision. He then explores alternative ways of carrying out supervision, and outlines six different models of supervision: directive, alternative, collaborative, nondirective, creative, and self-help–explorative.

Next Gaies and Bowers discuss inservice applications of clinical supervision from the perspective of the supervisor, focusing on the roles supervisors must play in settings where other forms of professional development, such as workshops, are limited or unavailable. They draw a distinction between the teacher as supervisor and as educator, suggesting that, as educators, clinical supervisors must do more than simply focus on technical aspects of classroom management. The discussion is supported by a description of professional development programs in use at the University of Cairo and in Yugoslavia.

Fanselow closes the section with a critical analysis of the view that major aims of supervision are to "evaluate" and to "help" teachers-in-preparation. He provides an alternative view of supervision as a means of encouraging teachers to see common classroom events from different perspectives. A number of practical techniques and procedures are suggested for realizing this alternative view.

10 Models of supervision: choices

Jerry G. Gebhard

As ESL professionals, it is likely that most of us have experienced teacher supervision, either as a supervisor, as a teacher being supervised, or as an outside observer. If we were to describe the roles the supervisor played in these experiences, they would probably fall into one or more of the following categories:

to direct or guide the teacher's teaching
to offer suggestions on the best way to teach
to model teaching
to advise teachers
to evaluate the teacher's teaching.

These categories were elicited from many teachers and teacher educators in several countries and appear to be a fairly representative sample. The purpose of this chapter is to demonstrate that supervision can be much more than this.

Six models of supervision are presented and discussed: (1) directive, (2) alternative, (3) collaborative, (4) nondirective, (5) creative, and (6) self-help–explorative. The first model is offered to illustrate the kind of supervision that has traditionally been used by teacher educators. This model has some serious limitations, however. The other five models offer alternatives for describing ways that we can define the role of the supervisor and supervision.

Directive supervision

In *directive supervision* the role of the supervisor is to direct and inform the teacher, model teaching behaviors, and evaluate the teacher's mastery of defined behaviors. There are at least three problems with directive supervision. First, there is the problem of how the supervisor defines "good" teaching. Second, this model may give rise to feelings of defensiveness and low self-esteem on the part of the teacher. Third, there is the problem of assigning ultimate responsibility for what goes on in the classroom. An experience I had as a teacher being supervised illustrates these problems:

I had taken a part-time job at a well-known language school, and as part of that job I was expected to be open to being supervised. One day a person I had never seen before walked in and sat down as I was in the process of teaching a reading lesson. I was trying out a few new ideas and wanted to see the consequences of not going over vocabulary before having the students read. Instead of presenting vocabulary, I was having the students read a story several times, each time working on a different task, such as underlining words which described the person in the story or crossing out words they did not know. The supervisor sat in the back of the room taking notes, and I became nervous. After about fifteen minutes of silence the supervisor came over to me. She smiled and whispered that she would like to meet with me at her office after class. She opened the meeting by leaning over, touching me on the arm, smiling and saying, "I hope you don't mind. I'm not one to beat around the bush." I sank a little further into my chair. She proceeded to tell me that I should always write difficult vocabulary on the board and go over it before the students read, that students should read aloud to help them with pronunciation, and that in every class there should be a discussion so that students have the chance to practice the new vocabulary.

This experience was one of several similar ones I had with that supervisor and others at the same institution. At the time I wondered what made the supervisor's way of teaching more effective than what I wanted to do. Now I know that it was not more "effective." It was simply different. It nevertheless appears that most people, including teachers, supervisors, school administrators, the owner of the neighborhood hangout, and the person on the street, believe that they can identify good teaching when they see it.

It is probably not, however, good teaching that these people see. It is, more likely, their *idea* of what good teaching should be. Most people would agree that good teaching means that learning takes place. But how do we identify what specific teaching behaviors cause the students to learn? Many years of process-product research have failed to identify specific teaching behaviors which are unambiguously linked to learning outcomes. Despite this, "the ultimate aim is still to end up with something helpful to say to teachers and their trainers" (Allwright 1983: 199). The search for effective teaching goes on. For these reasons, it is difficult to justify prescribing what teachers should do in the classroom.

A second problem with directive supervision is that it can make teachers see themselves as inferior to the supervisor, and this can lower their self-esteem. For example, after I met with the directive supervisor I referred to earlier, I felt doubtful about myself as a teacher. Another negative consequence of directive supervision is that it can be threat-

157

ening. While going to work I remember saying to myself more than once, "Oh, supervisor, don't come today. Please don't come today." I knew that the supervisor was not going to like what I had prepared. Rardin describes this state of affairs clearly when she notes that "threat can produce a 'half-in–half-out' engagement" (1977: 184). Although I wanted to fully engage myself in my own ideas of what the students could benefit from, I could not because of the overriding threat that the supervisor would disapprove.

In other words, threat can cause teachers to become defensive toward the supervisor's judgments. Rowe has pointed out that if we feel that we are being judged, we lose the "right to be wrong" (1973: 308). She believes that if we lose this right, we can also lose the courage to try new ideas, to explore more than one alternative, and to explore freely.

A third problem with directive supervision is that a prescriptive approach forces teachers to comply with what the supervisor thinks they should do. Blatchford (1976), Fanselow (1987b; and this volume, Chapter 12), Gebhard, Gaitan, and Oprandy (this volume, Chapter 2), and Jarvis (1976) have all strongly suggested that this keeps the responsibility for decision making with the teacher educator instead of shifting it to the teacher.

Alternative supervision

Copeland (1982) discovered in his research on teacher attitudes to supervision that some teachers feel the need to be told what to do when they first begin to teach. He attributes this to their insecurity in facing students without having the skills to cope with that situation. Teachers from a number of countries have also pointed out that if the teacher is not given direction by the supervisor, then the supervisor is not considered qualified. The roots of directive supervision grow deep.

However, there is a way to direct teachers without prescribing what they *should* do. This way is through a model that Freeman (1982) calls *alternative supervision*. In this model, the supervisor's role is to suggest a variety of alternatives to what the teacher has done in the classroom. Having a limited number of choices can reduce teachers' anxiety over deciding what to do next, and yet it still gives them the responsibility for decision making. Freeman points out that alternative supervision works best when the supervisor does not favor any one alternative and is not judgmental. The purpose of offering alternatives is to widen the scope of what a teacher will consider doing.

Although Fanselow's (1987b; this volume, Chapter 12) approach to teacher supervision includes much more than the generation of alternative teaching behaviors (see section on self-help–explorative supervision), he does offer suggestions about how alternatives can be used to guide the beginning teacher. One way is to have teachers try the opposite of what they usually do. For example, if students usually read silently, the teacher can generate a lesson in which students read aloud to the whole class or in pairs. Another way is to duplicate inside the classroom what goes on outside of the classroom setting. For example, the teacher can have students stand up when conversing. He also trains teachers to be aware of "leaden" (as opposed to "golden") moments – to identify consistent problems – and to try alternative behaviors to resolve the problem. For example, if students always come late to class, the teacher could offer coffee or another reward to those who come on time, or simply talk with the students or write notes to them about the importance of starting class on time.

The aim, as Fanselow makes clear, is for teachers to try alternative behaviors and to pay attention to the consequences. If teachers are provided with strategies that give them a way to understand the consequences of what they do, teachers can gradually rely on themselves to make teaching decisions.

Alternative supervision could have been used in the situation I described at the beginning of this chapter. Instead of prescribing what I should have done with my reading lesson, the supervisor could have had me describe (1) what I did that day and then (2) the opposite of what I did. She could have requested that I try the opposite to see what happens, which could have taught me a strategy of paying attention to the different consequences on the students' behavior of doing lessons differently. Or, the supervisor could have said something like, "I don't know what the best way to teach a reading lesson is. You will have to make those decisions for yourself. However, I can share my experience. Let me give you three ways to teach a reading lesson. You can try the one you like or try all three on different days. The first way you can teach a reading lesson is . . . "

Collaborative supervision

Within a collaborative model the supervisor's role is to work with teachers but not direct them. The supervisor actively participates with the teacher in any decisions that are made and attempts to establish a sharing relationship. Cogan (1973) advocates such a model, which he calls "clinical supervision." Cogan believes that teaching is mostly a problem-solving process that requires a sharing of ideas between the teacher and the supervisor. The teacher and supervisor work together in addressing a problem in the teacher's classroom teaching. They pose a hypothesis, experiment, and implement strategies that appear to offer a reasonable solution to the problem under consideration.

Going back once more to the supervisory situation I was in, collaborative supervision could have been used thus: Instead of telling me what I should have done, the supervisor could have asked, "What did you think of the lesson? How did it go? Did you meet your objective?" This would be said in a positive, interested, and nonjudgmental way. Then the supervisor could have more easily understood my ideas, the problems I saw in the lesson, and my objectives. It would have been possible for the supervisor to also have input, to make suggestions, and to share her experience. A decision about what to do next could have been made together.

It is worth mentioning that although the ideals of equality and the sharing of ideas in a problem-solving process can be appealing, the ideal and the real are sometimes far apart. Not all teachers are willing to share equally in a symmetrical, collaborative decision-making process. A colleague from the Middle East remarked to me that if, as a supervisor, he attempted to get teachers to share ideas with him, the teachers would think that he was not a very good supervisor.

Nondirective supervision

The essence of nondirective supervision is captured in the following observation by a teacher-in-preparation: "My supervisor usually attempts to have me come up with my own solutions to teaching problems, but she isn't cold. She's a giving person, and I can tell that she cares. Anyway, my supervisor listens patiently to what I say, and she consistently gives me her understanding of what I have just said." The same teacher also expressed the consequences of this type of supervision for her when she added, "I think that when my supervisor repeats back to me my own ideas, things become clearer. I think this makes me more aware of the way I teach – at least I am aware of my feelings about what I do with students."

Supervisors who listen and demonstrate an understanding of what the teacher has said are providing what Curran (1978), who bases his ideas on the work of Carl Rogers, calls an "understanding response." An understanding response is a "re-cognized" version of what the speaker has said. In supervision, the supervisor does not repeat word-for-word what the teacher has said but rather restates how he or she has understood the teacher's comments.

Applying a nondirective approach to the supervisory situation I described at the beginning of this chapter, the supervisor could have said something like, "You just explained to me what and why you did what you did in the classroom. Let me see if I understand what you said. You told me that you wanted to see the consequences of trying a reading lesson where the students read silently while doing tasks, such as underlining words which describe the main character in the story. You said that you did not write vocabulary on the board because you wanted to see if the students would come up with the words they wanted to learn. You also said that you wanted students to..."

According to those foreign and second language teacher educators who have discussed a nondirective supervisory approach (Dowling and Sheppard 1976; Early and Bolitho 1981; Freeman 1982), if the supervisor had been more nondirective when supervising me, I could have had the freedom to express and clarify my ideas, and a feeling of support and trust could have grown between the supervisor and me. I could have realized a freedom to try new ideas and to fully invest myself in what I was doing. I could also have had the chance to raise questions about myself as a teacher and about the consequences that my teaching had on the students. I could have gained experience in making decisions on my own, and I could have further realized my own responsibility for my teaching behavior.

Nondirective supervision can also have a different result. Some teachers report that it makes them feel anxious and alienated. One reason for anxiety may be due to the inexperience of the teacher. For example, I once supervised a new teacher through mostly nondirective means. At one point he asked, "But what do you think I should do in the classroom? How can I know what to do if I have no experience doing it?" If we follow the assumption that teachers benefit from what they think they need (Copeland 1982), then a nondirective model of supervision might not always be appropriate.

The way the supervisor understands nondirective supervision could also cause the teacher anxiety. Perhaps the supervisor has simply been using the surface techniques while ignoring the deeper philosophical principles. "To borrow only certain outward features of the approach without understanding what its real power is would be like using an airplane only as a car or a sophisticated computer only as a typewriter" (Blair 1982: 103–4).

At the deeper philosophical level, we need to understand the importance of working with the "whole person" of the learner (Curran 1976, 1978; Rardin 1977; Taylor 1979; Stevick 1980). Curran advocated such techniques as the nonjudgmental "understanding response" to break down the defenses of learners, to facilitate a feeling of security, and to build a trusting relationship between learners and the teacher. This trusting relationship allows the teacher and learners to "quest" together to find answers to each learner's questions.

161

Jerry G. Gebhard

Creative supervision

De Bono's statement that "any particular way of looking at things is only one from among many other possible ways" (1970: 63) serves as the basis of creative supervision. Each model of supervision presented thus far in some way limits our way of looking at supervision. The creative model encourages freedom and creativity in at least three ways. It can allow for (1) a combination of models or a combination of supervisory behaviors from different models, (2) a shifting of supervisory responsibilities from the supervisor to other sources, and (3) an application of insights from other fields that are not found in any of the models.

Working with only one model can be appropriate, but it can also be limiting. Sometimes a combination of different models or a combination of supervisory behaviors from different models might be needed (Freeman, this volume, Chapter 7). Freeman (1982), for example, selects a particular supervisory approach according to the type of information the teacher is seeking. If new teachers are trying to find out "what" to teach, he uses a directive approach. If they want to know "how" to teach, he uses an alternatives approach. If they want to know "why" they teach, he uses a nondirective approach. One supervisor I know likes to work with teachers through alternative supervision and will sometimes model the alternatives. Gradually he starts to use nondirective supervision as the teachers gain the ability to generate their own alternatives and understand the consequences of what they do in the classroom. Another colleague approaches supervision through a nondirective model; after she gains the teachers' trust, she begins to collaborate more with them. The number of combinations is endless.

A second way that a creative model of supervision can be used is to shift supervisory responsibility from the supervisor to another source. For instance, teachers can be responsible for their own supervision through the use of teacher centers (Zigarmi 1979). Teacher centers are places where teachers can go to find answers to questions, use resources, and talk about problems with other teachers or special "consultants" or "supervisory experts." Rather than the supervisor going to the teachers, the teachers can go to the teacher center. Another way to shift responsibility away from the supervisor is to have peer supervision, where fellow teachers observe each others' classes. In this case there is no supervisor. I have seen this done in Thailand at the university level where teachers were friends, had no reason to defend their teaching, and enjoyed trying out new ideas in their classes.

A third way that creative supervision can be used is through the application of insights from other fields which are not found in any of the models. For example, some teacher educators have adapted observation systems originally developed for research, such as Moskowitz's (1971) and Jarvis's (1968) adaptations of Flanders's (1960) Interaction Analysis, to help them observe and supervise practice teachers. Other teachers prefer Fanselow's (1977a, 1987b) FOCUS (Foci on Communication Used in Settings) because the five major categories and many subcategories within FOCUS can be used easily as a metalanguage to talk about teaching in nonjudgmental and specific terms.

The application of observation systems has been a valuable asset to supervisors. It allows them to describe rather than prescribe teaching, and observation systems provide a means through which teachers can continue to monitor and study their own teaching. But why stop there? Why not apply yoga and meditation techniques to teacher supervision? Leadership training from business management? Ethnographic interviewing techniques? Storytelling skills used in Hawaiian folklore? Use of metaphors in counseling? As Fanselow (1983) makes clear, we will never know the consequences of trying new ideas in the preparation of teachers if we keep doing the same things over and over again.

Self-help–explorative supervision

The self-help–explorative model of supervision is an extension of creative supervision. The emergence of this model is the result of the creative efforts of Fanselow (1977a, 1981, 1987b, and Chapter 12 in this volume), who proposes a different way to perceive the process that teachers go through in their development, one that provides opportunities for both teachers and supervisors (or "visiting teachers," as Fanselow, this volume, suggests supervisors be called) to gain awareness of their teaching through observation and exploration. The visiting teacher is not seen as a "helper" (which is the basis for other models of supervision) but as another, perhaps more experienced, teacher who is interested in learning more about his or her *own* teaching and instills in teachers the desire to do the same. The aim is for both the visiting teacher and teacher to explore teaching through observation of their own and others' teaching in order to gain an awareness of teaching behaviors and their consequences, as well as to generate alternative ways to teach.

The goal to "see teaching differently" is achieved not because the supervisor has helped the teacher to do so, but because the teacher has discovered a way to view his or her own teaching differently through self-exploration. The aim is likewise for teachers, including the visiting teacher, to construct and reconstruct teaching based on awareness gained from observations of teaching. As Fanselow (this volume) states, based on knowledge gained from the ideas of Paulo Freire, "When we observe others to gain self-knowledge and self-insight and when we generate our own alternatives based on what we see others do, we construct our knowledge" (p. 184).

As a part of the awareness-generating process, teachers visit each other's classes or gather to observe a fellow teacher's class in progress. During these observations teachers take notes in order to capture what is going on. Teachers also audiotape their own teaching or have their teaching videotaped. These tapes are later used as a way for teachers to study their teaching alone or with other teachers. In order to study the interaction in the classrooms they observe on tape, teachers take notes or make short transcripts from segments of the tapes (what Fanselow calls "vignettes"). (For a discussion of observation procedures, see Day, this volume, Chapter 4.)

Teachers practice describing the teaching they see rather than judging it. Language that conveys the notions of "good," "bad," "better," "best," or "worse" is discouraged, because judgments impede clear understanding. Judgments are also avoided because there is, as discussed earlier, little proof that any one way of teaching is more effective than another. (This claim is to be distinguished from research studies that have shown certain kinds of teaching activities to promote or inhibit second language acquisition.)

Part of the process of exploration is to classify or group aspects of teaching that are observed. For example, it is possible for teachers to group the kinds of questions they ask students into "yes/no," "either–or," "tag," or "Wh-." It is also possible to group or classify the target for each question by sex or by where students are sitting in the classroom (front, back, middle). Finally, questions can be classified according to content; for example, questions about language, personal questions, general knowledge questions. Such grouping provides a way for teachers to see teaching differently from how they previously viewed it. As Fanselow (this volume, p. 187) points out:

By seeing that there are many ways to group the same communications, we basically are developing a checklist of options and the multiple characteristics of each.

As such lists and groupings expand, ways to vary our teaching – use different options – become more and more evident. Each activity, and the groups it fits in, provides at least one more variable, with a distinct range of characteristics, that we can manipulate in our own teaching.

Teachers could create their own groupings, but it is recommended that teachers use the categories of others (found in their observation systems) to describe and study teaching. There are at least two reasons for doing this. First, as Lortie (1975) points out, the absence of a common technical language limits the teacher's abilities to communicate ideas about teaching. The language used in someone else's category or observation system can supply teachers with such a metalanguage. Second, a technical language not only provides a common language to talk about teaching, but affords teachers a way to be explicit and highly analytical. It is possible to view teaching not only through any one category but across categories, thus allowing teachers to see patterns in teaching.

There are several category systems that teachers can learn. Ullmann and Geva (1982) have designed a system called TALOS (TArget Language Observation Scheme); Allen, Fröhlich, and Spada (1984; see also Spada, this volume, Chapter 19) a system called COLT (Communicative Orientation of Language Teaching), and Fanselow's FOCUS. Each system provides teachers with a language to talk about teaching and a way to analyze the teaching they observe.

In my experience, use of observation systems to classify and talk about teaching seems to provide much awareness about teaching possibilities. For example, one teacher told me, "You know, when I use FOCUS to guide my observations of the teaching I see, I gain an incredible amount of knowledge not only about how other teachers view teaching, but also about how I can see my own teaching differently as well as consider what changes I can make in my teaching."

Gebhard, Gaitan, and Oprandy (this volume, Chapter 2) offer guidelines on providing opportunities for teachers to more systematically explore teaching. Teachers are encouraged to select some aspect of their teaching they are interested in learning more about, such as the consequences on classroom interaction of using space in different ways; how adding paralinguistic mediums (gestures, touch, use of space), nonlinguistic mediums (objects, silence), or linguistic visual mediums (print) changes the way students react to directions; the consequences of trying out different behaviors in treating student errors; or what happens when "input" is comprehensible and when it is not.

The guidelines include having student teachers video- or audiotape those portions of their teaching pertinent to their teaching interest; making transcriptions and coding the interactions relevant to the investigation; studying the coded transcriptions for behavioral patterns; describing how the teaching affects interaction; deciding on changes in teaching behavior that will break the pattern; implementing the changes while taping the classroom interaction; again transcribing, coding, and studying the interaction for patterns and consequences; and finally, comparing the consequences of the old as opposed to the new pattern. Although such investigative projects require time and interest, teachers who do them learn not only about their teaching, but also about a process that provides a means for them to explore teaching.

Returning to the supervisory situation I described at the beginning of this chapter and applying the self-help–explorative models, we see that the supervisor could have approached me with a proposal to join her

165

(and other teachers) in exploration. Rather than approaching me as an authority whose job it is to help me improve my teaching, she could have explained that she was simply another teacher who is interested in learning more about her own teaching by observing me teach. She could have asked me if I would like to videotape my teaching, learn an observation system so that we could have a common language to talk about the teaching we observe, and join her and other teachers in nonjudgmental discussion of teaching and its consequences. Perhaps in time I would have become interested, through her example, in doing investigative projects of teaching. We could have shared the joy of discovery, generation of teaching ideas, and awareness.

Conclusion

Many second-language teacher educators seem to limit their approach to supervision and their choice of supervisory behaviors. In doing so they risk restricting or, in the case of very directive supervision, even retarding teachers' progress in assuming responsibility for their own teaching and in developing their talents as professional teachers. This does not have to be the case, for there is a wide choice of supervisory behaviors that teacher educators can select from. Each supervisor will have to discover which supervisory behaviors work well. Unless we are willing to explore and use new behaviors in our supervisory efforts, we will never know the consequences that these behaviors can have on the professional development of teachers. It is up to us to continually apply this and other knowledge in our development of more and more sophisticated and productive teacher supervision.

11 Clinical supervision of language teaching: the supervisor as trainer and educator

Stephen Gaies and Roger Bowers

The role that effective teaching plays in the language classroom seems to be regaining, quite deservedly, much of the attention it had lost in some quarters of the profession during the last several years. Evidence of this trend is seen in a recent flurry of position statements and other documents which stress the priority of upgrading the preparation and ongoing guidance of language teachers.

This chapter focuses on one aspect of teacher education: namely, *clinical supervision,* which we define as the process by which teaching performance is systematically observed, analyzed, and evaluated. In this discussion, we limit the topic of clinical supervision in the following ways:

1. We discuss clinical supervision in its inservice applications exclusively. While clinical supervision is an important component of preservice preparation of teachers, we will be concerned only with its use in monitoring, guiding, and improving the performance of practicing teachers.
2. Our discussion of clinical supervision examines this component of teacher development from the perspective of the supervisor. We examine the roles that supervisors must play and the skills they must have to perform those roles, and we are less concerned, for example, with clinical supervision as it is perceived by teachers themselves.
3. Finally, our interest is in the roles supervisors must play in settings where other forms of teacher development – conferences and workshops, professional books and journals, and regular contact between teachers and the larger language teaching community – are limited or unavailable, and where directives and advice on language teaching come most usually from a highly centralized authority – for example, a regional or national ministry. To amplify this latter point, we should stress that we are not concerned here with clinical supervision in settings where preservice preparation aims at providing teachers with a broad repertoire of classroom strategies and techniques and where extensive teacher initiative in the areas of materials selection and classroom practices is a basic expectation of practicing teachers.

Having limited our scope in these ways, we can now introduce what we do cover. First, we examine the clinical supervision process in very general terms (from the perspective just described). In doing this, we emphasize what for us is a key distinction in the roles language teaching supervisors must play: namely, what we label the roles of *trainer* and *educator*. As trainers, supervisors are concerned with technical improvement: that is, in showing teachers that what they are doing can be done better. As educators, supervisors must be concerned with strategic change: that is, in showing teachers that what is done in the classroom might be done differently and in sensitizing teachers to alternative classroom practices.

This distinction is then further explored in two case studies, which in turn suggest the need for and propose a systematic means of preparing supervisors for these dual roles. By looking at these two case studies, one from Yugoslavia and one from Egypt, we argue that in language teaching programs in many settings, the question of preparing supervisors for the tasks they discharge needs to be seriously and systematically considered.

Defining clinical supervision

It is useful to begin our discussion with an exploration of these questions about clinical supervision:

1. *What is clinical supervision?* By clinical supervision, we refer to an ongoing process of teacher development that is based on direct observation of classroom teaching performance. Clinical supervision is a cyclical process consisting of three stages: a *preobservation* consultation between the teacher and supervisor, in which the general and specific goals of a classroom visit are established and in which the teacher and supervisor discuss the context in which the observation will take place – in other words, the general conduct and problems in the course as a whole; the *observation* itself; and a *postobservation* analysis and discussion, in which strengths and weaknesses are examined and proposals are made to improve subsequent classroom performance.

2. *What is the relationship between supervision and other components of inservice development?* There are a number of forms of inservice development and support. The best known include seminars, workshops, summer programs, professional meetings, and journals. These formats for professional development, to whatever extent they are available, have the advantage of reaching relatively large numbers of teachers efficiently and economically. The corresponding limitation of these forms of inservice development, however, is that they are

generally "selected and developed for uniform dissemination without serious consideration of the . . . needs of individual teachers" (Sergiovanni and Starratt 1983: 327). By contrast, clinical supervision is aimed at the needs and problems of individual teachers, and the supervision process itself is based on direct examination of individual teaching performance.

3. *What are the goals of clinical supervision?* In the most general terms, clinical supervision aims at promoting more "effective" teaching. As Acheson and Gall (1980) put it, the supervision process has as its goal helping teachers reduce the discrepancy between *actual* teaching behavior and *ideal* teaching behavior.

Implicit in this statement of the goal of clinical supervision is the premise that "effective" teaching can be described. This is an issue that has perhaps generated more debate and controversy than any other in our field (see Richards, this volume, Chapter 1, for discussion). It is, however, common practice, in the settings in which we are interested here, for there to be a fairly narrow and uniform specification of acceptable classroom performance. This specification generally prescribes the linguistic, methodological, and management skills that teachers are to exploit and constitutes a definition of "effective" teaching in a given setting.

The disparity, then, between what a teacher is expected to be doing and what the teacher has been observed to do, between the levels of linguistic, pedagogical, and managerial ability that a teacher is expected to have and the observed performance of the teacher, becomes the focus of supervision. The role the supervisor must play in this process, however, will depend on several factors.

The fundamental factor is whether what a teacher is *expected* to do is something that the teacher has been *prepared* to do. We contend that for the clinical supervision process, there is a fundamental and often ignored difference between teaching behaviors and attitudes that practicing teachers can reasonably be expected, on the basis of their preservice preparation, to be familiar with, and those that have not been introduced in the course of preservice or previous inservice development. In the former case, supervision is a remedial *training* process; in the latter, it is an *educational* one.

The training role of the supervisor is fairly obvious: It involves the use of classroom observation to identify deficiencies and to bring these to the teacher's attention. It involves showing the teacher that what the teacher has done can be done better. In their training role, supervisors may choose from a number of procedures: informal demonstration of the use of a technique, explanation of what should be done, or more elaborate demonstration teaching. The key point, though, is that one presumes that the teacher knows what ought to have been done – how a technique ought to have been exploited, how a lesson ought to be organized, how classroom control ought to be managed.

By contrast, there is the situation of teachers whose classroom performance falls short of what is expected for entirely different reasons. These can be thought of in general as problems that result from deficiencies or gaps in preservice preparation, but it might be useful to list some of the specific problems that fall into this category:

- the adoption of new texts that differ in one or more substantial ways from previous text materials;
- shortages of teachers with conventional preservice preparation, resulting in the use of personnel with no teaching preparation or a different area of specialization;
- the introduction of paradigmatic (methodological) or pedagogical reforms that inservice teachers have not been prepared to implement;
- the establishment of new goals for a language teaching program (for example, a shift toward developing aural-oral fluency); and
- the prescription of new teacher–learner role relationships in the classroom, such as result when a central authority recommends a shift away from frontal teaching in favor of more learner-centered classroom work.

In settings in which other forms of inservice development are available, responsibility for dealing with these problems is less exclusively that of the supervisor, and supervision can focus more exclusively on "quality control": on monitoring teachers' performance of what they themselves have been prepared to do in the classroom. When alternative forms of inservice development are not available, however, it is the supervisor who plays a crucial role in educating teachers to implement changes in the classroom. The supervisor, then, becomes the central link between what an educational authority intends to have happen and what actually takes place in the classroom.

Obviously, in pointing out the dual functions of training and education which supervision involves, we run the risk of overstating the distinction. Quite clearly, what supervisors do often involves a combination of the two roles, so that clinical supervision in any one instance will generally reflect a goal somewhere along a continuum between purely technical improvement of teacher performance and exclusively educational efforts on the part of the supervisor.

The distinction needs to be made, however, since it alerts us to an important need for adequate preparation of supervisors. Unless the preparation of supervisors gives sufficient attention to the dual roles of trainer and educator, the likelihood of planned change taking place smoothly and effectively may be seriously jeopardized. We contend that supervisors must themselves be prepared, and that this preparation should involve experiences and activities through which supervisors themselves are trained and educated for their roles. In other words, supervisors should be *trained* to provide training, and they should also be sensitized to and *educated* in alternative approaches to classroom teaching and learning. The first case study we report on may suggest why this should be so. The second case study may suggest how this is done.

Case studies

Yugoslavia

We first look at English as a foreign language (EFL) teacher supervision in Yugoslavia: more specifically, in the Republic of Slovenia. To do this, some background information on preservice preparation may be useful.

Foreign language teachers – including EFL teachers – undergo different preservice education, depending on whether they are preparing to teach at the primary or secondary level. Primary school teachers are prepared at teacher training colleges, which are oriented to primary school pedagogy. Secondary school teachers undergo a university education. Their program is more general – that is, less specifically geared to teaching – than that offered in teacher training colleges. The university program does, however, include some pedagogical subjects, and secondary school teacher trainees do a limited amount of classroom observation and practice teaching as part of their preservice training.

Inservice supervision is designed primarily to support new teachers at both levels and to provide assistance to the special needs of recent university graduates teaching in secondary schools. This supervision is shared by several different individuals. The director, or *headteacher,* of a school is responsible for orienting a new teacher to the teaching and administrative (clerical) procedures in the school. The headteacher's evaluation of a new teacher centers largely on the teacher's performance "as a worker": in other words, on how well the teacher functions as a member of the school staff. During the first year of teaching, a new teacher is paired with a *senior teacher* in the same school. The senior teacher helps the new teacher adjust to the demands of teaching, helps familiarize the teacher with school procedures, counsels the new teacher – both by anticipating potential problems and by helping the teacher deal with difficulties that arise – and provides a model for the new teacher to emulate.

The headteacher and the senior teacher are the internal components of the supervision process, and their primary roles are as monitor and counselor, respectively. The *regional foreign language advisor* is the external component of inservice supervision, and it is the foreign language advisor who does clinical supervision. Although the problem varies from region to region, in general clinical supervision takes place less frequently than either teachers or advisor would prefer. Classroom visits by advisors are in part evaluative; the advisor determines whether teachers are teaching according to accepted principles and whether they are following current methodological recommendations. Only rarely, however, do evaluations of teaching performance lead to the dismissal of a teacher; for this reason, in conjunction with the fact that there is no merit system in which an advisor's evaluation might play a role, an advisor's visit tends to be viewed mainly – both by advisors and teachers – as serving a constructive inservice development function.

The main problem foreign language advisors face in their roles as trainers is making sufficiently frequent classroom observations. Slovenia is divided into nine regions; each of these regions in principle has its own foreign language advisor. Currently, however, there are only five regional foreign language advisors in Slovenia: for Maribor, Celje, Ljubljana, Nova Gorica, and Kranj. The other four regions are looked after by these five advisors, who thus find themselves with many more schools to visit than is practical. Though the regions differ to some extent in size and number of schools, the responsibilities of the foreign language advisor for the Kranj region will give a reasonably representative idea of a foreign language advisor's supervisory responsibilities. In this region, the advisor supervises 50 English teachers and 15 German teachers in 28 primary schools, and a total of 48 language teachers (30 English, 10 German, 5 French, and 3 Russian) in 14 secondary schools.

The more serious problem currently facing foreign language advisors and teachers in Slovenia concerns the educational role that advisors are expected to play in implementing a recent series of curricular reforms. Within the space of a few years, three major curriculum changes have taken place in English language teaching in Slovenia. One was the adoption of a new series of secondary school texts. These texts reflect the second major curricular effort: a much greater emphasis on small-group and pair work in communicative tasks, a major step away from almost exclusively teacher-directed classroom activity. Finally, there have been directives to emphasize English for special (vocational) purposes beginning in the first year of secondary school English; by the third year, students are supposed to be working with materials geared very narrowly to their occupational or professional aspirations.

These reforms have both proponents and critics among secondary school teachers; nearly all teachers and advisors agree, however, that the responsibility for providing teachers with the information and new techniques necessary for these reforms to be implemented successfully falls almost exclusively on the foreign language advisors. There is general agreement among advisors that:

1. clinical supervision is currently not sufficiently frequent to accommodate the considerable amount of training and education that curriculum reform of this scope demands;
2. the supervisors themselves are unprepared to provide teachers with a clear specification of how their teaching behavior must change to accommodate these new language teaching directives and materials; and
3. perhaps most importantly, the sensitivity to and acceptance of the need for change that supervisors must impart to teachers is something with which the supervisors themselves are not entirely familiar.

Since English teachers in Slovenia *have* been encouraged for some time to take some degree of initiative in organizing classroom lessons and in choosing classroom activities, the perception of advisors that their role in educating teachers through clinical supervision is one for which they are insufficiently prepared points even more strongly to the need for adequate preparation of supervisory personnel. This in turn raises the following question: How can we prepare supervisors to fulfill more effectively their roles as trainers *and* educators in situations in which they constitute the main link between classroom teachers and decisions made at the highest levels of educational authority?

The second case study, in which we describe programs and procedures in somewhat greater detail, offers an example of a program of supervisor preparation that takes into account the dual role that language teaching supervisors must play.

Egypt

This section describes supervisor preparation programs introduced from 1981 at the Centre for Developing English Language Teaching (CDELT), Ain Shams University, Cairo, Arab Republic of Egypt; and in particular the Professional Diploma in Teaching English as a Foreign Language. Candidates for the diploma are all qualified and experienced Egyptian teachers of English. A major objective of the course is to train and educate them so that they can train others: They enter the course as teachers, and leave it as counselors and supervisors – generally within the *senior teacher* role described earlier. Techniques of clinical supervision are incorporated into the diploma course for two reasons. First, the course members must be provided with techniques whereby they can supervise teachers in the field and promote effective learning – this is Gaies's "training" function at one remove. Second, as future leaders in the field, they must be alerted to alternative strategies and techniques – the "educational" function. The first approach encourages the short-term view that what is already being done in the classroom can be done with better results; the focus is on feasible adjustments in teacher performance. The second approach encourages a longer-term perspective, that different things can happen in the classroom and will have different results; the focus here is on ideal directions of change in the national expectations for teacher performance.

There is a further reason why clinical supervision figures significantly in the program, and this rests upon the necessarily empirical nature of classroom observational techniques. Through the native speaker expertise provided by British and American agencies, CDELT seeks to make available to Egyptian educators current developments in teaching EFL in Britain and the United States. But it is Egyptian students and colleagues who have the critical task of assessing the relevance of these ideas to the particular conditions of the Egyptian classroom – a judgment that we, as outsiders, are neither equipped nor authorized to make. We do not believe that such a judgment can be made on purely theoretical grounds. The development of an "appropriate" or "intermediate" methodology must be based on clinical study of existing and suggested approaches and methods in the classroom contexts in which they are and might be applied. The analogy with the aid concept of "intermediate technology" is an instructive one.

Five principles underlie the clinical supervision component of CDELT courses. These are:

1. There should be a balance between theory and practice, between the "educational" and the "training" functions.
2. The feasibility of proposals for change in teacher performance should be judged against the real constraints of the teaching context.
3. The personal sensitivity essential to effective counseling and training is best developed within the security of a system or "paradigm" of counselor–teacher interaction.
4. Observation should be systematic and focused, with evaluation based on evidence available to the teacher.
5. Counseling should guide the teacher toward specified, measurable, and moderate changes in behavior.

Examination of these principles offers an indication of the strategy and content of the CDELT approach to supervisor preparation.

   1. *There should be a balance between theory and practice.* The diploma

is a full-time course of 24 weeks. It includes 20 weeks of coursework, in four blocks of 5 weeks each, and one 4-week block of practical experience, in the middle of the five blocks.

During the first two blocks, along with courses related to language improvement, there are lectures and seminars in introduction to linguistics, theories of English language teaching, and teaching methods. These satisfy the need to establish perceptions of what language is, what teaching is, and alternative approaches to the teaching of English.

In addition, the second block, leading up to the practicum, devotes substantial time to developing a familiarity with techniques for observation and evaluation, training and supervision. Trainees watch techniques in use, either by the trainer or by each other, and also experience their application in the peer context to the remediation of their own teaching performance.

The practicum is, unusually in our experience, a period not of teaching practice but of *training practice,* conducted in local state preparatory schools. Course members, working in twos or threes in a school with a small self-selected group of teachers, get extended practice in preobservation, observation, and postobservation techniques; they move from unstructured to structured observations; and they practice their skills in teacher counseling and training.

In the blocks that follow the practicum, the group reviews that experience, basing their discussions on the permanent evidence provided by a range of observational techniques. Additionally, attention is given to the production and peer testing of compact training materials centering on observed teacher deficiencies. Individual training skills, such as presentation and demonstration, are practiced using these materials.

Over the diploma course as a whole, therefore, we aim to incorporate into supervisor preparation the five essential aims of teacher education identified by O'Brien (1981: 54–63), which among them ensure theoretical appreciation and practical application:

Rationale (the explanation and justification of classroom procedures in relation to psychological, sociological, linguistic, and educational theory)

Experience (as teacher trainees, being subjected to the procedures of observation, evaluation, counseling, and training)

Observation (as detached observers, watching the processes of observation, evaluation, counseling, training)

Trial (practicing in simulated and real contexts the skills of observing, evaluating, counseling, training)

Integration (through practical experience in the counseling context, and

175

subsequent development of "action packages," integrating new techniques of teacher assistance into the existing pattern of supervisory duties)

2. *The feasibility of proposals for change in teacher performance should be judged against the real constraints of the teaching context.* It is important for those new to supervision and counseling to recognize their limitations and to avoid the stress and likely failure involved in trying to tackle problems that they are powerless to resolve.

The recurrent problems that teachers wrestle with and about which they are most likely to complain are, in fact, largely predictable, though the scale and perceived acuteness of problems will vary from individual to individual and system to system. Using techniques described in Early and Bolitho (1981: 71–85), we therefore help our trainees to recognize at the outset of their course what these recurrent problems are. They are simply asked as teachers themselves to set down, through individual introspection followed by group discussion and class review, the ten problems that most prevent English teaching in the schools from being effective. Consistently, the following figure in the list:

large classes
inadequate coursebook (too difficult, boring, irrelevant, etc.)
inadequate time (or unwieldy syllabus)
pressure of formal examinations
poorly trained teachers
poorly motivated teachers (underpaid, etc.)
heavy workload (therefore, lack of preparation)
low student motivation
mixed, including low, student ability
lack of resources (particularly visual aids, language labs)

Once these problems have been recognized, we can discuss which of them lie beyond the scope of the counselor/trainer, which can to some extent be alleviated, and which can be substantially resolved. Such discussion sets broad realistic terms of reference for the counseling/training process. It also incidentally offers the initial exorcism of unmanageable problems as a counseling technique, which they themselves can employ in future.

Teachers in third world contexts are often suspicious of new methodologies developed in what they assume to be different, supportive, well-resourced, and trouble-free environments. Their receptivity can be much expanded by the realization that most teachers anywhere suffer from the same largely predictable constraints, and that new methods are generally intended as steps toward minimizing such problems.

3. *The personal sensitivity essential to effective counseling and training is best developed within the security of a system or "paradigm" of counselor–teacher interaction.* In ideal terms, the relationship between counselor and teacher is a matter for private negotiation, in which the individual style of the counselor interacts with the personality and preoccupations of the teacher to produce a unique prescription for the counseling/training process in each case. This approach is in itself, however, a "counsel of perfection."

In practice, unlike the earlier report of the Slovenian experience, we find that our trainees at Ain Shams are prone to approach the counseling task in ways that are likely to prove unproductive. First, the role of adviser often goes hand in hand with that of assessor or inspector; so there is a tendency to jump to evaluation before the confidence of the teacher has been won or reliable and communicable evidence accumulated of teaching performance. Second, observational techniques will generally tend to follow traditional procedures. They will, for example, omit the preobservational phase; they will cover inadequate samples of teacher performance; they may deliberately exclude investigation of the early and often critical components of a lesson; and they may never have access to other than prescheduled and thus probably stage-managed "model" lessons.

In our supervisor preparation, therefore, we establish a definite procedure for observation–evaluation–counseling–training. The procedure is insisted on in the practicum, and we expect the new counselor to continue to apply it, on the assumption that with experience it will be gradually modified, in just the same way as the novice teacher initially works within carefully prepared lesson paradigms but learns in due course and with the confidence that comes from experience to be flexible and responsive to the student reactions of the moment.

Our paradigm is built on the assumption that the three stages of preobservation, observation, and postobservation are essential. We build these into a three-phase process through an analogy with the doctor–patient relationship and the three phases of diagnosis, consultation, and remediation. The paradigm we enforce is this:

DIAGNOSIS (H-O-R-A-C-E)

H – *Hear.* Listen to the teacher and what the teacher says about objectives, methods, content, procedures for evaluation.

O – *Observe.* Watch the teacher in action, in as representative a set of classroom situations as possible.

R – *Record.*   Use a variety of techniques to record for subsequent discussion the events and skills observed.

A – *Analyze.*   Use a variety of techniques to "make sense" of the data collected.

C – *Consider.*   Think about the findings, trying to *justify* all that has happened. Relate the events to the intentions and limitations of the *teacher;* the objectives and constraints enforced by the *system* (institution, etc.) in which the teacher works; and the principles of "good teaching" recognized within the *profession* at large.

E – *Evaluate.*   Only then reach a judgment of the teacher's performance. Praise where praise is due, and criticize in those areas where adjustment is not only desirable but also feasible.

CONSULTATION (S-S-S-S)

S –   *Sympathize.* Begin the postobservation discussion by showing that you recognize the constraints under which the teacher operates.

S –   *Select.* Avoid a comprehensive or global critique. Concentrate on one or two critical features of performance – areas where your advice is likely to be accepted and applied. (These areas may have been predefined during H if the teacher has invited attention to particular difficulties.)

S –   *Summarize.* Be brief in your treatment of a point, offering compact evidence for a manageable element of teacher behavior.

S –   *Study.* With the teacher, give that behavior close consideration – what happened, what did not happen, why, what alternatives exist.

REMEDIATION (T-T-T)

T –   *Try again.* Merely thinking and talking about what has happened will often make it possible for the teacher to modify their own behavior. The easiest remedy is therefore for the teacher, in his or her normal teaching context and unobserved, simply to try again – to pursue a similar lesson activity with a greater awareness of teaching performance and the options available.

T –   *Team-teach.* Some options may require demonstration. It is difficult, for example, to explain in words the characteristics of effective drilling, or the efficient organization of group work – such things are easier to demonstrate. The most effective demonstration is the one that takes place in the teacher's own classroom and students. The most productive relationship may be that in which counselor and teacher share a lesson, the counselor initially teaching those elements with which the teacher lacks experience.

T –   *Train.* For some purposes or in some contexts, training may be the most effective or economical or feasible strategy. This will generally take place outside the classroom. It may be extensive (full-time training, day-release, formal courses for groups of teachers). It will often be informal (staffroom discussion). Whatever its form, training should aim to incorporate the five elements of rationale, experience, observation, trial, and integration. At this point, individual clinical supervision ends and the treatment of common problems on a group basis through training programs takes over.

4. *Observation should be systematic and focused, with evaluation based on evidence available to the teacher.* Our trainees are offered a wide range of observational techniques on the argument that all techniques have strengths and weaknesses and that use of a variety of procedures tends to aggregate the strengths and neutralize the deficiencies.

We begin with relatively unstructured techniques of recording and analysis – a diary narrative maintained by the observer, an uncategorized teacher study, and a child study maintained over a period of time. Such techniques leave room for the unadulterated perceptions of the observer. They may encourage unsupported value judgments. They generally offer a sequential description of what has happened but omit consideration of what has not happened (and perhaps should have).

Semistructured techniques come next. These include the lesson analysis, working to an approximate prediction of the progression of a lesson. In Egyptian preparatory schools, where patterns are set by teacher training and the prescribed textbook, paradigms such as that of presentation/production/practice are largely applicable. An alternative semistructured technique employs rating schedules that allow the assessment over a fixed period of time of specific ongoing characteristics of teacher style.

Finally, practice in structured observational techniques requires the presentation and discussion of a range of refined category systems, generally concentrating on verbal interaction between teacher and learners. Techniques such as those developed by Flanders (1960, 1970) are used both on a count-coding and on a time-lapse coding basis. In some cases,

179

a transcript of the interaction allows subsequent detailed analysis of forms and functions.

Use of these techniques in the practicum is cumulative. Our trainees enter the schools with the full battery of techniques and instruments at their disposal. In the first week, they use only unstructured observation. In the second week, they add semistructured procedures. In the third week, they use these plus count-coding. During their final week, they use all available techniques. At each stage, they are free to select the particular features that they, with the teacher under observation, decide to focus upon. Weekly workshops back at the Centre allow for discussion of the advantages and disadvantages of each approach.

Emphasis throughout is on the need for value judgments to be supported by evidence in order to provide the teachers with information about their performance which, because of their preoccupation with the task, they are unable to collect for themselves.

5. *Counseling should guide the teacher toward specified, measurable, and moderate changes in behavior.* The final principle is that of modesty and caution. In consultation with the teacher, the counselor will be able to present evidence and advice on a discrete range of teacher behaviors. Within this, an "action plan" can be drawn up jointly with the teacher for the remediation phase.

Often, however, it is useful to present an action plan not simply in terms of the alteration of particular techniques and subroutines but rather as a gradual progression toward the application of new "methods" or the adoption of a new "approach." In pursuing strategic change of this kind, where we can assume continuity of contact between counselor and teacher and continuity of pedagogical development, we are at the point where the balance shifts from individual counseling to group training and from skills training toward a broader program of teacher education and curriculum renewal. Be that as it may, it remains important that the changes that a teacher is counseled personally to make should be small, manageable steps in the right direction – moves which though small in themselves nevertheless represent steps toward a new classroom regime; moves that can be theoretically justified as implying a more communicative approach, for example, or less teacher dependence, or more integrated skills development.

These then are the principles we apply and the procedures we impose in introducing our course members to the techniques of clinical supervision. By providing Egyptian teachers, trainers, and inspectors with these means of finding out what goes on in classrooms and what can go on, we hope to perform a triple task. First, by putting our group through this process of training and of education, we familiarize them with attitudes and procedures which as trainers and educators themselves they can use to support teachers in the field. Second, we are providing them with a practical understanding of current professional developments in language teaching. Finally, by resting our program firmly on the values of clinical supervision, we are offering empirical procedures for assessing the relevance to Egyptian classrooms and teachers of approaches developed elsewhere. By coming to grips not only with new ideas but with the evidence of what happens when they are introduced into the local context, they equip themselves with the tools for establishing an appropriate methodology that can set realistic national objectives for teacher training and education.

12 "Let's see": contrasting conversations about teaching

John F. Fanselow

Aims of supervision and observation

When I used to ask teachers to write down comments they recalled from conversations with supervisors or fellow teachers who had visited their classes or had watched videotapes of their teaching, the comments and exchanges between different supervisors/observing teachers and the observed teachers seemed very different from each other. Others have found this too. Gebhard (this volume, Chapter 10), in a review of different models of supervision – different ways of making comments or of having conversations about lessons between supervisors and teachers – uses these labels: *directive, alternative, collaborative, nondirective, creative,* and *self-help–explorative.*

Although the conversations I asked teachers to recall often indicated an overall tendency to be, say, more collaborative than directive, or more directive than nondirective, I consistently saw elements of many distinct models in the same sets of comments or conversations. I also began to notice that all the distinct models had the same aim: to provide a means for a more experienced person to help or evaluate a less experienced person. Two sources on supervision in second language teaching use the following words and phrases to characterize the purposes of the supervision models they describe: *functions as an arbitrator, commenting, evaluating, helping, provides* (Freeman 1982: 21); *to direct or guide, to offer suggestions, to model teaching, to advise teachers, to evaluate* (Gebhard, this volume, p. 156). All of these words indicate that the person doing the visiting, no matter whether that person is following a collaborative model, creative model, or any other, is there mainly to help or evaluate the practice teacher, fellow teacher, or inservice teacher-in-training.

On first thinking about it, what could be more reasonable than designing models of supervision that provide ways for experienced people to help or evaluate inexperienced people? But thinking about the idea of *help* in other contexts provides a different perspective. Haven't you

Reprinted from "Let's see: Contrasting conversations about teaching" by J. Fanselow, 1988, *TESOL Quarterly* 22, pp. 113–30. Copyright 1988 by Teachers of English to Speakers of Other Languages. Reprinted by permission.
Winner of the 1988–89 Fred W. Malkemes Prize from the American Language Institute at New York University and Language Innovations, Inc.

heard children shout to parents or teachers words like, "Let me do it –
don't show me," or "Don't give me the answer"? When referring to the
need of children to be allowed to do things on their own, Montessori
(1967: 309) made the plea, Let them fill their own buckets. As Alinsky
(1971) reminded us:

It is a human characteristic that someone who asks for help and gets it reacts
not only with gratitude but with a subconscious hostility toward the one who
helped him. It is a sort of psychic "original sin" because he feels that the one
who helped him is always aware that if it hadn't been for his help, he would
still be a defeated nothing. (p. 93)

The type of resentment Alinsky mentions is not necessarily universal.
Some people seem to like to be helped and expect to be told what to do as
well. For them, evaluations containing prescriptions of what to do are
welcome. In discussing the appropriateness of different models for teachers at various stages, Freeman (1982) highlights the value of help and evaluation by pointing out that beginning teachers, for example, seem to
prefer models and direction to collaboration. But even while pleading for
help from the cooperating teacher or supervisor, many practice teachers
assert, "The most valuable part of practice teaching was seeing other
teachers teach!" Seeing other teachers teach is not the same as being told
what to do by an evaluator, nor is it being helped by someone.

As a result of this keen interest that practice teachers and many inservice teachers have in seeing others teach, my fear that helping people
can lead to resentment toward the one providing the help, and the fact
that prescriptions from a supervisor's evaluations can be demeaning and
decrease the teacher's authority and responsibility, I see the need for an
aim of supervision and observation different from the ones frequently
practiced and described in the literature. Whereas the usual aim of observation and supervision is to help or evaluate the person being seen,
the aim I propose is self-exploration – seeing one's own teaching differently. Observing others or ourselves to see teaching differently is not
the same as being told what to do by others. Observing to explore is a
process; observing to help or to evaluate is providing a product.

Besides leading to resentment, help can also lead to "learned helplessness" (Abramson, Seligman, and Teasdale 1978). Helpful prescriptions can stop exploration, since the receiver, as someone in an inferior
position being given orders by someone in a superior position, may easily
develop the "ours is not to wonder why" syndrome.

A conversation reflecting the aims of the usual models might go like
this: "Here I am with my lens to look at you and your actions and tell you
or discover with you what is right and what is wrong and needs to be improved; I will then prescribe better activities or collaborate so we or you
alone can discover better activities." A conversation reflecting the aim of

observation I am suggesting might go like this: "Here I am with my lens to look at you and your actions. But as I look at you with my lens, I consider *you a mirror;* I hope to see myself in you and through your teaching. When I see myself, I find it hard to get distance from my teaching. I hear my voice, I see my face and clothes and fail to see my teaching. Seeing you allows me to see myself differently and to explore variables we both use." Although supervisors may consider their roles so set that empowering teachers to make decisions seems impossible, such redefinition is possible in any field. The role of managers in relationship to workers, for example, is presently undergoing change in many companies.

Although observing others does not automatically lead to seeing oneself differently, mainly because the aim of seeing others to help them is so usual, over time an increase occurs in comments like these: "That teacher said 'Ok, now' to mark changes in activity just as I do"; "How little each of us walks around"; "That teacher spoke to students at eye level some of the time; I do so only during breaks."

The model I am describing grows out of a range of sources, not only my examination of many transcripts of teacher-supervisor conferences. For example, Jarvis (1972) argued that in order for teacher preparation programs to be truly responsive, they need to shift "the responsibility for the decision-making to the classroom teacher ... It is perhaps time to train the teacher to analyze his situation and make his own decision for his situation" (p. 201). As Freire (1970) points out, learning "consists of acts of cognition, not transferrals of information" (p. 67). Each of us needs to construct, reconstruct, and revise our own teaching. He reminds us that for learning to take place we need to resolve the "teacher-student contradiction" (p. 67).

When we observe others to gain self-knowledge and self-insight and when we generate our own alternatives based on what we see others do, we construct our own knowledge and engage in the type of learning Freire has advocated. In a discussion of education, Abbs (1986) has this to say: "Authentic education is to be found in that act of intelligent exploration ... the first priority of teachers should be to secure the necessary condition for the autonomy of teaching and for the freedom to learn" (p. 21). Using the word *supervisor* – a person with super vision – hardly supports our autonomy. When I observe and when I invite others to observe me, I refer to all of us as *visiting teachers* to avoid the use of the word *supervisor*.

Practices

I and others have used various combinations of the following practices in pre- and inservice master of arts and adult education programs. Anyone genuinely interested in exploring, in seeing teaching differently, and anyone who believes that we can learn about our own teaching by seeing others can use the practices.

In my experience, trying to observe and supervise with the aim of exploring practices and of gaining insight into one's own teaching does not in itself enable us to stop treating observation and supervision as a means of helping and evaluating others. For people to begin to learn that they can see their own teaching differently by observing others, I and others have found the following practices for collecting, describing, and interpreting observations useful:

1. Short amounts of time have to be set aside for observation and discussion.
2. Segments from observed lessons need to be collected by note taking, taping, or transcribing.
3. The exchanges and activities in the segments need to be grouped in a range of ways.
4. Finally, what was done, as reflected in notes, tapes, and transcripts, needs to be related to notions, beliefs, and goals. Coupling this data collection and analysis with discussions of freedom and the need for each of us to construct our own knowledge helps many visiting teachers to decrease their suggestions to others, to increase their descriptive and analytical comments about the lessons observed, and to relate their insights to their own lessons.

Although allowing time for discussions of observations as part of a teacher's load is a policy I advocate, this policy is rare. Even in teacher preparation programs, there are not always long periods of time for discussions. Rather than putting off observations and discussions until sufficient time is available, thereby virtually ensuring that they will never take place, I recommend limiting observations and discussions to as little as five minutes.

Obviously, seeing five minutes of a lesson prevents us from seeing lesson development. But look how much we notice in one-minute commercials. In many classes, thirty questions are asked in a minute (Hoetker 1968). A dozen instances of feedback – both the treatment of errors and communications made after acceptable student moves – can be seen in a minute as well (Fanselow 1977b). In a thirty-minute period, hundreds of communications are made, each in split seconds (Jackson 1968).

Though short segments provide much data, short discussions force a limit to the number of communications that can be considered and the number of alternatives that can be generated. Since one or two communications often affect what is done and since many of our communications are unconscious, we can only hope to see and later try out one or two alternative communications per class period. Short time segments do not of themselves lead to fewer evaluative or helping comments or more exploration, however, and that is why the following activities are used.

Collecting and describing data

TRANSCRIBING AND NOTE TAKING

The first step in our observations, no matter how long, is to capture as many of the specific communications as possible by audio- or videotaping, by taking notes, and by drawing sketches or even taking photographs as communications are observed. Later, tapes can be transcribed to reveal details missed in notes and sketches.

Observers can take notes, sketch, and transcribe as they wish. Many put exchanges in dialogue form in their notes. But now and then, one will put teacher communications in the left-hand column of a page and student communications in the right-hand column to highlight them. Many write one line and pause, forgetting that the purpose of looking is to collect data, not to judge the teacher or think of ways to help the teacher. Some prefer sketches to notes, noting the position of teachers and students, their location, or expressions on faces of teacher or students. Others note what is done rather than what is said – movements, objects used, writing on the board.

Except for the instruction that observers are to write down only what happens, not comments about what happens, no directions are given about what observers are to note. Different observers often note different communications, reflecting differences in the values of the observers. Some observers write down things they are interested in seeing in their own classes that they cannot see while they are teaching. Though two observers are likely to capture some of the same spoken exchanges, they are not likely to have the same account of how the exchanges were said or what other communications were made. Discussing what took place and listening to tapes will make clear a central lesson of observation: What we see is not what takes place but what we value as important to see; observing is selecting.

While transcribing exchanges, drawing sketches, or otherwise noting or capturing specific communications, we cannot write comments such as these: "To make the class lively, this teacher needs more activities"; "This teacher should follow the responses with clearer feedback." When not taking notes or transcribing, we tend to revert to our usual pattern of thinking of ways to help or evaluate another. This is a sure way to miss seeing anything differently, a sure way to limit our observations by trying to relate them to our preconceived notions of good and bad teaching.

GROUPING ACTIVITIES

As data are collected, the observers, and in many cases the teacher observed, begin to group the communications. For example, if the teacher asks the students to give synonyms for some words and to draw sketches to show the meanings of other words, the two types of tasks are grouped. One possible grouping that emerges has to do with the fact that one task requires the students to speak and the other one requires drawing and silence.

A range of groupings of tasks and activities, rather than just one, is aimed for. Looking at the same exchanges again, we can group the questions on the basis of who was asked the question. Were students sitting in particular rows asked to perform some tasks more often than students in other rows? Were males asked to perform more of some types of tasks than females? How many tasks did students perform because the teacher requested them to, either by using names or pointing, and how many did they volunteer for?

The purpose of the questions and the grouping is not to imply that, for example, using names is better than pointing or getting volunteers. The questions are asked so that the same tasks or activities can be grouped and categorized on the basis of a range of characteristics. When we look at, say, a dessert menu, we see many characteristics. We have categories such as high calorie or low calorie, sweet or semisweet, high or low cholesterol, easy or difficult to prepare, for children or adults, and so on. By seeing that there are many ways to group the same communications, we basically are developing a checklist of options and the multiple characteristics of each.

As such lists and groupings expand, ways to vary our teaching – use different options – become more and more evident. Each activity, and the groups it fits in, provides at least one more variable, with a distinct range of characteristics, that we can manipulate in our own teaching. Each grouping also reminds us that communications have multiple dimensions, a fact that is hidden by one-dimensional terms often used to judge teaching, such as *great pace, nice grammar work,* or *fine communications.*

Data are also grouped by making lists. For example, one teacher may give the answer to a question after a student cannot answer, and another may give a clue rather than the entire answer. Thus, we have two specific items on a list of feedback possibilities. Clues, too, may be given in various ways. A teacher may sometimes say, "The word starts with a *g.*" Another time the teacher may say, "It has two syllables" or "It is a noun." One of the insights that come as lists are developed of what is observed in distinct areas of teaching such as feedback, group work, and so on is that the range of activities observed in any one class is often small, but across many teachers the range becomes great.

If transcribed communications are merely listed without being grouped or categorized, the list can become very long, of course. By grouping different communications on the basis of inferences we make about them, the value of category labels – technical language – becomes apparent. Thus, from the descriptive statement "Students gave synonyms," an observer and teacher might infer that memory was required but that no motor control was, as in the case of drawing sketches to show the meaning of words. Then, looking at communications from our own or other classes and seeing other activities that require memory alone or memory plus motor control, subsequent communications can be compared with the first ones in the category. The feedback activities listed, such as the distinct clues given, can also be compared and grouped. "Clues given with spoken words" versus "clues given with symbols on the blackboard" would constitute one way to distinguish clues, for example.

After a few discussions between observers (visiting teachers) and the teachers observed (visited teachers), the following general categories inevitably arise: questions that require students to share previous knowledge versus those that require information just presented; tasks done individually or in groups; answers for which the teacher is interested in the form of what is said versus the meaning; questions teachers know the answers to and those they do not know the answers to; communications containing experiences of students and those using language for its own sake; student-to-student communication and teacher-to-student or student-to-teacher communication. Observers are reminded to develop categories that refer to at least two dimensions of any item in order to keep in mind the aim of seeing multiple dimensions of any communication.

The categories for the lists made and the groupings can cover whatever areas that observers and teachers want, as long as the focus is on the data: transcripts, sketches, photographs, notes, and actual recordings as well, when possible. This concentration on the collection and grouping of data makes it difficult to think of helping or evaluating anyone.

Lortie (1975), among others, has said that one of the critical problems that teachers face is that they do not have a language to discuss what they do: "What students [practice teachers] learn about teaching, then, is intuitive and imitative rather than explicit and analytical" (p. 62).

Lortie (p. 73) maintains that the absence of a common technical vocabulary limits the ability to analyze as well as the acuity of the observations that teachers make.

Giving category names to the groups of communications and lists of activities provides a technical language, since those noting the similarities and differences between communications and activities constantly have to go back and forth between data and names applied to distinct types of data until they agree on a fit between the terms and the data. Once teachers and observers have developed some technical terms, coding systems developed by others can be introduced. The one I introduce most frequently is my own, called FOCUS (Fanselow 1987b). COLT (Allen, Fröhlich, and Spada 1984), TALOS (Ullmann and Geva 1982), or any other coding system can also be used (Long 1980).

Starting discussions with a published coding system can make the idea of categories clear earlier, but there are some disadvantages to their early introduction. If teachers and observers are unaware of the problem coding systems were designed to deal with, they may use the systems in a mechanical way. Starting with published systems can also imply that the observers and teachers working jointly may not be up to the development of categories. On the other hand, going through the steps of gathering data and grouping data often shows the value of a technical language. It is also more likely that somebody else's categories can be made our own if we develop some of our own along the way. When those doing the observing develop the categories, knowledge is being created, rather than buckets being filled (Montessori 1967) or information being transferred (Freire 1970: 67).

Interpreting data

Once a range of communications is captured in the form of data and once activities are listed, grouped, or categorized, interpretations can be made. It must be remembered, of course, that collecting data and listing and grouping them according to jointly developed categories or published ones are not activities free of interpretation. In initial discussions, as in initial collection and grouping of data, most participants interpret data in light of preconceived notions of good teaching. But at this stage, attention is given to showing how the data and lists of categories already reflect values, notions, or theories of teaching and learning. If the data indicate, for example, that the teacher smiled constantly, one participant may point out that a person noted smiles rather than frowns or shaking of the head. As the observer who noted the smiles equates smiles with friendliness, he or she realizes how a belief affected what was observed.

Since it is very common for us all to see, list, and group, as well as interpret, what we see in light of our preconceived notions about teaching, there is no way to prevent such "filtered" data collecting, grouping, or interpreting. But this effect can be counterbalanced. After one observer or teacher says that the teacher's smile showed that the teacher was friendly, other possible interpretations of a smile can be sought. Alternative interpretations emerge from asking what smiles have meant in our classes or by asking for possible negative meanings of smiles. Usually, a comment such as "Well, I often smile when nervous" comes forth. Or one will hear, "I smile sometimes when I want students to like me." Different data from the segment being discussed might also be noted: "The smile was fixed as I recall; I frowned a lot too – look at the sketch you made of me."

To encourage interpretations that are quite different from the normal ones that people with similar preconceived notions offer, participants are taught to ask each other to provide at least one interpretation that is seemingly outlandish or different in intent from the ones given. If all the interpretations are positive, possible negative interpretations can be sought. And if all are negative, positive interpretations can be sought. In the case of the smile, a negative interpretation might be that smiling can be used to keep control. Arguments about the superiority of a particular interpretation are not allowed in the beginning. Rather, the goal is simply to try to remind the participants that each event we see can be interpreted in ways different from our usual ways of doing it because we are each limited by the ideas of reality we have.

Another central lesson that emerges from multiple interpretations of the same event is that each event has more than one cause and that these causes need to be specified precisely. A replay of the videotape or a review of the notes or sketches may reveal some of the exchanges that took place before the smile, exchanges that were not seen because they seemed unimportant: the realization that the smile was perhaps the result of a number of small events that had happened immediately beforehand. By searching for different interpretations, observers and teachers are thrown back to the data, lists, and categories, not to seek support for what they thought when they started, but to seek support for the seemingly outlandish new interpretations. Seeing our own teaching differently is not going to happen if we are simply looking at other lessons and interpreting them in the same way we have been looking at lessons and interpreting them all of our lives.

Data and categories can also be interpreted in relationship to beliefs about teaching the participants have heard about. For example, participants can search for communications that are congruent or incongruent with Smith's (1971) admonition that "information about an error and aid in performing a task correctly are more helpful than discouraging comments about an inadequate performance" (p. 229). If a teacher is heard saying "Why can't you ever do it right?" the participants might respond at first by saying that the communication seems incongruent. *Seems* is used because "Why can't you do it right?", if said humorously and with a smile, could be congruent with Smith's advice. Such tentativeness among the participants is possible because of a self-developed realization based on engaging in the process of collecting data, listing specific communications and activities, and relating them to ideas over and over again in short segments of time.

Isolating beliefs about language teaching that can be related to data and categories is not difficult. Most articles and books are written to further beliefs or theories. By relating beliefs from the literature to what is actually done and observed in specific detail, participants clarify beliefs and see ways to translate the beliefs into practice. To translate Krashen's notion of "comprehensible input" (see Dulay, Burt, and Krashen 1982) into action, teachers and observers can first examine exchanges in a range of lessons and then group those that seem comprehensible and those that seem not to be. Barnes's (1976) ideas about "exploratory talk" and "finished talk," about "school knowledge" versus "action knowledge," can be understood, seen, and translated into action only when related to data gathered from lessons.

In addition to relating data and categories to beliefs about learning, we can relate them to goals. If our goal is to ensure that students can obtain literal and implied meaning from what they hear and read but we never ask any inference questions of them, then our practices are not congruent with our goal.

Relating data to notions in articles and books brings us to another activity that can be used in the observations and discussions of teaching: reading. Just as one goal of working in pairs and groups is to provide multiple perspectives, so reading is used to provide different angles. When our partners give us a different view of a lesson, we have to take our usual lenses off, for a few seconds at least, to try to see what they have seen. Published notions, both of ways of looking at teaching (Bateson 1972; Mehan 1979) and ways of teaching (Haskell 1987), show us different maps of similar territory that require us to try on a range of different lenses.

Self-observation and the notion of opposites

Transcribing, listing activities, grouping communications, categorizing and relating these activities to our notions, beliefs, and goals – all show the great number of different ways of seeing variables, relationships between them, and consequences, *if* these activities can be done in pairs or groups. However, often we cannot find even one person to observe us or to be observed.

The basis for getting multiple perspectives when we are in a group is simply to juxtapose different individuals' perceptions. This same idea of juxtaposing, of using opposites, can also be used to provide different perceptions when we are alone. If in our own classes we see the students always sitting in chairs during speaking lessons, we can ask ourselves to juxtapose – to give an opposite posture. In this case two opposites come immediately to mind. Students and teacher alike can sit on the floor, if the room is carpeted, or everyone can stand. Though much conversation outside of the classroom takes place when we are standing, the point of juxtaposing or contrasting opposite situations is to see situations not seen before, not to argue about the absolute superiority of a particular format. And although some may object to standing or to sitting on the floor, by precluding alternatives based on what people might think, we close off inquiry and tend to limit what occurs to our preconceived notions of good and bad teaching.

In addition to generating alternatives by looking at aspects of the classroom, we can compare the communications in a class with those we see outside of a teaching setting. Using our chair example, we can compare where we sit in a teaching setting with where we sit in a nonteaching setting, such as a dormitory room, living room, or park. Finding opposites to what we normally do in a teaching setting or comparing what we do in teaching and nonteaching settings can be extremely valuable in providing the alternative perspectives a partner would supply in pair or group work.

The idea of opposites can also help to broaden the range of interpretations. If the first and only interpretation of a teacher's smile is that the teacher is happy, and no other interpretations come up in a discussion, an opposite interpretation can be offered: "I have interpreted the smile as a good communication; now let me consider a smile a bad communication. Then what could it mean? What are some disadvantages of smiling?"

In second language acquisition research, learner errors were first attributed to the first language of the learners. Then, some began to explain the errors on the basis of developmental stages. Different types of errors were later considered to be caused by different types of tasks used to elicit the sentences that contained the errors (Ellis 1985). What are these but opposite interpretations of the same data? Most fields are enriched by multiple interpretations of the same data, and these multiple interpretations can be generated by considering opposite interpretations to those usually provided.

Even with the concept of opposites to provide different perspectives, self-observation is limited. It prevents us from getting distance from our teaching and seeing our teaching through others. Though transcribing our own teaching gives us some distance from what we do, since the written record removes our voice, the transcriptions often remain too much a part of ourselves.

Meanings

Given the aim I advocate for conversations about teaching, labels often used to classify conversations about teaching, as well as the words in the conversations, take on new meanings. "Ask questions more rapidly" is *not* necessarily a prescription or an offer of help in a conversation in which exploration and seeing teaching differently are the goals. The meaning need *not* be, "Do this because I who visited your class know more than you do and you need help." Rather, the meaning can be, "Try this to see how it alters what has been happening. I am going to ask questions more rapidly too; perhaps different reasons to ask questions both slowly and rapidly will become apparent. We can compare tapes when we have some descriptions of both quick and slow questions." On the other hand, when a visitor in the role of a person in charge says, "You might try a slower pace," though the modal *might* is used, the meaning can be a "helpful" prescription. The message can mean, "I know, and I want you to do what I say." Exploration can be inhibited or completely stopped because the underlying intention of the words can be to show who is in charge.

Even a comment such as "The quick questions were great" can be seen as a description rather than as a judgment if the aim is exploratory. In such a context, the *great* could refer to the execution of the direction rather than to the technique itself.

Words in our conversations, to be judgments, must imply that the speaker or hearer is attributing good or bad, superiority or inferiority, to a practice. If "good lesson" is said or heard to imply that you or a teacher you visited did what was prescribed – what the speaker or hearer considers to be the right way to do it – then a judgment is probably being made in our communication. The words must be heard in relationship to the aim of our conversation and the role of those having the conversation. In the conversations I advocate, judgments are avoided because they tend to close off exploration. They tend to end, rather than continue, a process.

Some label an emphasis on data and description *objective*. I avoid both the terms *objective* and *subjective*. The meaning of *a lot* in "You asked a lot of questions" is not subjective because of *a lot*. Nor are 42 and 2 objective in "You asked 42 questions in 2 minutes." Both statements can be judgments or descriptions, depending greatly on what the speaker's and hearer's aim is and the role each is assuming. Again, if the words are used to see differently, as a means to explore – suggesting the importance of comparing the asking of 42 questions in 2 minutes with 22 in 2 minutes or a few with a lot – then they are both simply descriptive. If the words are used because the speaker or listener – the visited or visiting teacher – is against frequent questions or feels that asking a lot of questions is *not* the thing to do, both groups of words are likely to be judgments. Both can be implied, helpful prescriptions to use fewer questions if they come from, or are addressed to, a teacher who believes "good" teachers do not ask frequent questions.

There is a reason that explanations or proof to support categories or interpretations have not been mentioned. Observers do not request explanations like "Why did you smile?" And teachers do not give such explanations: "I smiled because I thought at that moment the class needed reassurance." These exchanges tend to lead to arguments and can be seen as veiled attempts to support or strengthen the authority of one of the participants. In the model presented here, explanations are replaced by what a person did; what the characteristics were of what was done; how these related to beliefs, theories, or goals; and multiple interpretations of the data and groupings and the relationships among these.

Trying to see how the same words that for so long meant one thing can begin to mean something else is, of course, not something accomplished only by going through a series of steps. Nor indeed is seeing differently – exploration – a point to reach, but rather a tendency, a movement toward.

This tendency, this movement toward, as well as the tendency back toward the usual conversations, is noted by recording the discussions among teachers and observers – visited and visiting teachers. The exchanges in the discussions are dealt with in the same way as exchanges from classes: Short transcriptions are made, communications are grouped and coded, and multiple interpretations are made. They are related to the beliefs upon which this model rests – the trust that can come from joint effort without external evaluation; exploration; multiple perspectives; multiple causation; the idea that much of what we do in classes, just as outside the classroom, is beyond our awareness; and the notion that helping another from a superior position can lead to resentment and dependence.

The discussions of the observations often show confusion, struggles to group and categorize data. They also contain examples of simple causation ("The repetition of the sentence made them learn it"), prescriptions ("You should never put the directions up on the board when they are in their books"), and all the other normal types of conversations we usually have about teaching. But now and then the teaching act is discussed in a way that is congruent with the beliefs of this model.

Conclusion

Judgments and predictable prescriptions are *not* limited to conversations about teaching. In a critique of Vincent Canby's movie reviews, Carney (1986) reminds us that using words like *charming, sincere, buoyant, funny,* and *clever* to review films "amounts to an alarming aesthetic" (p. 30). He goes on:

One is accustomed to seeing invocations of charms, etc., as measures of value ... in ads for Calvin Klein, Christian Dior, Clinique, and Club Med. But these are hardly the supreme values that one would expect in a serious reflection on art... They are, indeed, precisely the values such a reflection should question. (p. 30)

If we discuss teaching with words implying judgments like *exciting, boring, flowed smoothly* – all variations of *good* and *bad* – we limit our perceptions in the same way that such one-dimensional, uncritical words limit our perceptions of film and other forms of art.

The usual conversations, full of prescriptive clichés designed to help or evaluate, no doubt provide more certainty than conversations whose purpose is to see our own and others' teaching differently and to explore reality. In fact, Canby's *buoyant, funny,* and *clever* might be welcome in many conversations about teaching. Conversations between Socrates and others in the Socratic dialogues could not be described in this way! These characters reflect more complexity in their conversations – movement from strongly held opinion to floundering uncertainty to a confused not knowing. Similar stages occur in conversations aimed at seeing teaching differently – exploring. An authentic quest for learning and meaning requires that these stages take place. Neat, pat answers to complex problems were not a part of the Socratic dialogues, nor are they a part of conversations exploring teaching. As Abbs (1986) reminds us in a discussion of Socrates:

To adopt the Socratic view of education would be to reaffirm that education in our culture is primarily concerned with critical reflection... with sustained inquiry into the various forms of meaning, with the lifelong process... that goes well beyond the enclosing pressures of the ego and the ephemeral clamourings of party politics. (p. 21)

To observe others and ourselves with the purpose of helping implies not only that we know that one set of practices is consistently superior to another, but that we know what needs to be done in each distinct setting. It also implies that there is a simple cause–effect relationship between a communication and a result: "Smile and the class will be relaxed"; "Speak slowly and the class will understand." To help another or ourselves means we know what should be done and what practices produce what results. If experience in classes has taught us nothing else, we have learned that each day we and our students are different as a result of ongoing experiences and that practices that seemed to have particular consequences one day have different ones another day.

To *help* means we have something to give another, a product to sell. The whole thrust of the point of view and activities presented here is toward the value of process, not product, and toward the construction of our own knowledge, not the acceptance of the knowledge of others in some type of package, as a product. Freire's (1970: 59) use of *banking* as a metaphor for education that stresses product highlights the aim of many conversations about lessons we observe: the passing of information from one person to another. As Mehan (1979) says:

In sum, providing people with prearranged packages of information is oppressive, for it fails to treat people as responsible for their own lives. Furthermore, these imposed programs often have little to do with the participants' own preoccupations and practical circumstances. Providing people with ways of looking, on the other hand, reminds the participants that they are capable of acting on the world, and that these actions can transform the world. (pp. 206–7)

The model for visiting teachers presented here, like the ideas of Mehan and Freire, all come together in Bronowski's (1956) discussion of the purposes of art and science. For the words *science* and *works of art* in the following quotation, one might consider substituting the words *observation* and *lessons and conversations about lessons,* respectively.

The discoveries of science, the works of art are explorations – more, are explosions – of a hidden likeness... When a simile takes us aback and persuades us together, when we find a juxtaposition in a picture both odd and intriguing, when a theory is at once fresh and convincing, we do not merely nod over someone else's work. We re-enact the creative act, and we ourselves make the discovery again. At bottom, there is no unifying likeness there until we have seized it, we too have made it for ourselves. (p. 19)

When we collect and interpret data from observations and reconstruct our teaching, we are, of course, reinventing the wheel. But why not? Why deny others or ourselves this pleasure? By providing pat prescriptions to *help,* we not only deny others or ourselves the excitement of constructing knowledge, we also imply that we ourselves or those we work with cannot construct knowledge. Moreover, helping can stop exploration. Again, Bronowski's (1956) comments are appropriate. To him, the process of exploration is the "habit of truth": "In science and in art and in self-knowledge we explore and move constantly by turning to the world of sense to ask, Is this so? This is the habit of truth, always minute yet always urgent" (p. 43).

Questions and tasks

Chapter 10 (Gebhard)

1. Compare the six models of supervision presented by Gebhard with Freeman's (Chapter 7) three options for intervention in practice teaching. What points of similarity and difference can you find?

2. List the roles and functions that you feel supervisory teachers play in your own situation.

3. Summarize Gebhard's chapter by completing the following table:

Model	Distinctive features	Strengths	Weaknesses
Directive			
Alternative			
Collaborative			
Nondirective			
Creative			
Explorative			

4. Make a list of all the practical suggestions made by Gebhard that you might suggest to teachers being supervised or that you might experiment with in your own situation.

Chapter 11 (Gaies and Bowers)

5. What is the distinction drawn by Gaies and Bowers between the training and educative functions of clinical supervision? Do you agree with their characterization?

6. What effects do you think that the curriculum changes in Slovenia would have on the skills and knowledge required by teachers? What implications does this have for supervisors?

7. How are the five principles underlying the preparation of supervisors realized at the University of Cairo?

Chapter 12 (Fanselow)

8. What reservations does Fanselow have about the supervisor as "helper" or "evaluator"?

9. Scan Fanselow's chapter and make a list of all the ways in which classroom data can be used by supervisors.

10. Select a segment from a classroom video (or, alternatively, use a live lesson) and carry out Fanselow's suggestions on grouping and categorizing activities. What insights does this yield? How useful do you think these techniques might be for clinical supervision?

11. What suggestions does Fanselow make that might help student teachers link theory and practice?

General

12. What suggestions are made in the three chapters in this section for using classroom data in clinical supervision?

Part V Self-observation in teacher development

The unifying theme in this section is that of the teacher as self-observer. Bartlett (Chapter 13) articulates a view of reflective teaching. Proponents of reflective teaching suggest that experience alone is insufficient for professional growth, and that experience coupled with reflection is a much more powerful impetus for development. Related to the notion of reflection is the concept of criticism. The critically reflective teacher is one who moves beyond the search for instructional techniques alone (asking "how to" questions) to a concern for "what" and "why" questions. The latter questions, it is suggested, give teachers a greater power over their teaching. Bartlett provides a number of suggestions for teachers who wish to become more critically reflective about themselves as teachers.

In the next chapter Bailey presents the use of diaries and journals in teacher education programs. Diaries have been well established in the literature as a research tool, and here their use is extended to the field of teacher development. Also included is an extended review of the literature on diary studies. Bailey then presents a five-step procedure for carrying out a study, and makes a number of practical suggestions to guide the potential diarist.

The final chapter in this section also deals with the use of journals in teacher training, although from a somewhat different perspective. Porter et al. make a case for teachers-in-preparation to keep a journal on the courses and seminars that form the formal part of their graduate training. The chapter is motivated by three educational principles. The first of these relates to the connection between writing and learning in which writing acts as a stimulus to the generation and exploration of ideas. Second, writing is seen as a social as well as a cognitive activity. Third, in keeping with communicative language teaching, journal writing stimulates greater learner involvement in the learning process. The chapter is illustrated with extracts from the journals of two student teachers and the written responses given to the student teachers by the instructors.

All three chapters see self-monitoring and self-evaluation as key components in teacher preparation programs, for they aim to take participants beyond training to education. Techniques are described that enable teachers-in-preparation to document and submit to critical scrutiny their teaching practices and the assumptions and beliefs upon which these practices are based.

13 Teacher development through reflective teaching

Leo Bartlett

Since the early eighties a number of approaches to teacher development have been proposed and implemented in classrooms. These approaches include the teacher-as-researcher, action research, clinical supervision, and the critical pedagogy perspective, among others. Another form of inquiry intended to help teachers improve their practice is reflective teaching. It was popularized by Cruickshank (Cruickshank and Applegate 1981; Cruickshank et al. 1981) and Zeichner (Zeichner 1981–2; Zeichner and Teitlebaum 1982; Zeichner 1983). They have reported on projects attempting to assist both preservice and experienced teachers to teach 'reflectively'.

Cruickshank and Zeichner define the term *reflective teaching* differently. Cruickshank defines reflective teaching as the teacher's thinking about what happens in classroom lessons, and thinking about alternative means of achieving goals or aims; he sees it as a means to provide students with 'an opportunity to consider the teaching event thoughtfully, analytically and objectively' (Cruickshank and Applegate 1981: 4). The purpose of reflective teaching is to engender good habits of thought (Cruickshank 1984). The focus is on teaching as a craft or apprenticeship. Teaching is defined in the narrow sense inasmuch as what happens in the classroom is decided by people and events inside the classroom alone. Reflection is reduced to the psychologistic process of thinking. According to this mode of thinking and defining reflection, the development of teaching techniques is regarded as the most important means for helping teachers to improve their practice.

Zeichner and Liston (1985) propose a quite different perspective. They argue, 'A reflective teacher is defined in this literature as one who assesses the origins, purposes and consequences of his or her work at all levels'. Work at different levels refers to Van Manen's (1977) three levels of reflectivity. The first of these levels corresponds broadly to Cruickshank's conception of reflective teaching. But Zeichner and Liston (1985) are more interested in what might be called the practical and critical level of reflectivity or orientation to inquiry into teaching (Carr and Kemmis, 1986). His leaning is toward the critical when he says that a program of reflective teaching is for students who are willing and able to reflect on the origins, purposes, and consequences of their actions, as well as the material and ideological constraints and encouragements embedded in the classroom, school, and societal contexts in which they live. These goals are directed toward enabling teachers to develop the pedagogical habits and skills necessary for self directed growth and toward preparing them, individually and collectively, to participate as full partners in their making of educational policies. (p. 4)

In this chapter I want to discuss reflective teaching as a means of improving classroom practice. The first section looks at the idea of reflective teaching which is aligned with Zeichner's conception. In the next section, a process for becoming reflective is proposed using examples from second language teaching. The last section considers questions teachers might ask of themselves in becoming more reflective teachers.

Thinking about reflective teaching

To grasp what it means to be a reflective teacher, we need to consider what it means to be a 'teacher' and what the word *reflection* implies. Both of these concepts have a large literature.

The idea of teaching

When we teach language we engage in certain actions. Often we read about improving classroom teacher behaviours; but behaviours are different from actions. Identifying an action involves knowing its intended purpose. For example, when an athlete raises a fist in triumph, no one would equate this action with that of a Nazi salute. Hence, one important consequence is that actions are intentional and are to be understood in the social context of their occurrence.

Intentional actions are not guided by intention conceived as some kind of pure mental concept in the head of the actor. A teacher's actions are influenced by intentions in the social settings and by the beliefs and chains of reasoning that are held before and after the occurrence of the action. The point in all this is that if we want to improve our teaching through reflective inquiry, we must accept that it does not involve some modification of behaviour by externally imposed directions or requirements, but that it requires deliberation and analysis of our ideas about teaching as a form of action based on our changed understandings.

The linking of what we think (intend) and what we do (act) applies to ourselves as individual teachers. But teaching is much more than this. Teaching is essentially an interactive process among a group of people learning in a social setting usually described as 'the classroom'. Interaction has been defined by Simpson and Galbo (1986) as

all manner of behaviour in which individuals and groups act upon each other. The essential characteristic is reciprocity in actions and responses in an infinite variety of relationships; verbal and non-verbal, conscious and unconscious, enduring and casual. Interaction is seen as a continually emerging process, as communication in its inclusive sense. (p. 38)

Implicit in this description of teaching as an interactive process is the need to develop shared understandings in a community of knowledge users and developers. Gore (1987) describes this in the following terms:

The sharing of experience in reflective teaching potentially has two outcomes. First, students may come to value their practical knowledge instead of viewing it as inferior to the scientific knowledge produced by researchers [of teaching]...A second possible outcome of the shared experiences provided by reflective teaching is strong collegiality. (p. 37)

We can enlarge the idea of collegiality and teaching to something more than the events that occur *inside* the classroom. The term *teacher* can be redefined as someone who engages learners, who seeks to engage each person wholly – mind, sense of self, range of interests and interactions with other people in learning (Duckworth 1986). Teaching becomes pedagogy when teachers engage learners in events inside and *outside* the classroom. Furthermore, teaching as pedagogy becomes a quest, a research endeavour which can be improved best through addressing both everyday experiences and the societal events that influence them.

The idea of reflection

Improvement of teaching may be achieved through reflection. Reflection is more than 'thinking' and focuses on the day-to-day classroom teaching of the individual teacher as well as the institutional structures in which teacher and students work. The description by Kemmis (1986) best summarizes the meaning of reflection:

Reflection is not just an individual, psychological process. It is an action oriented, historically-embedded, social and political frame, to locate oneself in the history of a situation, to participate in a social activity, and to take sides on issues. Moreover the material on which reflection works is given to us socially and historically; through reflection and the action which it informs, we may transform the social relations which characterise our work and our working situation. (p. 5)

Reflection therefore has a double meaning. It involves the relationship between an individual's thought and action and the relationship between an individual teacher and his or her membership in a larger collective called society. The first relationship involves the subjective meanings in teachers' heads. The second relationship explores consciously the relationship (which may be a part of unconscious knowledge) between individual teaching actions and the purposes of education in society. This dual meaning of reflection may be described as 'critical critical'.

Becoming a critically reflective teacher

Becoming critical means that as teachers we have to transcend the technicalities of teaching and think beyond the need to improve our instructional techniques. This effectively means we have to move away from the 'how to' questions, which have a limited utilitarian value, to the 'what' and 'why' questions, which regard instructional and managerial techniques not as ends in themselves but as a part of broader educational purposes. Hence we need to locate teaching in its broader cultural and social context. An analogy might be drawn from the communicative use of language. In a narrow, immediate sense, language is a medium of communication in the classroom, something the adult immigrant, for example, has to learn in order to survive as a citizen in a new country. In the broader sense, however, language broadcasts the new culture into which the immigrant enters, and perhaps redefines the immigrant's culture of origin.

Asking 'what' and 'why' questions gives us a certain power over our teaching. We could claim that the degree of autonomy and responsibility we have in our work as teachers is determined by the level of control that we can exercise over our actions. In reflecting on 'what' and 'why' questions, we begin to exercise control and open up the possibility of transforming our everyday classroom life. The process of control is called *critical reflective teaching*.

It should be noted that the word *critical* does not mean 'criticising' or being negative; it refers to the stance of enabling us as teachers to see our actions in relation to the historical, social, and cultural context in which our teaching is actually embedded. Becoming a critically reflective teacher is intended to allow us to develop ourselves individually and collectively; to deal with contemporary events and structures (for example, the attitudes of others or the bureaucratic thinking of administrators) and not to take these structures for granted.

Reflective teaching as a form of critical inquiry is located in a socially critical orientation to teaching. Apple (1975) describes this orientation in the following way:

It requires a painful process of radically examining current positions and asking pointed questions about the relationship that exists between these positions and the social structures from which they arise. It also necessitates a serious in-depth search for alternatives to those almost unconscious lenses we employ and an ability to cope with an ambiguous situation for which answers can now be only dimly seen and will not be easy to come by. (p. 127)

Becoming a critically reflective teacher within this orientation therefore involves the realisation that as second language teachers, we are both the producers *and* creators of our own history. In practical terms this means we shall engage in systematic and social forms of inquiry that examine the origin and consequences of everyday teaching so that we come to see the factors that impede change and thus improvement.

We can be assisted in the process of becoming critically reflective by asking ourselves a number of general 'what' and 'why' questions. They might include:

What counts as knowledge in second language teaching?
How is knowledge in language teaching organized?
How is what counts as knowledge transmitted? How is access to such knowledge determined?
What kind of multicultural society or cultural system uses this knowledge legitimately?
Whose interests are being served by the production and legitimation of this knowledge?

Some other, more specific questions might include:

What caused me to want to become a second language teacher?
Do these reasons still exist for me now?
What does it mean to be a teacher?
Is the teacher I am the person I am?
Where did the ideas I embody in second language teaching come from historically?
How did I come to appropriate them?
Why do I continue to endorse them now in my teaching?
Whose interests do these ideas serve?
Who has power in my classroom and how is it expressed?
How do power relationships in my classroom influence my interactions with students?
How might I teach differently?
What is the nature of knowledge that guides my teaching of content?
Who creates this knowledge?
How did this knowledge emerge during the evolution of teaching?
Whose interests does this knowledge about language teaching serve?
How do I / can I personally work to uncover the contradictions in my teaching?

How does what I do affect the opportunities in life of students?

What connections do I make with organisations outside the school or centre to demonstrate my active role in society?

Do I wish to uncover the 'hidden curriculum' – the inconsistencies – in my teaching?

These questions need to be systematised into a set of procedures to help us to become critically reflective teachers.

A process for reflection

Several processes of inquiry, each driven by its own theoretical understanding of reflection, have been proposed. However, most follow the ideas first formulated by Dewey (1933) when he said in his book *How We Think* that it was necessary

first that the pupil have a genuine situation of experience – that there be a continuous activity in which he is interested for its own sake; secondly, that a genuine problem develop with this situation as a stimulus to thought; third, that he possess the information and make the observations needed to deal with it; fourth, that suggested solutions occur to him which he shall be responsible for developing in an orderly way; fifth, that he have opportunity and occasion to test his ideas by application to make the meaning clear and to discover for himself their validity. (p. 174)

Dewey's statement reinforces the need to consider a number of principles that guide a process by which teachers can become reflective. They are summarised briefly here:

1. The issue upon which the teacher reflects must occur in the social context where teaching occurs.
2. The teacher must be interested in the problem to be resolved.
3. The issue must be 'owned' by the teacher – that is, derived from his or her practice.
4. Reflection on the issue involves problem solving from the teaching situation in which the teacher is located.
5. Ownership of the identified issue and its solution is vested in the teacher.
6. Systematic procedures are necessary.
7. Information (observations) about the issue must be derived from the teacher's experience of teaching.
8. The teacher's ideas need to be tested through the practice of teaching.
9. Ideas about teaching, once tested through practice, must lead to some course of action. There is a tension between idea and action

TABLE I. CYCLES OF REFLECTION WITHIN DIFFERENT REFLECTIVE TEACHING PROGRAMS

Reflective teaching program	Before lesson	Immediately after lesson	Later after lesson
Cruickshank Peer teaching Any stage of teacher education	PREPARE	⇄ REFLECT group – shared: verbal	
Zeichner School teaching Final year of teacher education	PLAN ⇄ PREPARE ⇄	REFLECT self or supervisor: verbal or written	⇄ REFLECT group: verbal
Gore Peer teaching First semester of teacher education	PLAN ⇄ PREPARE ⇄	REFLECT group – shared: verbal	⇄ REFLECT self: written critique ⇄ REFLECT | self or | group: | written in | journal or | verbal |

Source: Gore and Bartlett (1987).

which is reflexive; once it is tested the action rebounds back on the idea which informed it.

10. Hence, reflexive action may be transformed into new understandings and redefined practice in teaching.

These statements indicate that not only must reflective teaching be reflexive but also that there is a cycle of activity in the process. Table 1 shows that the three programs cited in this chapter all have cycles of reflection before, during, and after lessons in which the teacher engages in reflective teaching.

These cycles of activity could be redefined as containing the five elements of mapping, informing, contesting, appraising, and acting. They are represented in Figure 1. It is important to understand that all elements constitute the process of reflective teaching, but the elements are not linear or sequential. That is, in reflecting on your teaching you may 'pass through' the cycle several times (hence the process becomes reflexive); one element is not always or necessarily followed by the next element

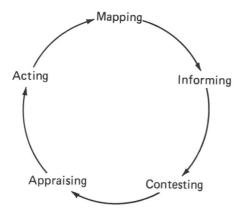

Figure 1   The elements of a cycle for the process of reflective teaching. (Adapted from McTaggert and Kemmis 1983; Smyth 1987.)

in the cycle; and an element *may* be omitted in moving through the cycle, especially when different courses of action are adopted.

Let us consider each element or phase separately.

Mapping

'WHAT DO I DO AS A TEACHER?'

Mapping involves observation and the collection of evidence about our own teaching. Probably the best means of observation is to record our practice. This may be done by audio or visual means (tape-recording a lesson, using photography, etc.), but the best means would seem to involve some form of writing. In writing, we begin not only to observe, but we take the first step in reflecting *on* and *about* our practice.

The emphasis here is on our individual observations. One of the better known ways of recording is to keep a diary or journal. Kathleen Bailey in this volume (Chapter 14) provides many excellent ideas and practical suggestions about diaries as potential tools for teacher training in second language teaching. Holly (1984) and Tripp (1987) also describe in some detail how to start and what to do in keeping a journal which may be descriptive or thoughtfully analytical about teaching. The emphasis in this phase of reflection however is on description. Hence, the journal is more like a ship's log, where what happened and who is involved form the main part of the record.

Our writing will be about our routine and conscious actions in the classroom; conversations with pupils; critical incidents in a lesson; our personal lives as teachers; our beliefs about teaching; events outside the classroom that we think influence our teaching; our views about language teaching and learning. The description of our particular orientation or approach to language teaching is all-important in this phase of observation and information gathering. Some of the specific questions listed earlier (for example, 'Is the teacher I am the person I am?') are relevant.

Some important points seem worthy of mention in writing for reflection. First, focus on a specific teaching problem which can be improved. Keep the problem 'small'; that is, keep your observations focused on a particular aspect of teaching. If you are addressing the problem of questioning, for example, see if you can identify one aspect of the topic (delivery, your response to students, the number of questions you ask relative to the number that students are allowed to ask). Write in your own language of everyday experience, voicing your descriptions and concerns freely. Your record may be brief or lengthy depending on time available and your inclination to write. Begin writing immediately after teaching a lesson or sequence of lessons. The aim is to raise your consciousness of your teaching through writing: This is the first step to 'sussing out' the meaning behind your ideas.

Informing

'WHAT IS THE MEANING OF MY TEACHING?'

'WHAT DID I INTEND?'

Having mapped our images and ideas about our teaching, about ourselves, about the content of our teaching, and about other persons inside and outside the classroom whom we think influence our teaching, we turn to look for meaning behind the maps. This phase, like others in the cycle, cannot be neatly separated from other phases; but by consciously focusing on it, we make sure we exhaust the possibilities and opportunities for reflecting.

In effect, we revisit our first record – our maps – add to them, and make meaning of them. Informing may occur after a teaching sequence or lesson. It may be accomplished by the individual teacher or in discussion with others. Hence, the element of mapping may be meant to be as much the basis for shared discussion and understanding of the meaning of teaching for our colleagues and students as much as it is for the individual self.

The element of sharing or collaboration with colleagues offers the possibility of extending one's insights about oneself as teacher to oneself as an individual member of a larger community. This supports the idea of teaching as interaction: the idea that teaching cannot be separated from one's students, one's culture, one's expectations about life, and how one wants to participate in society.

It is possible now to distinguish between teaching routine and conscious teaching actions and unmask the principles behind them. Questions such as 'Who defines knowledge about our teaching?' appear relevant. For example, if we assume we select the subject-matter content of teaching, what is the basis of our selection? If there are curriculum guidelines, how is our selection contingent upon them? Are our purposes in selecting content to develop a working citizen or an educated citizen or a person actively participating in changing society?

This phase in reflective teaching begins the search for principles that underlie our teaching, the search for reasons which are the basis for our theory of teaching. It also begins the first steps toward identifying our uncertainty about our taken-for-granted and most preciously held ideas about our teaching and its broader purposes. Certainty is embedded in our thinking, as it is for many people in our contemporary society. Our search is not for the correct or most *certain* solution, but for the *best* possible solution based on informed choice.

Contesting

'HOW DID I COME TO BE THIS WAY?'

'HOW WAS IT POSSIBLE FOR MY PRESENT VIEW OF TEACHING (WITH REASONS) TO HAVE EMERGED?'

This phase involves contesting our ideas and the structures that hold them in place. This is most effectively achieved through sharing with our colleagues (including teachers, students, parents, and community members) our understandings and reasons we have for teaching in particular ways.

Contesting ideas and reasons for teaching is meant to uncover our assumptive worlds. As we become experienced teachers we make our histories, which contain assumptions about best ways of teaching. Should we focus on the individual student, for example? What assumptions do we make when we regard the individual as more important than the class group? What does it mean for the relationships between ourselves and our students? the nature of learning? assessment of learning? Questioning our assumptive worlds may mean dislodging 'unquestioned' ideas about our teaching. In mapping and informing, we considered our espoused theories about teaching. In contestation, we confront and perhaps begin to dislodge the complex system of reasons (theory) for our teaching actions.

Contestation involves a search for inconsistencies and contradictions in what we do and how we think. A contradiction exists when our reasons for an action or the premises on which a course of teaching action is founded cannot all be realized simultaneously. Hence, if we pursue one course of action or premise we must repress another: by accepting one, we reject another. If we believe that a given piece of behaviour will have positive consequences for some and negative consequences for others, then we hold an interdependent or dialectical view of action or behaviour. We might illustrate this by considering the issue of teacher talk. If we believe that the amount of talking we as teachers do does not disadvantage others, we hold an independent view of classroom speech. If, however, we believe that teacher talk advantages us while disadvantaging our students, we hold an interdependent or dialectical view of classroom speech.

Another way to describe this example is in terms of individualistic or reciprocal power relationships: 'Who has the power in my classroom?' 'How is it expressed?' 'How do power relationships in the classroom influence my interactions with students?' 'How does what I do benefit students?' 'What disadvantages may result?' If we accept that every teaching action has both advantages and disadvantages for our students, we might then ask whose interests are being served. Quite often our teaching may appear to be in the best interests of students when in fact it is ourselves or the institution which has most to gain.

There are varying levels of contradiction in our teaching. Some are quite visible; others are less visible. Quite often our wish to improve our teaching may be distorted by visible institutional requirements; for example, the requirement to demonstrate improved grammatical or communicative competence in student learning as defined by the syllabus. Not to demonstrate improvement in such competencies may be to demonstrate our professional inadequacy to colleagues or administrators whose views about the purposes of second language teaching may be quite different from ours. Our interpretation of syllabus requirements as regards assessment can also become a complex mix of desires to improve our teaching, to enhance our professional status, to ensure student gains in learning, and to provide appropriate opportunities for students to learn. There are visible and invisible agendas each with their own contradictions in our teaching.

Appraisal

'HOW MIGHT I TEACH DIFFERENTLY?'

Contestation of teaching practice logically leads to a search for alternative courses of action. Appraisal begins to link the thinking dimension of reflection with the search for teaching in ways consistent with our new understanding. A handy way of appraising is to ask the question 'What would be the consequences to learning if I changed . . . ?' Hence, with regard to measuring proficiency, we might understand whose interests are being served in assessment of student learning if we more frequently negotiate what will be learned; or we might negotiate the criteria upon which students will be assessed. Most importantly, we might ask ourselves whether criteria for making assessments are made public for students; and whether we attempt to make public our assessments against these criteria. When we search for more participatory styles of goal-based or democratic assessment procedures, we are appraising possible courses of action.

Acting

'WHAT AND HOW SHALL I NOW TEACH?'

Paulo Freire (1972) has proposed that reflection without action is verbalism: action without reflection is activism – doing things for their own sake. Acting is listed here chronologically as the last phase in the process leading to reflective teaching, but it is not the final phase. There is a continuing dialectical relationship among the preceding phases and the idea of acting out new ideas about our teaching. We 'rearrange' our teaching practice after mapping what we do, unearthing the reasons and assumptions for these actions, subjecting these reasons to critical scrutiny, appraising alternative courses of action, and then acting. Although there is nothing magical or imperative about this cycle, it offers a systematic approach to the process of making committed choices as the basis of 'good' teaching.

Conclusion

Reflective teaching, like most teacher-based forms of self-inquiry, is not an easy process. It involves a major shift in emphasis in our thinking and acting. Becoming reflective forces us to adopt a critical attitude to ourselves as individual second language teachers – to challenge our espoused personal beliefs about teaching. Becoming reflective through testing our practice systematically also challenges us to think about the influence we directly or indirectly exert on the formation of society in our role as teachers. How we present language through the curriculum and through our teaching has profound cumulative effects on the way our community and wider society changes. Becoming reflective also extends beyond ourselves, making possible a similar form of self-inquiry in students. It may allow them to break the chains of alienation imposed on them not only by the routine of everyday experience but also by the oppressive ignorance of language in the society into which they have been inducted. Students are no longer seen as receptacles of prepackaged knowledge but are given the language of possibility to challenge the very constructs which may relegate them to the status of mere objects in a 'new' culture. For teachers of students of diverse ethnic backgrounds, becoming a reflective teacher offers a very real challenge.

14 The use of diary studies in teacher education programs

Kathleen M. Bailey

A diary study is a first-person account of a language learning or teaching experience, documented through regular, candid entries in a personal journal and then analyzed for recurring patterns or salient events. Throughout this chapter I will use the labels *diary* and *journal* interchangeably. However, here the term *diary study* has a meaning that is intentionally different from its use in some of the early case studies in the second language acquisition research literature (e.g., in the anthology edited by Hatch 1978), where adults kept written records of child second language learners' linguistic output. In contrast, here the term emphasizes first-person authorship.

As a research genre, diary studies are part of a growing body of literature on classroom research (Allwright 1983; Gaies 1983; Long 1983; van Lier 1984, 1988; Bailey 1985; Chaudron 1988; Allwright and Bailey 1990). They are examples of participant observation that fall within the "anthropological approach" to classroom research (Long 1983: 18) in the hermeneutic (interpretive) tradition (Ochsner 1979). My concern here, however, is not so much with diary studies as a mode of research but rather as potential tools for teacher preparation. (See Blass and Pike 1981 for a similar approach.)

The first purpose of this chapter, then, is to briefly review some of the insights gained by teachers and teachers-in-preparation who kept language teaching diaries and analyzed the results. Second, I will offer some guidelines for teachers-in-preparation who would like to keep teaching journals, and to teacher educators who are considering suggesting this option to their students.

Literature review

To date, diary studies in language research and pedagogy have generally taken one of three broad focuses. They have been used to document (1) language learning experiences, (2) student teachers' reactions to academic courses, and (3) language teaching experiences.

Language learning diaries

Some teachers-in-preparation and experienced professional educators have kept journals of their experiences as language learners. Although most of the resulting diary studies are lengthy, unpublished manuscripts, a few have found their way into accessible volumes in psychology and applied linguistics (see, for example, Moore 1977; Schumann and Schumann 1977; Bailey 1980, 1983; Schumann 1980; Danielson 1981; and Schmidt and Frota 1986). The actual topics of these first-person accounts of language learning vary widely, but each has sought to investigate issues not normally accessible through outside observation. For instance, Schmidt documented his internal struggle to "notice the gap" between his utterances and those of Portuguese native speakers – a cognitive process that would have been invisible to another researcher.

Some studies have involved the analysis of several different language learners' diaries by one researcher. In an investigation of learning strategies, Asher (1983) analyzed the diaries of eight teenage students of French, with entries made before and during a trip to Switzerland. Brown (1985) analyzed sixty-one diaries kept by older and younger adult learners of Spanish, and compared their records with those she made as an observer. Bailey (1983) examined eleven diaries in an investigation of competitiveness and anxiety among adult second language learners. These second-person analyses of first-person language learning journals have yielded interesting insights that were not always obvious to the original diarists.

In a different use of the diary process, Porter et al. (this volume, Chapter 15) discuss the use of journals by teachers-in-preparation to document their reactions to reading materials, lectures, seminars, materials-development projects, classroom observations, and some initial teaching experiences in their teacher preparation courses. In reviewing the contents of these journals, Porter et al. conclude:

> The journal encourages students to go beyond learning course content in isolation and to strive to link this information to theories and knowledge beyond the particular assignment and the particular course. The journal thus enables students to develop a professional approach toward learning and to write as members of the larger language learning community. In sum, it teaches them to do what we do as professionals – to work to integrate new ideas with what we already know and to talk with each other as we do so. (p. 240)

This approach parallels the use of dialogue journals (Spack and Sadow 1983) in teaching second language composition skills. I will refer to diaries used to document participants' reactions to teacher preparation courses as *academic journals*.

Porter et al. include teaching experiences in their list of topics to which student teachers respond in diaries. In this context, the teachers-in-preparation develop individual written accounts of their classroom experiences and their subsequent reflections on the teaching/learning process. Some diaries have been kept by teachers as part of their preservice graduate education, while others have been written by practicing teachers, for inservice self-evaluation.

In one of the earliest studies, Telatnik (1977, 1978) did her master's thesis research on the introspective journal as a self-evaluative tool. The findings deal predominantly with her struggles to articulate her philosophy of teaching and to define good teaching. The main difficulty she faced arose in trying to mesh her own ideas about effective teaching, based on her experience and her belief system, with the experts' and theorists' ideas she encountered in her graduate program.

The question of teacher power emerges in a diary study conducted by Butler-Wall (1979), who kept a record of her teaching in an upper-intermediate, university English as a second language class. Other major themes that emerged in Butler-Wall's diary study were feedback, harmony, and community, as they relate to classroom language teaching.

Deen (1987) kept a diary of her experiences as she taught a project-based course in Dutch as a second language at the same time that she was taking a graduate seminar on project-based language teaching. Deen's diary study combines her own observations about the course she was teaching with written comments from the professor of the graduate seminar.

Ho (1985) conducted a diary study on the use of English and/or Chinese to teach remedial English classes in secondary schools in Hong Kong, in order to investigate the "teacher's actual feelings and frustrations experienced in making the language choice" (p. ii). (She also collected survey data about other teachers' classroom language choices.)

Among my own graduate students, I have used the diary study approach as one option for the classroom-centered research project required in the practicum, the course in which the graduate students complete a practice teaching assignment. Over the years, the resulting journals have focused on issues related to lesson planning and creativity, time management, problems faced by nonnative teachers of English, classroom control, group work, and difficult student–teacher relations. My sense of the results is that, while these journals were not necessarily always gems of ethnographic investigation, they were often extremely useful exercises for the teachers-in-preparation, both in generating behavioral changes and in developing self-confidence.

Since I am not at liberty to cite any of these unpublished diaries, I will draw on the studies listed earlier in discussing the possible benefits

Kathleen M. Bailey

of keeping a teaching journal. First, however, it is useful to summarize the procedures involved and consider some remaining questions about diary studies.

Keeping a language learning or teaching diary

The procedures for keeping a diary are relatively simple, technologically speaking, but the process does require discipline and patience. The following suggestions may help preservice or inservice teachers who wish to conduct diary studies.

The steps involved in doing a diary study are depicted in the flow chart in Figure 1. It should be noted that diary studies, both as qualitative research and as teacher-preparation tools, are still evolving. The steps depicted in Figure 1 have been followed with more or less devotion, depending on the individual diarist's purposes and personality. For instance, some diary studies have not included a language learning or teaching history (step 1). Compiling such an account is particularly useful for teachers-in-preparation because, in many cases, we teach as we have been taught: The patterns that emerge in our current classroom behaviors may have been formed (or at least clearly modeled) long ago. Some diarists have not rewritten their uncensored private journals for public review (step 3). In actual practice, events that are embarrassing or painful when they occur often lose their sting after weeks of reflection, and can be discussed openly and objectively in the analysis. However, teachers-in-preparation can be especially sensitive to criticism and perceived failure. Even if my graduate students choose not to edit their private journals, I suggest that they remove or staple shut any pages they don't want me to read.

The main point is that the original journal entries must be candid if the diarist is to benefit from reviewing them. The novice teacher must feel free to reflect, experiment, criticize, doubt, express frustration, and raise questions in the journal. Otherwise its main benefits in teacher development – personal development and insights about teaching – will be negated.

In talking about how teachers-in-preparation can use intensive journals, I specifically want to separate the two phases of conducting a diary study: (1) making the (daily) diary entries and (2) analyzing the raw qualitative data provided by these entries. Although simply keeping the diary and not analyzing the results may be helpful to the individual diarist, the finished document does not constitute a diary study per se unless analysis has been undertaken. Unfortunately, it is beyond the scope of this paper to review the procedures for analyzing qualitative data such as those yielded by the diary entries. Interested readers are

218

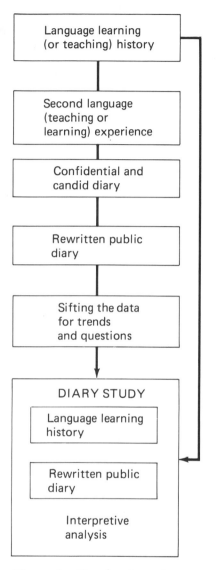

Language learning (or teaching) history	1. The diarist provides an account of personal language learning or teaching history.
Second language (teaching or learning) experience	2. The diarist systematically records events, details, and feelings about the current language experience in the diary.
Confidential and candid diary	
Rewritten public diary	3. The diarist revises the journal entries for the public version of the diary, clarifying meaning in the process.
Sifting the data for trends and questions	4. The diarist studies the journal entries, looking for patterns and significant events. (Also, other researchers may analyze the diary entries.)
DIARY STUDY / Language learning history / Rewritten public diary / Interpretive analysis	5. The factors identified as being important to the language learning or teaching experience are interpreted and discussed in the final diary study. Ideas from the pedagogy literature may be added at this stage.

*Figure 1   Conducting a language learning or teaching diary study.
(Adapted from Bailey and Ochsner 1983: 90.)*

referred to Bogdan and Taylor (1975), Crippendorf (1980), Spradley (1980), Bailey and Ochsner (1983), or Matsumoto (1987) for further information. The following suggestions about starting a diary study are given, first, as potentially useful ideas collected from several teachers and teachers-in-preparation who have kept diaries and, second, as a way of illustrating some of the typical procedures involved.

First, if a diarist is taking or teaching a regularly scheduled language class, it is important to set aside time each day immediately following the class to write in the diary. The diary entries should be written in a pleasant place free of interruptions. Some diarists who are comfortable with word processors have used these to write and record their diary entries. A few people have preferred to tape-record their entries, since they found writing to be cumbersome. However, in choosing this option, one must consider the data analysis phase: Will it be necessary to transcribe the tapes in order to analyze the data? If so, many hours will be added to the analysis. Thus, a diarist must decide on a balance between overwhelming quantity and the possible depth of quality added by electronic recordings.

Second, the time allotted to writing about the language teaching or learning experience should at least equal the time spent in class. A learner or teacher immersed in the target culture will probably find it impossible to record everything that happens in a day, so it may be helpful to focus the diary entries on some particular aspect of interest.

Many diarists have reported great difficulty in getting started, partly because honestly focusing on one's own behavior can be an uncomfortable process. Telatnik (1978: 2) reports:

At first it was very slow work. For almost two weeks I used only ten or twenty minutes of my hour. It was difficult both to write and to know what to write. Without realizing it, I was editing my thoughts before I put them down on paper... It was not until the fourth or fifth week that I was able to read the journal and say, "Oh, so *that's* what I do."

Thus it is important to set up the conditions for writing so that the actual process of writing is (or can become) relatively free – not a chore to dread, or one that interferes with learning, teaching, or preparation time.

The next point is related both to Telatnik's comment and to recent writings about the "process approach" to composing (Flower and Hayes 1977; Mayher, Lester, and Pradl 1983). In recording entries in the original uncensored version of the diary, one should not worry about style, grammar, or organization – especially when writing in a second language. The goal is to get complete and accurate data while the recollections are still fresh. For this reason, the original diary entries often read like "stream of consciousness" writing. (The data presentation can be polished later, if and when the journal is edited for public consumption, perhaps with input from classmates or colleagues.)

Some of the language learning and teaching journals that have been kept to date are full of fascinating but unsubstantiated insights. Potential diarists thus need to reflect carefully as they are writing their diary entries. In writing an assertion, a diarist should ask "Why? Why did I write that? What evidence do I have for the statement I just made?" If the answers are not readily apparent, these questions can be kept in mind as the language experience continues, since they may prompt additional insights for future entries. Wherever possible, it is important to support reflective comments with examples from class sessions or actual language data.

This advice on keeping a journal is based on common sense and the experience of several people who have kept and analyzed diaries. Other procedures may work equally well for different diarists, as long as one tries to be systematic, thorough, and honest.

Remaining questions

READING OTHER DIARIES

Should a diarist read other language learning or teaching diary studies while keeping a journal? Some researchers have been concerned that this practice might lead to a "contamination" of the data. While this issue is certainly a problem in "pure research," in which the researcher tries to influence the setting under study as little as possible, it is much less of a concern in applied research, and even less so in "action research," in which the researcher actively sets out to generate change by conducting the study.

In teacher preparation practicums, I have often asked students to read aloud selections from their teaching journals, with the result that other students in the class have found parallels with, and gained insights into, their own issues. Furthermore, their classmates have sometimes offered comments which helped the individual writers interpret their own records or benefit from the teaching experience in ways that had not occurred to them directly.

DIARIES AND LANGUAGE LEARNING THEORY

Should a diarist read about and comment on theories regarding language learning or teaching while keeping a diary? The concern is that this process might mold the diarist's insights to fit the theories. Again, perhaps in conducting "pure research" one would want teachers keeping diaries to avoid reading the research literature in the field, to keep from biasing the results. But for purposes of teacher preparation, the examination of current theories in the context of one's own classroom is very helpful. A comment from Telatnik's (1978: 1) analysis of her teaching journal brings this issue into focus:

Even after my years of experience and training, I was uncertain about what worked and what did not work and why. I was challenged from all sides by

221

Kathleen M. Bailey

what one expert or another said was *the* correct methodology or the correct theory. But, because they were "experts," I thought I should accept what they said even though my own experience did not always support their theories.

Telatnik's position echoes the comments of Porter et al. (this volume, p. 235), who note that using academic journals encourages the teachers-in-preparation to make connections between the content of their graduate courses and their own teaching.

TIME MANAGEMENT

A third concern with data collection is the time factor. Keeping and analyzing a language learning or teaching diary is a laborious procedure (Butler-Wall 1979: 4). The value of using tape recordings must be balanced against the time the data analysis will involve and the purposes to which it will be put. In a paper comparing diary studies with participant observation, Brown observed that "field notes produced with the aid of an audiotape tended to be 50% longer than those produced solely from notes by hand" (1985: 127). Presumably this doubling factor would pertain to the diary entries as well.

TAKING NOTES IN CLASS

Another question is whether a diarist should try to take notes in class during the actual language learning or teaching experience. For students, the note-taking process might be distracting enough to interfere with their actual language learning. For teachers, it would be well nigh impossible to make notes during the teacher-fronted portions of lessons, though brief notes could be made during group work or individual students' presentations, which would certainly add to the immediacy of the journal entries written after class. In point of fact, a diarist is a participant observer, and this role implies a delicate, Janus-like balance: One must both participate and observe. In general, the luxury of making running field notes during the actual events under investigation is limited largely to nonparticipant observers. This is why so many of the diary studies are as much retrospective as introspective (Allwright 1988: 248–9).

USE OF OTHER DATA

The issues of note taking and tape recording lead to the next question. To what extent can other data (e.g., test scores, compositions written in the target language, supervisor's observations of the teaching process) be used to augment the researcher's insights? (This question is related to the practice of triangulation in qualitative research – see van Lier

222

1988.) Some of the language learning diaries have made excellent use of external information. For example, Schmidt and Frota (1986) incorporated an error analysis based on taped conversations during Schmidt's acquisition of Portuguese. In the teaching diaries, Ho (1985) used survey data to augment her diary study of teachers' language choice in remedial English classrooms in Hong Kong. Telatnik (1978) has incorporated supervisors' observational input in the interpretation of her teaching journal entries:

[My supervisor] commented once that, during a lesson she observed, she was slightly confused about how an exercise I had the students do was supposed to go. But she said she understood once we got started. This chance remark, in the light of my journal entries expressing my displeasure with sluggish lessons, made me realize that sometimes I gave unclear instructions.

In this case, it was the combination of keeping a diary and receiving outside input that led the teacher/diarist to an insight about her teaching.

THE EFFECT OF DIARIES ON THE LEARNING PROCESS

A final question has to do with the extent to which keeping a diary (i.e., of examining one's own language learning or teaching experience) influences the experience. An evolving self-assessment seems to be a natural part of the process. Brown (1985: 131), in her examination of the diaries kept by sixty-one adult learners of Spanish, notes that many second language learners "gave evidence in their journals of being aware of their progress. It may be that the awareness would have come without the journals, but writing it down made it very evident." She concluded that "the journal keeping itself makes a difference in the learning situation" (1985: 130).

The teachers' diaries reveal a similar pattern of awareness raising. Again, Telatnik's comments (1978: 7–8) are revealing:

After having analyzed myself daily I tended to see other people's analysis of my teaching more objectively. Having learned to be honest and objective in my own recording, I found it easier to be more honest and objective about others' comments... With Observer X, who criticized my authoritarian, teacher-dominated approach, I began to become less defensive. My resentment passed when I accepted the fact that I *did* run a teacher-dominated classroom and that was exactly what I wanted. I no longer secretly raged through our discussions. I even managed to glean from our sessions a few techniques on encouraging student participation.

Thus, once again we see a distinction, possibly even a conflict, between the use of diary studies as research tools and their use in teacher education. Whereas a researcher would be concerned about the diary-keeping itself influencing the phenomena under investigation, in teacher

Kathleen M. Bailey

education the diary's awareness-raising function can be extremely helpful. In fact, van Lier (personal communication) has suggested that, ironically, the best diary from an educational point of view might be the
worst from a research perspective.

Benefits of conducting a diary study

While many diarists have commented on the usefulness of conducting
a diary study, such remarks come from a self-selected sample: People
who choose to conduct diary studies probably have different psychological profiles from those who dislike the idea. Certainly, none of the
published accounts contain comments from potential diarists who aban-
doned the process because they found it more tedious than helpful. The
following ideas should be interpreted in this light.

Deen (1987: 15–16) has commented directly on the benefits of conducting a diary study:

The study showed the role the diary played in defining a personal philosophy
of teaching and it reflected problems with building an image of what a
classroom looks like and what the teacher's roles are in project-based
learning...Keeping a diary helped me very much in clarifying my thoughts
and feelings about learning and my way of handling problems that came
forth from doing real learning.

Butler-Wall (1979: 6) notes that keeping a diary helped her

to sort out recurring issues, important questions, and points to keep an eye
on in the future...Already some interesting themes are emerging which
promise to lead to certain insights available from no other source than
introspection.

Thus the very act of recording one's impressions seems to be helpful for
some teachers.

Bartlett (this volume, page 209) has commented on the writing process
in his discussion of reflective teaching:

Probably the best means of observation is to record our practice. This may
be done by audio or visual means (tape-recording a lesson, using
photography, etc.), but the best means would seem to involve some form of
writing. In writing, we begin not only to observe, but we take the first step in
reflecting *on* and *about* our practice.

However, I would argue that simply writing diary entries does not yield
the maximum potential benefit of the process. In order to really learn
from the record, the diarist should reread the journal entries and try
to find the patterns therein. Butler-Wall makes this point very well
(1979: 10):

Much of the time I actually did not know what was going on in the classroom. Because I tended to equate positive affect with learning, I looked no further to find out if any learning was in fact taking place. A review of the diary entries suggests that this would have been wise. It seems that a diary is more than the sum of its parts; although I was the one who recorded every individual item, I did not realize what I had recorded until I had recorded many items.

My own experience in keeping a language learning diary bears out Butler-Wall's realization. When John Schumann (then my professor) first read my French class diary, he asked if I was a competitive learner. I assured him (naively, but quite honestly) that I was a very cooperative, group-oriented language learner. John's only comment was, "Look again, Kathi." A subsequent analysis of the diary entries revealed numerous manifestations of competitiveness (Bailey 1983), which I had not noticed in my original review of the entries.

Again, Butler-Wall's comments are insightful:

One of the uses of diary studies is to clarify issues . . . These issues emerge when one looks at the data again and again – to see what is included, what is left out, what kind of language is used, what kind of perspective is taken, what kinds of reactions are noted, what kind of tone is adopted, what kinds of connections are made, what the cumulative weights are, what the parts add up to, what projections can be posited, what the cycles can reveal. (1979: 13)

Thus, in reworking, rethinking, and interpreting the diary entries, teachers can gain powerful insights into their own classroom behavior and motivation.

Conclusion

Several diarists have mentioned that it is probably not a good idea to force anyone to keep a journal. Some people are simply not comfortable with self-examination and introspection, and the issues that emerge can be painfully revealing. For teacher-educators considering assigning a diary study, I would advise using it as an option among several possibilities. Some student teachers may be much more amenable to transcribing tape recordings of their own lessons, and analyzing the resulting data for linguistic or discourse-level units instead. This more objective approach simply provides a different "window on the classroom world" (Brown 1985).

Nevertheless, for teachers who do undertake the diary study process, it can be as rewarding as it is humbling. One discovers strengths and previously unnoticed talents in the cumulative entries. For novice teachers in teacher preparation programs, who will not always be in a position to receive outside feedback from an educator, supervisor, or cooperating teacher, the diary study process can be invaluable. One of our responsibilities, as teacher educators, during preservice preparation is to provide beginning teachers with usable tools for self-evaluation, for ongoing development in the absence of our input. The mechanism of the diary study can do just that.

15 An ongoing dialogue: learning logs for teacher preparation

Patricia A. Porter, Lynn M. Goldstein, Judith Leatherman, and Susan Conrad

The use of journals in teacher preparation courses is motivated by three current ideas in education. The first is the importance of the connection between writing and learning. In this respect, writing can be viewed as a discovery process – a way to explore ideas, generate and connect ideas, change preconceived notions, and connect abstract ideas and experiences. (See, for example, Murray 1968; Flower and Hayes 1977; Emig 1978; Perl 1979; Langer 1986.) Journals have been used increasingly in content courses and in writing courses to exploit this writing–learning connection. Mayher, Lester, and Pradl (1983) discuss the use of learning logs or content journals in high school classes such as biology and chemistry: "One of the most effective ways students can use writing as an aid to learning is to keep a running account of what is going on as they work in a particular course. Teachers can skim these logs and find out what students understand or don't understand about the material" (p. 82). They suggest that when teachers ask students to introspect about learning, comment on the class, and communicate about what they are learning, students get more involved in the course and make connections between themselves and the course material.

A second idea that motivates the use of journals is that writing is a *social* activity as well as a cognitive activity (Cooper 1986). Writing is seen not as a solitary pursuit but as discourse among people with shared interests. Teachers-in-preparation are exploring new ideas but they are also exploring the ways in which members of the language teaching profession talk and write about these ideas. Journals help these student teachers to become members of this discourse community by giving them opportunities to write within it and to get responses from their teachers, who are active and practiced members. These exchanges give students both a real audience within the community and a developing sense of being a member of the community.

The third idea is the current focus in language teaching on a communicative approach, which implies more learner involvement in the learning process (see, for example, Breen 1985; Richards and Rodgers 1986). Teacher educators committed to a communicative approach em-

The authors of this paper are two teachers who assign journals in their TESL training courses and two students who wrote journals while in training.

phasize the need for second language students to be active language learners, to get more involved in the learning process by taking responsibility for their role in it. Student teachers are encouraged to find ways to use learner input in the curriculum, to focus their classes to meet learner needs, and to make their teaching more "process" than "product" oriented. In spite of all this, in teacher preparation courses the predominant mode of instruction tends to be the traditional teacher-centered format, with teacher-generated curricula and an emphasis on evaluated products as a measure of learning. In other words, the actual teacher education process is not in accord with the recommended method. The use of journals in teacher education courses makes preparation more closely parallel to the type of teaching expected of student teachers.

Procedures for using journals

The journal assignment

Journals can be used in all types of teacher preparation classes, from those of a theoretical nature, such as a survey of sociolinguistics or of second language acquisition (SLA), to those of a more practical nature, such as a survey of methodologies, a materials-preparation class, or a practicum involving extensive observation and/or teaching. At the beginning of the term, the journal is assigned as an integral part of the course: Students are asked to regularly write and hand in their journals. Since this type of journal is new to most students, a list of suggestions for what to write about is helpful. For example, for a theory-oriented class with extensive readings, the following suggestions are useful:

1. *React* to class discussions.
2. *Describe* class discussions.
3. *Ask* questions about readings/discussions.
4. *Relate* readings/discussions to your own experiences.
5. *React* to something that you read.
6. *Describe* something that you read.
7. *Argue* for/against something you read/discussed.
8. *Explore* pedagogical implications of readings/discussions.
9. *Describe* new knowledge you have obtained.
10. *Fit* new knowledge into what you already know.
11. *Question* the applications, motivations, uses, or significance of what you have learned.

For an applied class with less emphasis on readings, some *additional* suggestions are:

12. *React* to class demonstrations, observations, teaching/tutoring experiences, etc.
13. *Make connections* between course content and previous experiences you have had as a teacher, tutor, language learner, etc.
14. *Argue* for/against a particular technique or procedure.

The journal can be used in connection with students' "products," such as lesson plans, research reports, term papers, and even oral presentations and examinations. If used this way, these suggestions are appropriate:

15. *Describe* your progress or problems with the current assignment/exam.
16. *React* to my evaluation of your last assignment/exam.

(These suggestions are adapted from Mayher et al. 1983: 24.)

To make the journal most effective, four journal "ground rules" need to be established. First, the journal is not a personal diary, although students are encouraged to write about personal experiences as they relate to the content of the course. It is necessary to discuss this since many students may have written personal diaries or may have assigned them to their second language students. Second, the journal is not a place simply to take notes. Many students equate writing about readings or class discussions with note taking, and need to understand that the journal is a place to go beyond notes by exploring, reacting, making connections, and so on. Third, the journal entries are not intended to be polished pieces of writing. If the writing task is likened more to free writing than to a final product, students will have less trouble with the assignment. Finally, the journal deserves the same serious attention as any other course assignment, even though it is not graded.

How often the students hand in their journals depends on the nature and structure of the course. If the journal is used primarily as a cognitive tool for students to write about new and difficult concepts encountered in readings and class lectures and discussions, as in a theoretical course, then the journal can be collected only several times during the term. Many students need time to process what they are reading and make connections among a number of readings. If the journal is used in a practical course, where there is apt to be less reading and more focus on the demonstration of techniques, procedures, and materials, then the journal can be collected more frequently – every week of a quarter or semester course, more often in an intensive training course. No matter how often the journal is handed in, writing every week is productive since the journal is meant to be ongoing. How much students write per entry can vary. On the whole, at least one paragraph per entry seems a minimum to develop an idea, but some teachers may want to require more if this amount leads to a superficial treatment of issues.

The teacher's response

The teacher's response plays an important role in the effectiveness of the journal. The teacher should write a response to each entry, sometimes brief, sometimes lengthy. The response may focus on answers to questions, sources students can go to, praise for good insights, points of agreement or disagreement, or even personal experiences or opinions related to issues raised in the journal. Since students are concentrating on the content, as in other journals, the teacher's response should not extend to correction of grammatical errors; however, incorrect uses of technical terms or important new concepts should be pointed out. Students appreciate generic comments such as "Good point," "I agree," "Good grief!", "What a wonderful way to put it," because such comments sprinkled throughout their entries make them feel listened to and encouraged. But in general, teacher responses must be text-specific to create an ongoing dialogue. Text-specific comments are those that relate directly to the content of the entry and would not apply to any other entry. The following exchanges demonstrate text-specific responses to student entries:

Student (from an SLA course):
You know, I'm not bothered by early studies being ill-conceived or not proving what they were supposed to prove. 1. I think they still provide valuable info. 2. They served as a springboard for later studies. 3. For students of SLA they make clear the purposes of more complex studies. It sort of reminds me of in high school and college lab classes how we had to repeat the research of prominent scientists. We knew the results, but the act of thinking the problem out was valuable.
Instructor:
I can't agree more with you. The early studies do provide the foundation – it's only in hindsight that we see the "holes" and problems.

Student (from a Methods course):
This week I asked X to observe my grammar class at the institute. His comments, like yours, have made me realize that my planning/sequencing is a bit off. For example in the grammar class I presented the present perfect and its uses and went from the most abstract to the simplest. How's that for being up-side down?
Instructor:
Well, no one springs into the world *knowing* how to teach grammar! I still have trouble deciding what and how to teach it (after 17 years). I'd be interested in your reactions to our verb chapters in the English 208 materials. Maybe some of the information there would be of use to you as background (e.g., the major uses of the various tenses).

In addition to individual written responses, teachers might wish to write their own journal entries, and then distribute these or read them to the class (see, for example, Spack and Sadow 1983). Such an entry would not be presented as a model to copy, but as one example of a critical and thoughtful reaction. This procedure reinforces the idea of the social uses of writing, that is, that the teacher and the students are part of a community. One teacher used this procedure in a second language acquisition course in which students kept journals on their ongoing study of a second or foreign language. During the semester, the teacher visited Thailand, a country in which he had previously lived. When he returned, he wrote and distributed to the class his reflections on his use of Thai – vocabulary, discourse patterns, comprehension, and the possible reasons for his surprising fluency after an absence of twelve years.

Another kind of response, also in addition to individual written responses, is for the teacher to regularly give "public feedback" on journal contents. While reading the journals, the teacher makes notes of interesting or controversial points or questions that come up; then the teacher can begin the following class session with a brief mention of these issues, without identifying the authors, and discussion can follow. This "public feedback" on journals not only allows for student input into the curriculum and lets students know what their classmates are writing about, but can also lead to meaningful class discussion.

Benefits of using journals

The use of journals in teacher preparation courses benefits both teacher and student in numerous ways. In this section we describe these benefits, supporting our contentions with excerpts from the students' journals and from final journal entries they have written evaluating the journal as a learning tool. These excerpts are coded as to type of course (Sociolinguistics, SLA, Methods).

1. An obvious benefit is that *students can get help with areas of course content where they are having difficulty.* In the journals, students ask about terms, concepts, and even entire readings that they do not understand. The teacher can then provide individual help where needed. In one instance, a student wrote about a contradiction between what she found in the readings and what she observed in her own teaching:

People must still believe that contrastive analysis is useful. For example, all the language departments here have such a course. There is no denying that first-language interference is a problem in language acquisition. I teach and we practice age: "J'ai quinze ans, J'ai seize ans" but still they say and write "Je suis quinze, Je suis seize." After all these years I know what errors will occur, but I don't seem able to stop them. Maybe I have to keep reminding myself of Schumann's pidginization process and just accept these errors as natural and inevitable. (SLA)

Her journal entry gave the teacher a chance to clarify the role of contrastive analysis in second language acquisition theory:

Teacher's response:
I don't think that the current position belittles interference's role in SLA. What it does do, however, is say the following:
1) We can't predict transfer errors, we can only (possibly) explain them.
2) Often transfer errors occur when two languages are similar rather than different.
3) We need a psycholinguistic definition to explain "difficulty" when a nonnative speaker relies on his/her first language.
4) We need an adequate theory of grammar (maybe markedness theory) in which to do contrastive analysis.
5) We need to see transfer as part of the larger process of relying on old information.

In addition, the teacher can be alerted to unexpected areas of difficulty. For example, a teacher perceived a clear difference between teaching standard English to native speakers of nonstandard English and teaching English as a second language (ESL) to nonnative speakers. Therefore, she did not anticipate the following question from a student in her sociolinguistics class:

Why should teaching standard English be any more "impossible" than teaching any other foreign language in the classroom if appropriate methods are used? (Sociolinguistics)

This question gave the teacher an opportunity to write a response outlining what these differences are.

If a learning problem is common to a number of students, then the area can be addressed in class and planned for in subsequent semesters. For example, in a methods class several students expressed confusion in their journals about the meanings of *approach, design,* and *procedure:*

If I were asked to define my approach, I might be a little hard pressed. Yes, I could probably come up with appropriate "buzz" words, but do I always know how to implement my approach? Does this sound weird? Maybe you could suggest some articles on how to define one's own approach. (Methods)

Could you please talk about the clear definitions of Approach, Design, and Procedure? (Methods)

As a result of these questions, the teacher spent additional class time explaining these concepts and planned for the following semester to discuss this topic in greater depth before giving assigned readings.

Finally, because it is a safe place, students take advantage of the journal to talk about learning problems, and consequently many more learning problems get addressed. Students are often reluctant to ask such questions publicly during class and often are too busy or too shy to see the teacher during office hours. As one student summed it up:

Whenever I've had a question I could always put it in my journal and you answered it. I would never ask a question in class. I don't like to talk in class and I rarely ask questions, and I don't like to take up your time . . . (Methods)

2. A second benefit of using journals is that *they promote autonomous learning,* encouraging students to take responsibility for their own learning and to develop their own ideas. For example, the following excerpts show how one student used the journal not only to express her confusion about standard dialect learning but to find her own way out of this confusion. Over the course of several weeks, this student explored the issue, finally coming to the realization that standard dialect learning is not so much a linguistic endeavor as a sociolinguistic endeavor.

It is very interesting to see that language (English) and social classes have strong relationship. A society like Japan, it is not said that there are any significant relations between one's academic achievement [and the language one uses] and a social group he belongs to. (Sociolinguistics)

As I wrote after reading Cazden and Dickenson's article, I remember writing composition in Hiroshima dialect in the 1st or 2nd grades. But I gradually realized, without teachers mentioning me, that we had to use different form as spoken in T.V. in writing composition and I don't think anyone had a hard time adopting that form. Is it because American dialects are more complicated in grammar and phonology that they have serious problems introducing Standard English? (same journal)

If a Japanese child is put into an American school without any knowledge of English, I heard he will acquire English within a few months. I wondered why black people can't learn Standard English. However, reading this article, I came to realize that they don't because with the established social institutions they see no need to. (same journal)

Taking responsibility for learning also involves critically evaluating course content. In this next excerpt, the student both questions current theory and develops an alternative view.

After our discussion today about personality, I've decided that the theories (in relation to SLA) are all iffy. I think that there are people that fit into the stereotypical mold at either end of the continuum, but most are probably anywhere in the middle. There are too many varying situations/contexts possible in or during the learning process to make any definite generalizations. For instance, you consider yourself to be "always" an analytical type learner, and yet in your Japanese Silent Way experience you changed. So I think it's possible to be field independent at one time, or in one situation, and field dependent at another or in another. (SLA)

Patricia A. Porter et al.

Autonomous learning is promoted by the very act of writing because writing both stimulates and shapes ideas. The following excerpts demonstrate that students both recognized and benefited from this process.

One more reflection before I go back to actually writing this journal: Looking back through the journal I see I've sort of settled into writing sentences and paragraphs more than just notes. At the time I didn't consciously think of it, but I see now I needed to write sentences to help me make complete ideas. In notes I can just put down a concept and not say anything about it. In sentences I have to relate it to something or give it some significance in some way. (Sociolinguistics)

Not only did I learn a lot from your comments every week, but oftentimes I benefitted simply from the thought and effort required to put an entry together. (Methods)

Looking back through my journal I did learn a little bit about how I learn and writing plays a big role. By writing things down I look at them and the words seem to trigger off thinking. (Methods)

3. A related benefit is that through the exchange of ideas that occurs between students and teachers in the journals, *students gain confidence in their ability to learn, to make sense of difficult material, and to have original insights.* The traditional relationship between teacher as all-powerful knower and student as apprentice learner moves toward a relationship of greater equality, of colleagues in a profession where each has something of value to contribute. For example, one student wrote:

In Wolfram's article we see that Puerto Ricans with more contact with blacks show more use of characteristics of Black English and also tend to minimize the troubles between Black and Puerto Rican groups. There's a quantitative difference between Puerto Ricans with a lot of contact and with a little contact – that is, all the Puerto Ricans showed some use of Black English characteristics. One way to consider this difference is in light of LePage's contention about social factors influencing speech only to the degree that these factors represent groups with which the speaker identifies himself. Can we say that the Puerto Ricans who use more Black English identify themselves more with the Blacks, and they have more contact because they identify with the Blacks? So it isn't a matter of more contact causing more use of Black English characteristics. Rather, the language use and having more contact are both signs of the same thing: identifying with the Black group. I haven't really thought this out, just kind of playing with the idea. (Sociolinguistics)

The teacher's response was:

This certainly is how I view it – and it's exactly what motivated me to do my dissertation research.

234

In a follow-up discussion, the student reported that this exchange made her realize she could think on her own, that critically evaluating research was not "a strange bizzare process" that only Ph.D.'s could do.

4. The fact that students take more responsibility for their learning leads to a fourth benefit of journals: *more productive class discussion.* Class time can be used for discussion of the implications and issues raised by assignments, rather than just "going over the facts," because students have written and thought in depth about the readings, observations, and materials. One student described it this way:

When I had written about the readings before class, I brought more to the class: I came to class already knowing what I did and didn't know. I said more because I felt more confident: I had already formulated questions and made connections between the material and my experience, and I was interested in getting other students' reactions to my ideas. (Sociolinguistics)

5. A fifth benefit is that *the journal encourages students to make connections between course content and their own teaching.* One student told how a particular article had influenced her teaching:

Since I've read the first Pica and Doughty article, I've tried to change my group work so that I'm doing 2-way activities. Now the non-vocal students show their "information" to the group and still do not speak. I feel less happy about the group work than I did before because I'm getting the same types of communication as I got before but now I have more contrived activities than I had before. (SLA)

The teacher responded:

Do you have any ideas why this is so? Has Y observed? Does he have any suggestions?

Another student found that through her journal writing she developed greater empathy with her own ESL students. She described the connection she had made between her own feelings about writing a journal and the feelings her students may have about their writing:

After reading back over my journal, it was interesting to relive situations and see the progress of my personal development as a teacher and learner. One of the themes that stood out was how "exposed" I've felt. I've kept a personal journal for several years and it was a new experience to have someone read and react to what I've written. It is really scary to reveal yourself like that.

And that is something they've tried to make me aware of at work – how terrifying it is for so many non-literate or partially literate students to write, because it exposes them, not only their lack of literacy, but also their thoughts and feelings. I remember my mentor telling me that for many of the students writing is like putting themselves down on paper. Even though my writing skills are far beyond most of these students, I can now understand their feeling of being "exposed." (Methods)

6. A sixth benefit is that the *journals create interaction beyond the classroom, both between teacher and student, and among students.* In the first place, the journal itself allows for an ongoing dialogue between teacher and student that might not occur given the institutional constraints of most programs. Some students captured this idea in their summary comments at the end of the semester:

Even though you and I didn't personally converse much during the course of the semester, I still feel like I have had more personal interaction with you through this journal than I have had with any other professor of memory. (Methods)

For me, it's like a correspondence with someone who is at once mentor, colleague and friend. (Methods)

Of course, the sad part is that our conversations will stop. Your comments (and interest) became a real motivating force. I benefitted in many ways from your additions, suggestions, and support. (Methods)

This dialogue is especially important for those students who are hesitant to speak up in class. As one student put it:

I'm not exactly a shy person but large groups of people always intimidate me and I tend to observe more than participate vocally...So, this journal is a good idea for students like me, who are hesitant to say a lot of things in class. (Methods)

In addition, the ongoing dialogue seems to create a positive atmosphere in which students feel free to talk to the teacher outside of class. For example, one student sat in the library writing this entry:

Most of the class discussion clarifies ideas and issues brought up in the reading. Often questions on the study guide I couldn't answer before class I can answer afterwards. However, the summary of the Tarone article left me totally confused. I couldn't even formulate a question I was so confused! From talking to others after class, I found I wasn't the only one. Perhaps a written summary would help. Wait! Why am I writing this? I'm going to go talk to you about it. (Sociolinguistics)

At this point the student went to the teacher's office and discussed the problems she was having with the article.

Finally, the journal leads to more student–student interaction. Students talk to each other about their journal entries, sometimes out of curiosity about what other students are writing and often out of their continual involvement with the course content. One student described it this way:

Writing in my journal would lead me to talk to people about a topic that had come up and that would help me see other perspectives. It was a very enriching experience. (Methods)

7. A seventh benefit, one consistent with the motivations for using the journals in the first place, is that *journals make the class more process oriented,* in effect matching our training methodology with the second or foreign language methodology we wish to promote.

The increased interaction described earlier is very much a part of a process approach. Yet another feature of a process approach is that student input can in part shape the curriculum. By reading journals regularly, the teacher is in touch with the current state of the learners' knowledge: The teacher has some hints about what is difficult for students, what is interesting to them, what they need to get more information about, what they are ready to learn about, what is controversial to them, and so forth, and the teacher can then make the class more reflective of learners' concerns. One student recognized this and commented on it in the journal:

I've also been thinking about the advantages of using learning journals in teaching a class. When you take notes on the journals and bring up larger issues in class, you give the class much more immediacy and relevance to the students. (Methods)

The teacher can use this information about learner concerns to restructure the class for the timely presentation of particular information. For example, in a methods class the syllabus included "teacher feedback" as a topic in week ten. But the students were observing ESL classes regularly, and in week three they had a number of questions about feedback techniques they were seeing. In response, the teacher gave an introduction to feedback techniques and issues at that point in the semester in addition to covering the material in greater depth during week ten as planned.

Student input via journals can also restructure the course content. An example from a methods class emphasizes how the process can work. In class, students had demonstrated listening activities that they had designed. In response to the content of the dialogue in one of these, one student wrote a beautifully reasoned five-page journal entry questioning why ESL teachers tended to emphasize the negative factors in American culture in their lessons: for example, showing films of American teenagers as vandals, discussing the internment of Japanese during World War II, making jokes about the president, and so on. (This student had seen examples of this in many classes and had discussed this concern with other students before writing about it in her journal.) The teacher brought the issue up in class and it generated a great deal of passionate discussion, which, incidentally, did not end on a note of consensus. But the teacher felt it was an important consciousness-raising session for both new and experienced teachers, and one that certainly hadn't been planned for in the syllabus. The journals that followed the discussion, as was typical, contained even more discussion on the topic by those who hadn't presented their ideas in class.

Another feature of a process approach is that the teacher has a deeper context in which to evaluate the student. For example, when students use the journal to describe their preparation of course assignments, the teacher can not only intervene and help out but also can evaluate the work with a much greater depth of understanding. Spack and Sadow (1983), in writing about the benefits of working journals in composition courses, describe it in this way:

As teachers, we become aware that each of our students' papers has its own history – we learn about the difficulties and successes they have encountered from inception to completion. This awareness has influenced the comments we write on the papers we do correct and grade; we evaluate not only the product, but also take into consideration the knowledge that writing is an enormously complex activity. (p. 586)

The kind of context a journal entry can provide is illustrated in this student's description of her experiences in preparing a lesson plan.

Finally the lesson plan is done...I had originally planned to adapt materials from others' works, then I decided to write one of my own both out of laziness and a desire to challenge myself. I did it although the dialog I created sounds less than native. I did manage to read it to my husband (at 12 midnight). He pointed out that overall it was an interesting piece, but he felt there were too many ums and uhuhs which made the dialog a bit unnatural to him. He also thought it might be too colloquial. I did not accept this though. So, I'll be waiting to hear your opinion on the dialog.

Also my decision to write on this topic (cross cultural marriage) was somehow inspired by my own experience. As a result, I consider the creation less rigid than if I had written something totally unfamiliar. There did not seem to be a lot of hesitation during lesson planning having all those good examples in front of me. After I read the draft, I felt that the teacher's words were a little rigid, so I tried to recall what you said in class and practiced out loud to myself. I added many functional words to make the sentences flow better.

Finally I thought my third multiple choice was a bit tricky. The students have to be very attentive to get the right answer. Is it a bad thing to do? (Methods)

Here, the teacher had a wealth of material as background to the product: the student's concerns about the naturalness of the dialogue and of the teacher's language, the validity of the questions. The teacher knew why the student chose her theme, how she made use of the information and samples she had been given, and how much difficulty she had in actually writing the lesson. Thus, the teacher was able to read and evaluate the lesson plan with this background in mind. After the lesson plan was returned, the student responded with this entry:

Your criticism about the dialog is right – it does sound as though Tom was lecturing on cross-cultural marriages. I think this problem largely resulted from my Chinese thinking style. I grew up in an environment where all written works were meant to be educational, every piece of work conveyed some sort of moralistic message. Although personally I resent certain ways in which moral standards are imposed, my writing oftentimes reflects the lingering influence of my culture. Of course when that influence affected a dialog between two Americans, the dialog had turned out to be rather unbelieveable. Thank you for pointing out this weakness in my dialog. I will try to adjust more. Originally, I did have some questions by Tom and answers by Amy, but I crossed them out for fear the material would be too long. When the two things – length and appropriateness – contradict each other, how should we handle them? (same journal)

This response turned out to be an important learning experience for the teacher, who hadn't in fact made the connection between the student's "cultural conditioning" and the content of her dialogue. As can be seen, the student's response led to further questions for the teacher to answer.

Even when the journal is not used to describe preparation of work, the entries regularly contain information that helps the teacher understand the students better. For example, in this entry, the student supplied vital information about her pattern of class participation.

Reading articles on biculturalism and on bilingual (biculture) education, I was surprised to find myself influenced by or binded by Japanese culture. When I think of questions I want to ask during class discussion, I always think whether or not it would be a mutual question among classmates. If so, it's worthwhile to ask. But if not, it isn't good to waste valuable time just because of me. I consider myself as a person who is not so group-oriented as other Japanese who tend to behave in groups. However, when I realized that my way of thinking stated above is the result of putting the group first and an individual second, I was surprised to find myself still under the Japanese culture. (Sociolinguistics)

Conclusion

Teacher educators may find themselves concerned about the amount of time journals entail for both themselves and their students. However, we as teachers and students strongly recommend the addition of a journal to teacher education courses even if this involves eliminating some readings and/or assignments from the syllabus of an already developed course. The benefits described here demonstrate that journals provide opportunities for ongoing learning that most course assignments do not. Throughout the course they allow for a dialogue between teacher and students; they allow students to learn through writing without being evaluated on the writing itself; and they alert teachers to student concerns and needs, and allow for these needs to be met in the course.

The journal encourages students to go beyond learning course content in isolation and to strive to link this information to theories and knowledge beyond the particular assignment and the particular course. The journal thus enables students to develop a professional approach toward learning and to write as members of the larger language teaching community. In sum, it teaches them to do what we do as professionals – to work to integrate new ideas with what we already know and to talk with each other as we do so.

Questions and tasks

Chapter 13 (Bartlett)

1. What are the characteristics of "reflective" teaching as defined by Bartlett? What definitions are offered? In what ways does the concept attempt to go beyond the notion of "effective" teaching?

2. "If we want to improve our teaching through reflective inquiry, we must accept that it does not involve some modification of behaviour by externally imposed directions or requirements, but that it requires deliberation and analysis of our ideas about teaching as a form of action based on our changed understandings" (Bartlett, p. 203). To what extent is such an attitude feasible in your own situation? What problems can you anticipate in attempting to foster such an attitude?

3. Construct a questionnaire from the questions raised by Bartlett on pages 206–207. Get some colleagues or teachers-in-preparation to complete the questionnaire and summarize the responses. What common themes and/or points of difference emerge? How might these be fed back to the participants in the survey?

4. According to Bartlett, what is the significance of cultural and social setting? Are there aspects of a particular social and cultural setting that might be inconsistent with the notion of "reflectivity"?

5. Apply the process of mapping, informing, contesting, appraisal, and acting to your own teaching. What insights emerge? How would you modify this process for use with teachers-in-preparation?

Chapter 14 (Bailey)

6. List the advantages and disadvantages of keeping a diary as a professional development tool.

7. Using the procedure suggested by Bailey, keep a diary for a week (or get colleagues or teachers-in-preparation to keep diaries). Review the diary or diaries and note the insights that emerge. What problems or difficulties occurred?

8. How much time can or should teachers-in-preparation realistically devote to keeping a diary?

9. What is meant by the remark that "the best diary from an educational point of view might be the worst one from a research perspective" (p. 224)?

Chapter 15 (Porter et al.)

10. What suggestions do Porter et al. make for turning journals into an ongoing dialogue? Why is such a dialogue considered important?

11. Review the excerpts from journals and the responses provided by the teacher educators. Do the responses provide content or do they fulfill an affective function? What responses would you have given?

12. List and comment on the seven advantages of learning logs advanced by Porter et al.

13. Review the chapters in this section as a whole. What points of similarity and difference do you find in relation to the following:
  – teaching as a process
  – teaching as introspection
  – teaching as a social event
  – the self-directed teacher
  – teacher education as an interactive process.

Part VI   Case studies

In this section case studies of teacher education programs or aspects of such programs are presented. Each reflects a particular response to some of the issues discussed in this book, and shows how some of the approaches and procedures discussed by the different authors in this collection can be implemented.

In a major statement on the design of a teacher development program, Lange (Chapter 16) situates language teacher education within a general movement in education in which programs are school-based, involve practicing teachers, and develop professionals. Characteristics of the "good" and the "reflective" teacher are articulated and discussed, and a case is made for a broad focus on professional development rather than one that focuses narrowly on training. Lange also argues strongly for the notion that the base discipline for language teaching should be education rather than linguistics. He then examines six characteristics of the future "technological society" and develops from them a model for teacher development organized on nine core features. According to Lange, programs should be field-based, problem-centered, technology-driven, developmental, competency-based, expertly staffed, use experimental sharing, contain a critical mass, and be open-ended. A teacher development program based on the model is then presented and evaluated.

In the next chapter Johnson describes a program that focuses on the teacher's use of language in the classroom, particularly in settings where English is used as the medium of instruction. The program initially involves a focus on the performance of specific teaching acts and related communicative tasks that recur across the school curriculum. The program makes innovative use of the language laboratory as a convenient setting in which teachers engage in communicative and analytical tasks. Later, teachers evaluate their own classroom language through collecting data on their own classroom language use.

Dubin and Wong outline in Chapter 18 a procedure that enables the teacher educator working in a foreign language context to take as a point of departure the participants' perspective, rather than importing the latest word in theory and practice from the outside. The first part of the chapter addresses general principles in inservice training, and the second part presents a case study in which these principles are contextualized.

In the final chapter, Spada describes a major observation instrument, the COLT (Communicative Orientation of Language Teaching) scheme, which has been developed for analyzing classroom processes. While instruments such as the COLT scheme have been developed to provide data for classroom research, they are also invaluable for teacher education, as they can be used to provide objective, quantifiable data on what is actually happening in language classrooms. With appropriate training, teachers-in-preparation can use such schemes to obtain insights that are not readily revealed by unstructured observation. This is particularly valuable when it comes to self-analysis, because student teachers can record, describe, and document changes to their own classroom practices during the course of their professional preparation, and thereby document their own professional growth.

16 A blueprint for a teacher development program

Dale L. Lange

Teacher education in the United States is changing. It is clear that the social pressure brought to bear on teaching and education from the plethora of reports, critiques, and suggestions from broad segments of the society is having an effect. If the 1988 meeting of the National Holmes Group in Washington, D.C., is any indication, teacher developers are moving dramatically toward the renewal of teacher education. The collaboration of school districts and universities in the establishment of professional development schools and the description of schools for the twenty-first century to provide a context in which "tomorrow's teachers" would function are bold steps of the Holmes Group (Quality Schooling... 1988). Individual universities are also reorienting their efforts in the preparation of teachers away from the typically university-controlled program to those which are school-based, involve practicing teachers, and develop professionals. The contextualization and description of an experimental program in second language teacher development at the University of Minnesota provides an example of one university's change in direction.

The general need for change

Reports on education and teaching

The year 1986 was a "watershed" year for teacher education. Two major reports on teacher education appeared at that time (Carnegie Forum 1986; *Tomorrow's Teachers* 1986). These reports evidence a general failure in the American educational system. The blame for this decline has been pointed directly at schools, teachers, and teacher educators. In addition, the President's Commission on Foreign Languages and International Studies (1980) strongly criticized second language education. In short, the situation described in these documents is seen as reprehensible and requires "immediate" fixing. There have been many suggestions for improving the situation, including suggestions for second language education (Lambert 1987; Lange 1987a).

Both the Carnegie Forum and the Holmes Group provide recommendations for the renewal of teacher education. While their major recommendations are similar, they differ in the concepts of differentiated staffing, certification, financial elements, and implementation. Only the general flavor of the recommendations of these reports is given here.

The Carnegie and Holmes reports argue for the elimination of undergraduate teacher education, offering it only at a graduate level. They both contend that professional schools of education must develop rigorous standards for entrance into teacher education. They also discuss the need for career ladders and a national board of standards that would examine the competency of teachers. They recommend ways in which teachers can become more professional – in particular, by associating university programs closely with schools. In this way, developing teachers in a university program can relate theory to practice in actual schools. Both reports agree that professional autonomy, authority, and responsibilities of classroom teachers must increase greatly.

Research on the effective teacher

As an outgrowth of concern in the sixties that "teachers didn't matter," a twenty-year period of research evolved that examined teacher effectiveness and other aspects of schooling. Hawley et al. (1984) summarized research on effective teaching, school leadership, the learning environment, learning resources, and parental involvement. In a section on effective teaching, the authors characterized the coaction of several groups of teacher strategies as "effective" in developing successful student learning. They suggested that these teacher strategies may be highly significant to second language education because they mesh positively with the tasks (Candlin and Murphy 1987) required for students to learn and function with any aspect of the four syllabi conceived as being important for second language programs (Stern 1983). In other words, these strategies respond more fully to the interaction of teaching and learning than any single "method." Further, the applicability of these strategies may be important in any educational context.

According to Hawley et al. (1984), effective teachers function with five different yet interacting categories of behavior that direct student attention to learning. First, *effective teachers engage students with academic learning time,* where *learning time* signifies that portion of allocated time in which students are *successful* at working on tasks that are associated with desired outcomes (Fisher et al. 1978).

In the second category, *effective teachers credit student learning that meets desired outcomes.* Ultimately, all students desire to be praised for their work, and all students probably desire to be successful. Effective teachers combine these two wishes. They find a way to reward all students, binding successful performance on specific tasks to desired outcomes and goals. The rewards can be provided in competitive, cooperative, or individualized learning situations, according to type of task.

Third, *effective teachers engage students interactively*. Teachers using this strategy direct student attention to the task(s) to be completed; enthusiastically, they explain what, how, and with what expectations the material is to be learned. As the student proceeds with the task, the teacher monitors progress and decides either to continue or to adjust instruction. Teacher assistance is always available. Students are rewarded for completing the task and are informed of the progress that must still be made. This circle of interconnected teacher behaviors has proved most important, but may be limited when requiring students to learn more than basic skills and information. Cognitive and metacognitive behaviors may be required for higher-order learning (Jones et al. 1987; Marzano et al. 1988). In addition, students need to understand the learning process. For example, they need to be able to access knowledge; understand how to use prior knowledge; and have the metacognitive skills to monitor and adjust their performance (i.e., apply corrective strategies) if their initial procedures are inappropriate. Similar kinds of behavior will be required of second language students with the communicative syllabus. As an example, Tarone (1980) outlines categories and subcategories of paraphrase, transfer, and avoidance which fit into the kind of strategies people need and may learn in attempting to communicate orally. O'Malley, Chamot, and Walker (1987) discuss the application of cognitive processes to second language acquisition in a broader form. Second language education is beginning to realize that not all aspects of language learning and acquisition can be explained through a linguistic examination of the issues. Richards (this volume, Chapter 1) particularly recognizes the contribution of research on teaching to teacher preparation in this regard.

In a fourth category, *effective teachers maintain and communicate high expectations for student performance*. Teachers apply this behavior to all students. In other words, effective teachers communicate not only to the "good" students but consistently to all students that they will be treated fairly. The indication is that everyone will share in the learning resources, particularly instructional time and the opportunity to perform.

Finally, *effective teachers maximize learning time by the use of instructional settings appropriate to the tasks being pursued*. Effective teachers analyze both the tasks and their students to determine whether the task is best handled by large groups, small groups, or individually. The resulting decision helps determine an appropriate instructional strategy or constellation of strategies.

The reflective teacher

A reflective teacher knows the art and craft of teaching, and considers it carefully both during and after interaction with students. As used here, the *craft* of teaching relates to the teacher's specific knowledge of the subject matter, knowledge on teaching that subject matter, and knowledge on teaching in general. The *art* of teaching involves the combination of knowledge and experience in the many decisions that teachers make as they interact with learners. Reflection on teaching occurs both during and after teaching, as teachers think about the decisions they make and will make. The important question is how both the art and craft of the reflective teacher are transmitted to those who intend to teach.

In most traditional teacher development programs, the only form of "reflective teaching" is student teaching. Student teaching may last anywhere from three to ten weeks in undergraduate programs to an entire year in a graduate internship. Reflecting upon teaching, as a specific task, may not take place in a systematic fashion, however. Some programs employ microteaching, where single learning tasks are prepared and taught to students or are simulated with peers (Clifford, Jorstad, and Lange 1977) as preparation for student teaching. The practice may not be widespread, but it does involve more direct preparation, planning, and thinking about teaching. Both kinds of clinical experience could potentially include more extensive reflection on the act of teaching.

Within the framework of clinical or laboratory experiences in teacher development, there are two approaches to reflective teaching. One is technocratic, the other more philosophic. Reflective Teaching as technocracy (note the capital letters) is a specific approach used by Cruickshank, Holton, and their colleagues (1981) and Cruickshank (1985). It constitutes teaching one or more of thirty-six fifteen-minute lessons, unrelated to any school subject matter, to four to six peers. The teacher then evaluates the extent to which the peers learn and determines the value of the teaching/learning experience. This process is somewhat mechanistic, focusing specifically on what happened in teaching, why it happened, and how else the goals of the lesson could have been achieved.

A more philosophical approach to reflective teaching (note the absence of capital letters) is suggested by Gore (1987). While responding to the more empirical/analytical approach of Cruickshank, Gore elucidates the positive characteristics of reflective teaching that apply to any teaching situation. When applied to second language education, this "process" can be conveyed as the integration of several areas of knowledge and practice, exemplified by certain characteristics, listed below. *Reflective teaching* requires the interaction of:

1. Competence in a second language
   - ability to listen, read, speak, and write in the language to be taught
   - knowledge about language, language use, and culture, and their interrelationship
   - knowledge of how second languages are learned and acquired

2. Understanding of how the target language is taught
   - knowledge of both the theoretical and practical bases for teaching any subject
   - knowledge of both the theoretical and practical bases for language teaching and learning in schools
3. Practice in the application of knowledge about the subject and teaching in teaching situations
   - planning how to teach about language, language use and culture in an integrated fashion
   - development of alternatives in teaching any aspect of language, language use, and culture, and their interrelationship
   - practice in teaching the integration of language knowledge, language use, and culture through peer teaching, tutoring, microteaching, and student teaching
4. Opportunities to reach an understanding of both the art and the craft of teaching
   - observation of how others teach in tutoring, peer-teaching, microteaching, and student-teaching situations
   - discussion of the observations in an environment where experimentation and error is the norm, where risk-taking is encouraged and expected
   - discussions that relate theoretical assumptions about language, culture, teaching in general, and language teaching to actual situations
   - discussions that relate the personal values and assumptions of teachers to their assumptions about teaching
   - discussions that relate the climate and culture of the particular school to teaching individual students and groups
   - opportunities to replan, reteach, and reevaluate lessons taught after examination and discussion
5. Evaluation of teaching
   - examination of the appropriateness of assumptions about teaching strategies for the particular school, individual students, and groups
   - knowledge and use of existing tools for the evaluation of student progress in learning and use of language
   - knowledge and use of the several means for the examination of the effectiveness of teaching
   - knowledge and use of the means by which the effectiveness of teaching is examined in a particular school context

The interaction of these five elements of the reflective process benefits developing teachers, inservice teachers, administrators, students, and parents – all of whom interact with the school and community culture. The reflective process allows developing teachers latitude to experiment

Dale L. Lange

within a framework of growing knowledge and experience. It gives them the opportunity to examine their relations with students, their values, their abilities, and their successes and failures in a realistic context. It begins the developing teacher's path toward becoming an "expert teacher" (Berliner 1988).

"Professional development" – not "training"!

While the title of this section resembles sloganism, the concern it raises is not easily dismissed. All of the issues associated with either the broad or the narrow view of teaching as contained in the terms *development* or *training* cannot be attended to here. A brief examination of the matter will be sufficient to make it part of the context.

Teacher development is a term used in the literature to describe a process of continual intellectual, experiential, and attitudinal growth of teachers (e.g., Joyce and Weil 1980; Lange 1983; Sprinthall and Thies-Sprinthall 1983), some of which is generated in preprofessional and professional inservice programs. I have argued for the use of the term, distinguishing it from training and preparation as encompassing more and allowing for continued growth both before and throughout a career (Lange 1983). The concept is similar to that of Larsen-Freeman's (1983) "educative process." In using the term *development,* the intent here is to suggest that teachers continue to evolve in the use, adaptation, and application of their art and craft. It is the continuance of that evolution that teacher education programs seek, but rarely establish.

In the never-ending reform of teacher education (Joyce and Weil 1972; Soltis 1987), it appears that a different framework has materialized recently (Keith 1987). Instead of a linear approach to the "problem," illustrated by the statement, "If you fix teacher education, you fix education in the schools," Keith suggests an interactive framework instead. This framework considers the structure and organization of schools, and promotes schools as places in which to work and establish connections among teacher education, teachers, schools, and learning. This context allows renewal to proceed beyond the "usual more/less, longer/shorter, harder (never easier), quantitative earlier reform proposals" (Keith 1987: 23).

In this context, teaching is directly connected with its use in schools. The school–university relationship changes the nature of the questions asked about teacher preparation; it focuses questions differently: "How can the school–university collaboration make experiences for developing teachers more educative?" rather than "How much more of this [foundations] or how much of that [clinical experiences] is needed to train a teacher?" For example, instead of simply learning the elements of effective teaching, education students would use this knowledge as *one*

250

aspect in lesson and program planning, teaching, and examining the results within the framework of the school, its curriculum, its culture, and its environment. Schools would be used in which high levels of responsibility for curricular control and decision making are clearly in the hands of teachers. This would allow the teacher development program, the developing teacher, other teachers, and the school system to collaborate in teacher preparation. Such preparation would result from directing critical decision making, reflective, and evaluative processes toward the self, teaching, students, other teachers, the school culture and environment, and the community. If successful, it can prepare a teacher for continued growth. It would not require the teacher to choose between what Jackson (1986: 104) has characterized as two important historical trends within teaching, "learning to learn" and "choosing to learn." Huebner (1987: 21) might even say that such teachers would be prepared for "the making of meanings and values." In all of these senses, teachers would be *developed*, not trained.

The context established here represents major shifts from the established routine and expectations in teacher development. In part, these shifts resulted from both political and social action, culminating in the many reports on the quality of both education and teacher education, as well as the several major recommendations for renewal. The shifts are not only related to general forces, however, but to direction within the profession itself. However, the final response ultimately rests with the individual action of teachers.

Need for change in second language teacher development

The need for change in teacher development in second languages is not necessarily viewed any differently from that described in the previous section. It simply has not been studied as carefully, as indicated by Bernhardt and Hammadou (1987), who suggest that second language educators know little about the process and the preparation of foreign language teachers. If the ten years of literature examined in their review (1977–87) can be used as a fairly accurate impression of the total picture, the research data base in second language teacher education at all levels is pitifully small. Some of the characteristics of the data base are as follows:

1. Seventy-eight articles were written on foreign and second language teacher education in the years 1977–86, including English as a second language (ESL). The topics of these articles included global position statements, teacher behaviors, teaching assistant and university pro-

fessorial preparation for teaching, inservice opportunities, supervision, and methods course curricula.

2. Only eight of the seventy-eight articles were data-based research.
3. Of 129 potential citations on teacher education in the first two editions of the American Education Research Association's *Handbook of Research on Teaching* (Gage 1963; Travers 1973), only references to two researchers in those volumes appear in the second language teacher education literature during this decade, those being to John B. Carroll and Barak Rosenshine. Further, while there were articles on foreign language education in first and second editions of this handbook (Carroll 1963; Birkmaier 1973), the third edition (Wittrock 1986) does not contain such information, but does include one article on bilingual education (Filmore and Valadez 1986). None of the three editions of this important publication devotes a specific chapter to the teaching of or the preparation of teachers for ESL.

Bernhardt and Hammadou conclude from their analysis that minimal attention is paid to the development of teachers in second languages either conceptually or research-wise. Since both the number of topics and the depth of penetration into those topics in teacher development in their survey is limited, there has to be concern for the quality of preparation of teachers at all levels.

In many senses, second language teacher development is not a unified field. It is separated into at least two basic approaches, as represented by ESL and foreign language education. The ESL approach is basically theoretical in nature, somewhat an artifact of history, although it has attitudinal ideological aspects. As the need for ESL teachers became more crucial in the late 1960s, formal programs for teacher preparation developed within departments of linguistics, not departments of education. The programs reflect, therefore, the nature of that environment. Richards and Hino (1983), in a survey of master's graduates working in Japan, found that the most frequently studied courses in master's programs were structural linguistics, phonology, contrastive analysis, transformational grammar, and first and second language acquisition. By contrast, little attention was apparently given to "education" topics: curriculum development, instructional practice, and evaluation. Attitude has played a large role in determining such emphasis. Because, as a field, Education draws from a variety of areas of inquiry, and because it has a history of shortcomings in applying such inquiry, it has been avoided in favor of Linguistics, which has been perceived as a *science* that could be directly applied to language teaching. It would ensure "high quality" preparation of ESL teachers. The connection to Education was not made.

At least one aspect of ESL teacher development could not be avoided, however. The clinical experiences practicum seems to be an integral

A blueprint for a teacher development program

aspect of ESL graduate programs. Another survey (Richards and Crookes 1987), this time directed toward institutes of higher education that offered graduate programs in ESL, assessed the nature of the practicum. The study confirmed that a wide variety of clinical experiences were in use, that their importance was being increasingly recognized, and that their effectiveness has yet to be determined. These experiences seem to provide the main opportunity to translate the theoretical learning of students in these programs into practical application for the classroom. Although the study did not specifically examine the amount of time given to clinical experiences, that time may be limited, particularly in graduate programs. As a result, teachers may be learning more "on the job."

Teacher development in ESL is also offered at the undergraduate level, although the largest numbers of programs are probably at the graduate level. But it is probably fair to characterize programs at both levels as theoretically oriented toward linguistics and language acquisition with but a modicum of attention given to teaching and learning.

Foreign language teacher development has similar shortcomings. It has a basic orientation to methods of teaching. Unfortunately, the latest bandwagon "methodologies" come into prominence without much study or understanding, particularly those that appear easiest to immediately apply in the classroom or those that are supported by a particular "guru." Although concern for method is certainly not a new issue (Kelly 1969), the current attraction to "method" stems from the late 1950s, when foreign language teachers were falsely led to believe that there was a method to remedy the "language teaching and learning problems." Audiolingualism is no longer the reigning theory of language learning (Blair, 1982; Oller and Richard-Amato, 1983; Larsen-Freeman 1986), but it has been deeply ingrained in foreign language teachers' routines as basic practice. The obsession with methods makes the connection between university teacher development programs difficult, particularly in clinical experiences aspects, because the practice in schools is different from the more theoretical and "up-to-date" approach of college/university teacher development programs.

Foreign language teacher development has its own attitudinal problem, particularly in relation to linguistics. Theory of language acquisition, the application of linguistic knowledge to language teaching, and the relationship of psychology to linguistics are not necessarily viewed as important to foreign language teachers. The excuse often given is that these fields apply to teaching ESL and to ESL students, but not to foreign language learning. "That body of research and theory doesn't apply to us; our classrooms are *totally* different," is the claim. An example of this attitude can be seen as foreign language teachers struggle against the concept of communicative competence.

Whether there are specific data to demonstrate the extent or quality of clinical experiences, foreign language educators pride themselves on the practice opportunities they offer developing teachers. In other words, the feeling is that foreign language teacher education gives developing teachers plenty of practice in developing their art and craft before they are hired in a school. Some of these opportunities come from requirements for observation, tutoring, and microteaching in courses of general introduction to teaching, but these same processes and those of peer teaching and student teaching are also part of the program of "practice" specifically related to the foreign language program. In spite of the perception of foreign language educators, the suspicion of this writer is that if the situation were to be studied (cf. Richards and Crookes 1987), many of the same practices and vagaries would be found. Foreign language education should not boast.

There are many similarities and some differences between ESL and foreign language education. It is not being argued that they merge, but that they "touch" each other. The benefits of such a connection could be helpful in at least three ways. ESL and foreign language specialists could:

1. Direct efforts to considerations of and research into the nature of the effective teacher in second languages;
2. Devise and examine models of developing effective teachers;
3. Explore ways in which the effects of teaching on learning in either field could be more readily shared and discussed.

These kinds of undertakings could help both fields understand teacher development better and contribute to a broader knowledge base. Both fields have much to learn from each other. Some consolidation of effort between them could strengthen both.

The remainder of this chapter is devoted to the development of a model in second language education, its application, and evaluation.

The model: general framework

In their two articles, Mulkeen and Tetenbaum (1987; Tetenbaum and Mulkeen 1986) discuss six very broad characteristics of the future "technological society." From these characteristics, implications are drawn for teacher education, and a model of teacher development is organized on nine core features.

Characteristics

1. *The twenty-first century will be knowledge-based.* Social problems will be highly complex (hunger, overpopulation, needs for and supply

of energy, urban decay, etc.). Thus the issue for society as a whole must be on how to organize to make wise, informed, and intelligent decisions.

2. *The twenty-first century will see an increased information flow.* Scientific and technological knowledge doubles every 5.5 years. An overview of the contribution of research in instructional methods and conditions to knowledge about classroom learning (Walberg, Schiller, and Haertel 1979) relates positive results from over 2,000 controlled studies. Some of these results are being used in classroom teaching. Since 1979, however, there are about 4,000 more that have not been considered.

3. *The twenty-first century will see rapid change and impermanence.* Individuals will never be able to "complete" their education. They will also not expect to enter a job or profession and remain in it without retraining.

4. *The twenty-first century will see an increase in decentralization of organization, institutions, and systems.* Societal structures from business and industry to religious institutions and schools will experience decentralization of power, because problems are generally solved in groups of people who collaborate and share expertise and perspectives.

5. *The twenty-first century will be people-oriented.* People are the nation's most important asset. Individuals' need for self-determination and input into the decision-making processes that affect them are important for the cultivation of experimentation, innovation, and individual entrepreneurship in our culture.

6. *The twenty-first century will see major demographic shifts.* This condition is particularly true for the United States' ethnic and racial composition. The single largest, fastest-growing minority population in the country is Hispanic in origin. The differential birthrate suggests that the United States will produce more blacks, fewer whites, as many Hispanics as blacks, and more Asians.

Implications

1. The teaching profession must attract some of the "best and brightest." Entrance standards to teacher education programs must be rigorous.
2. Teachers will have to become facilitators, not repositories of knowledge. They will need preparation in a variety of alternatives in pedagogy and curriculum development (Schubert 1986).
3. Lifelong learning must be a construct in every teacher development program.
4. Experimentation, risk taking, autonomy, and flexibility must be key elements in the development of a model of schooling that places responsibility for learning on students, giving them freedom to try, test, innovate, and create.

Dale L. Lange

5. Schools must allow teachers to take responsibility for professional decisions that affect the classroom.
6. Teacher development programs must be more responsive to the needs of minority students in multicultural settings.

A model and its core features

From these characteristics and implications, Tetenbaum and Mulkeen (1986) develop nine core features. The model accounts for a continuing, integrated program of teacher development in several teaching centers. These features are as follows:

1. *Field-based.* Preservice teacher development takes place on-site in schools, in cooperation with collegiate teacher development programs; such schools are known as teaching centers.
2. *Problem-centered.* The theory and the practice of a curricular and instructional program are organized around the resolution of identified, real problems in actual classes, in real schools.
3. *Technology-driven.* Computers, videotape, videodisk, and satellite hookup are key components of a problem-resolving mode of instruction in providing an informational data base, the means for analyzing that information through a variety of spreadsheets, and the means for sharing decisions through word processors.
4. *Experimental sharing.* In this model, neophyte and experienced teachers, master teachers, college/university supervisors, and professorial staff share in the identification and organization of resolutions to curricular and instructional problems.
5. *Developmental.* The teacher development instructional program meets the needs of an increasingly sophisticated developing professional.
6. *Competency-based.* The teacher development instructional program, while focusing on the resolution of curricular and instructional problems, is oriented toward knowledge, skills, and attitudes that are appropriate to each experiential level identified, taught, practiced, and evaluated.
7. *Expertly staffed.* Problem resolution in such a program comes about because of a constellation of staff who work together: school staff, university faculty, representatives of agencies, consultants from the community, and the like.
8. *Critical mass.* A high concentration of professional staff within a school setting whose responsibility is to develop teachers through problem resolution using risk taking and experimentation makes the process possible.
9. *Open-ended.* The open-endedness of the model suggests that professional development is never-ending and lifelong.

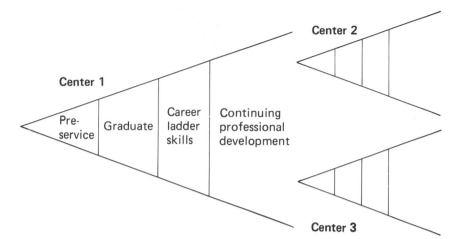

Figure 1   Mulkeen and Tetenbaum's model for an integrated teacher development program. Centers 2 and 3 signify a replication of Center 1 in other contexts. (Reprinted with permission of educational HORI-ZONS quarterly journal published by Pi Lambda Theta national honor and professional association, Bloomington, Ind.)

Figure 1 demonstrates the application of several principles and core features of the model.

The second language framework

Lange (1979) outlines seven principles that apply to the development of both pre- and inservice teachers. In addition, the American Council on the Teaching of Foreign Languages 1987 teacher education guidelines are briefly reviewed. Both contribute to the second language framework.

1. *Teacher self-selection and teacher selection are ongoing processes.* The process of teacher selection is based upon information about the applicant (grade point averages, IQ, language proficiency, personality, teaching aptitude, evidence of work with children), preprofessional counseling, and a decision-making process whereby a team of faculty members and the candidate make the final decision for entrance.

2. *Teachers are cognitively and experientially aware of the intellectual, scientific, and artistic history of their world.* Before their selection as preservice teachers, individuals should demonstrate knowledge of and experience with different categories of the intellectual, scientific, and artistic endeavors of humankind. A broad liberal arts background, ori-

ented toward the language and culture of the major, contributes to an understanding of the native and the nonnative cultures.

3. *Teachers are proficient in the language and are experienced in the cultural environments of the language they teach.* There is general agreement that teachers need to be competent in the four language skills (listening, reading, speaking, writing). Advanced language competence in all language skills cannot be accomplished in the university classroom. Work, travel, living, and/or study experiences in a setting where the language is used could provide opportunities for the development of such competence. Such experiences would also necessitate confronting another culture and force students to focus on their feelings, attitudes, and beliefs about their own culture. Similarly, some experience with the learning of a second language should also be a *sine qua non* for ESL teachers.

4. *Teachers are knowledgeable about processes to help students develop their own experience with the cultural environments of the language(s) they are learning.* Lange (1979) has described a ten-item process for handling the resolution of differences in attitude, *Weltanschauung*, and perceptions created by the meeting of two cultures. This process has been further described by Crawford-Lange and Lange (1984).

5. *Teachers examine developments in second language teaching and learning through experience in order to understand both cognitively and affectively the implications of those developments for students.* In order that understanding of the continuing development of foreign language teaching develop, a framework of language teaching is constructed to situate developments into appropriate roles. In this manner, theoretical constructs and research findings in language learning, acquisition, and teaching can be examined in relation to practice. This framework can serve to organize the clinical experiences portion of any preservice teacher development program. Teachers need to know and understand the connections between theory and practice. They also need to experience these associations through a program of clinical experiences, such as microteaching, tutoring, observation, peer observation, and student teaching, where reflection can be exercised.

6. *Teachers and students contribute to a growing understanding of language teaching.* In creating "the professional teacher," development programs help their clients create a classroom climate where dialogue between teacher and students is important to the resolution of personal, social, and learning problems. Such a climate is especially important to language learning. Dialogue can become a source of "data" that can help determine what *works* in helping students voice their opinions, feelings, and perceptions. In this regard, teachers and students learn from each other.

7. *The student–teacher relationship allows for both student and*

teacher to understand each other's needs and goals in developing a program of second language study. Some modification of the industrial or product model of education must emerge relatively quickly, because concentration on the knowable, observable, and achievable does not prepare students to cope with the processes, the results, and the uses of change that determine today's culture in the United States. There is overemphasis in U.S. culture on a model of accountability that does not fit the development of higher-order thinking, emotional maturity, and a system of values for our students. Likewise in learning a foreign language, the product model leads to low-level functioning in grammar: rules, vocabulary, memorized language.

Another concern is that teachers dominate students; only teachers know what is best, what should be learned. Here, a resolution is proposed based on the work of Freire (1970, 1973). It is described in a very general sense. In this approach to learning, teachers and students have equal importance, although their experience and input may be different. Teachers provide opportunity, resources, support, encouragement, and expertise. Students have the major decision-making role in determining what to learn in order to empower their lives. Both students and teachers function in a climate where social and personal problems find resolution by the group; the atmosphere is helpful and respectful; resolutions are not imposed.

Using this model, the goals of a program of language and culture learning (Crawford-Lange and Lange 1984) are determined through dialogue between students and teacher. The goals would actually relate to the problems posed for the students by the culture and its most important means of expression, language. In this way, the understanding of another culture through language becomes the major purpose for foreign language learning. But most of all, there is balance between the product orientation and the need to process the product into a broader context: Language is placed in its original context, which comprises both a specific as well as a broader cultural base.

A more specific set of guidelines for teacher education is being prepared by the American Council on the Teaching of Foreign Languages. The last important statement of this kind was developed by Paquette (1966). In draft form, the guidelines focus on three basic areas: personal, professional, and specialist development. Personal development includes communication skills, acquisition and use of knowledge, and leadership. Professional development involves an understanding of the need for foreign language study, of child development and learning, curriculum development, instruction and the instructional setting, and foreign languages in the elementary school. The guidelines for specialist development focus on language proficiency, culture and civilization, and language analysis. Although not yet approved or widely discussed, these guidelines will be useful to institutions as yet another framework for developing second language teachers.

The resulting program

Having presented the characteristics of society in the twenty-first century, implications for teacher development, and a responding model, we now turn to a more concrete, though only partial, response: a postbaccalaureate program of teacher development at the University of Minnesota, Twin Cities Campus. Offered in the 1986–7 academic year by the Second Languages and Cultures Education program, this model is only partial because it is still in development. It was initiated in the fall quarter of 1987. It represents only a preservice phase (Lange 1987b). This model program not only provides professional preparation, but also allows for research within the process of such development. The resultant "data base" can be used to examine teachers as they develop within the program, and also for follow-up studies on developing and continuing teacher competence. The data base also allows for a detailed evaluation of program effectiveness.

Another important general feature of this program is that it has not been targeted to any one specific language. Programs in many universities relate only to the development of teachers in one language. Because teacher development in second languages at the University of Minnesota is located in the College of Education and not in a language department,

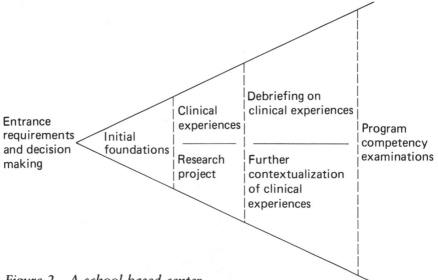

Figure 2   A school-based center.

TABLE I. TIME LINE FOR POSTBACCALAUREATE PROGRAM

First summer (3 months)	Academic school year (9 months)	Final summer (3 months)
Educational foundations Courses to meet general state requirements	On-site clinical experiences Second language teacher preparation courses Special topics seminars Reflection and debriefing seminars	Remaining state requirements Debriefing Exit exams Research report

the same program serves the most commonly taught languages: French, German, Spanish, and ESL taught in schools in the United States. It also accommodates Chinese, Hebrew, Japanese, Latin, Russian.

The model has the following basic elements: Entrance Requirements, Educational Foundations, Clinical Experiences, Research Component, and Exit Requirements (see Figure 2).

General description of the program

A postbaccalaureate program should be at the graduate level and it should concern the development of teachers who are mature enough to experience the relationship of theory to practice and who are professionally capable of resolving questions related to that experience. In its current form, the program is fifteen months long. Students begin coursework in June of one year and finish in August of the second year. The two summer sessions at the beginning of the course build foundations upon which the nine-month clinical experiences are built. In the nine-month period from September to June, the Second Languages and Cultures program offers courses and experiences that are committed to the development of competencies in analyzing and resolving questions of both a curricular and instructional nature. Such questions are addressed through on-site courses, seminars, and clinical experiences conducted and supported by master teachers, university supervisors, classroom teachers, and university professorial staff. Some foundational work follows the clinical experiences portion of the program during the following summer, allowing for practice to inform theory. Table 1 summarizes the stages of the program. Licensure is recommended at the end of this program. Many of the credits amassed will apply to a Master of Education degree, the details for which have not as yet been fully worked out.

Dale L. Lange

Program elements

1. ENTRANCE REQUIREMENTS AND DECISION MAKING

Program admission criteria can serve to evaluate the development of teachers within the program as well as predict success beyond program completion. Those who apply have already completed a Bachelor of Arts degree with a major in the language they intend to teach. Entrance decisions are made by a committee of faculty in the program area and admissions counselors. The decision for acceptance is based on a constellation of qualities:

1. *Preprofessional skills.* The Preprofessional Skills Test battery, developed by the Educational Testing Service, responds to the State Board of Teaching mandate that all teachers must be competent in the basic skills of reading, writing, and computation.

2. *General aptitude.* To meet this requirement, applicants must take the Miller Analogies Test, a test of general verbal ability.

3. *A writing sample.* All applicants must respond to a similar set of general questions relating to why they have chosen teaching as their career, and particularly why they chose to teach a second language.

4. *Grade point average.* Applicants must have a minimum of 2.8 overall and 3.0 in the major.

5. *Pre-education preparation.* The Bachelor of Arts degree with a major in a language is the basic requirement. However, if applicants have had extensive study (1–5 years) in a context where they have used the language in which they are to be licensed, and can prove the required proficiency, they are considered viable applicants. For applicants in ESL, the situation is generally more complicated. If applicants have not pursued courses leading to licensure either as undergraduates or before admission to the postbaccalaureate program, they must fulfill specific requirements for licensure during the program.

6. *Background experience.* Persons applying to the program are required to have worked with children or adolescents in youth groups of various kinds: church, community, recreation.

7. *Second language proficiency.* Before consideration for admission, applicants must be tested in the language they are going to teach. ESL applicants whose native language is not English are given an ACTFL-type oral interview. They are the only ESL applicants tested in this manner.

8. *Cultural awareness.* Through transcripts and other evidence, applicants demonstrate awareness of the country (countries) where the second language is used. First priority for entrance is given to those applicants who have actual living or study experiences in a country where the language is used.

262

There is a single application date in the academic year. For 1987–8, there were twenty-seven applications. Twelve students were admitted and nine chose to participate. They were distributed in the following manner: one ESL, three German, two French, and three Spanish.

2. EDUCATIONAL FOUNDATIONS

An indication of the "becoming" nature of the postbaccalaureate programs at the University of Minnesota is found in the concept of educational foundations. There is some agreement on what the content of the foundations might be, but the delivery system has not yet been determined. The topics below represent the content.

   * = regularly scheduled courses
  ** = second language courses
 *** = special seminars

Computer Literacy***/*
Concepts of Learning Important in Schooling: Cognitive, Affective, Psychomotor*
Culture and Role of Schools in American Society*
Curriculum of Schooling: Contents, How Developed**
Classroom Management and Organization**
Getting into the Profession: Job Interviews, Placement Service, Resumés, and the Like***
Drug Awareness*
Effective Teaching/Effective Schools***
Exceptional Children*
Evaluation of Learning and Its Interpretation**/*
Human Interaction in Schooling**/*
Multicultural Education***/**/*
Nature of Adolescents / Young Adults in Relation to Schooling*
Personal Wellness: Emotional, Physical*
Professionalism: Personal, Ethical, and Legal Issues*
Students, How Are They Similar/Different?: Behaviorally, Intellectually, Physically, Sexually, Socially*
How Do We Prepare for Them Instructionally?**/*
Processes of Research in Education***/*

Some of these topics are mandated by the legislature through the State Board of Teaching: multicultural education, exceptional children, drug awareness, personal wellness, and human interaction in schooling.

3. CLINICAL EXPERIENCES

The courses, seminars, and clinical experiences in Second Languages and Cultures are offered on-site, within a school district. They comprise an

Dale L. Lange

TABLE 2. CLINICAL EXPERIENCES, SECOND LANGUAGES AND CULTURES

Level	Activity	Content
1. Awareness	Observation	Classroom process
2. Practice	Tutoring Leading small-group activities Microteaching: student, peer	Student–teacher interaction Management: classroom, instructional, curricular Planning Curricular and instructional goals and student outcomes
3. Induction	Student teaching	Evaluation of learning achievement → proficiency Evaluation of instruction

academic year-long course on the examination of curricular and instructional problems with second language teaching and learning, a seminar for clinical experiences, and a seminar on special topics. Examples of the content of the latter include the student research project; current research on listening, reading, speaking, and writing in second language education; and the teaching of reading to non-English proficient students for the ESL group.

The clinical experiences program, displayed in Table 2, consists of three phases: awareness, practice, and induction. In the *awareness* phase, students observe students learning and teachers teaching, not only in language courses, but throughout the entire curriculum. Program participants are also required to closely examine the culture of the community and its relationship to the district. In the *practice* phase, teachers tutor one-on-one, lead small groups, and microteach (both peer groups and in class). In the *induction* phase, teachers are responsible for both the curriculum and the instructional program over two six-week periods. In these contexts, developing teachers learn to resolve the teaching and learning problems they face on the practical level through strategies suggested from a theoretical framework, as well as by their peers and experienced colleagues. They learn to evaluate themselves through these same processes and strategies. The clinical experiences seminar is heavily involved in reviewing the observations students make in these phases. The intensity of the three phases of clinical experiences is visualized in Figure 3.

4. THE RESEARCH COMPONENT

Since the program is at the graduate level, students are required to complete a project that examines the relationship of theory to practice, using a chosen research mode. In this regard, students complete a research project of their own choosing. In that project, they demonstrate

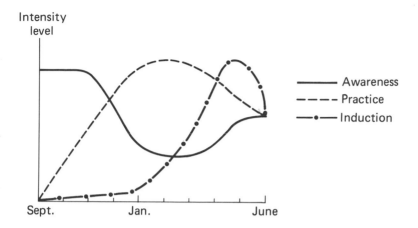

Figure 3   Relative intensity of the three levels in the total clinical experiences.

their understanding of research processes in the resolution of a teaching/ learning or curricular problem. The process includes the determination of a problem, the relation of the problem to a theoretical as well as a practical background, the design of a study, the gathering and analysis of data to demonstrate the resolution of the problem, a statement of resolution, and a formal report of the process. This component is part of the nine-month academic year program in a school setting. In this first year students are examining issues important to them, including the relationship of homework to success in language learning, the relationship of time spent in a job outside school to success in language learning, and the effect of different kinds of written feedback from the teacher to the student who is writing in English.

5. EXIT EXAMINATION

The exit examinations for the first year of the program were contextualized, simulated problems. They required students to bring theoretical, practical, and experiential knowledge together for the resolution of the problems posed. Although students were given choices among problems, they were required to deal with situations that involved instruction, curriculum, evaluation, and research. These examinations required written responses only. There was no oral examination.

The team

A team of university and school personnel runs the program. That team includes Second Languages and Cultures Education staff, two University of Minnesota teacher supervisors, one of whom coordinates the clinical experiences seminar, a school postbaccalaureate coordinator who is a teacher in the school district, and cooperating teachers in different languages in the various schools of the district.

In establishing the necessary cooperation from the school district for the creation of the partnership, the following arrangements were made. The school postbaccalaureate coordinator is released from duty on a "one hour each day" basis to make arrangements, observe students, and communicate with cooperating teachers and university personnel. Cooperating teachers are rewarded with university credit for their participation in the program, including an ongoing seminar where the university and the school district personnel work diligently on problems connected with the program and the partnership.

Research agenda

The postbaccalaureate program allows the faculty to focus on research in teacher development. For long-term study, the focus of the questions is on program and teacher development:

1. Within the predetermined characteristics of entrants to the program, what are the qualities of each admitted cohort? How do different cohorts of this program compare?
2. What is "effective teaching" in a second language?
3. What aspects of effective teaching contribute specifically to the preparation of teachers in a second language?
4. Assuming that indicators of effective teaching in second languages can be ascertained, do admission criteria have any predictability of indicating teacher effectiveness after the program has been completed?
5. What is the relationship of these same qualities to success in teaching after initial licensure?
6. By what means do we evaluate the effectiveness of a teacher development program?
7. What happens to those licensed in second languages once they have completed the program? Are they still effective teachers at one, three, five, and ten years later? Why? Why not?

Evaluating the program and the process

By what means can we evaluate such programs? It is useful to compare the postbaccalaureate program to elements of the models of Mulkeen and Tetenbaum, and Lange. Further evaluation of the curriculum as indicated by Short (1987), as well as a more complete evaluation process suggested by Cooper (1983), provide direction for the future.

One method of evaluating the process as translated into the program described here is a logical one. Have the implications from the model of Mulkeen and Tetenbaum and the principles stated by Lange been included? A check of the program description and elements suggest at least three deficiencies. Most of the other features of both models are detected in the description of the program, its elements, staff, or research agenda.

The first deficiency is related to a core feature of the Mulkeen and Tetenbaum model. The University of Minnesota program is certainly not technology-driven. Videotaping of students in classrooms is the only element of technology used. In this regard, the program must decide how it will work with technology in the future.

The second, mostly unfulfilled aspect is related to Mulkeen and Tetenbaum's concern for the inclusion of minority students. This is a problem related to the demography of the state of Minnesota. There are only Caucasians in the current program. Efforts are being made at the University of Minnesota to recruit more minority students in programs. This subject is a matter for continuing concern.

The third imperfection in the program is Lange's seventh principle, which suggests a different kind of teacher–student relationship. Though this aspect may be difficult to achieve in the climate of today's schools, it must be a strong candidate for ongoing consideration.

While this comparative approach to the evaluation of the University of Minnesota program is momentarily convenient, it is obviously not complete, largely because the program is new. Other evaluation processes need to become part of this or any other attempt at the renewal of teacher development. Although not intended as a curriculum evaluation plan per se, Short (1987) enunciates a clear set of guidelines for the development of teacher education curricula which could easily suffice as elements of a curriculum evaluation process in this context. These guidelines cluster under four categories which are interrelated: the formulation and adoption of policies for the development of a teacher education curriculum; the development and revision of a curriculum plan; the conceptualization and design of a curriculum plan; and the identification of a unifying concept or theme in the enactment of a curriculum plan. These guidelines should be considered extremely useful for the guidance and evaluation of any design and implementation for teacher education renewal.

The Cooper (1983) approach to the evaluation of teacher development programs is of course broader than that derived from Short. The proposition involves an examination of both the processes by which development occurs as well as expected outcomes, a "goal-attainment approach." Teachers who have been developed by the program are examined at the beginning of the program to ascertain the current status of their knowledge. Upon completion of the program, they are evaluated again to locate deficiencies, for which a modified plan for the student or for the program could be determined. Data to be collected for this evaluation include teacher characteristics and demography, teaching effectiveness, program characteristics and effectiveness, school and community contextual information, and pupil outcomes. While this process emphasizes the collection of hard data, the approach to evaluation is one that is flexible enough to include information of a qualitative nature.

Conclusion: will it work?

The conditions relating to the development of teachers for the future have been reviewed. The context has been set. Two sets of contributing principles to that development have been examined. A general model of teacher development has contributed to the specific development of a preservice teacher development program in foreign language education, the five basic elements of which have been displayed. All of these conditions, principles, and models are associated with the development of future foreign language teachers. Many of these principles are not new. In fact, they have been ideals of the past and have been discussed in the literature. Here, they have been operationalized. It is upon this operationalization that we can build the future.

Will it work? Will the program described here succeed? This question cannot be answered here, obviously. Teacher renewal faces many problems: lethargy, tradition, bureaucracy, and fear of change, among others. But the context that has been portrayed argues solidly for different directions. Those who are willing to take risks will provoke change. The groundwork has been installed. The mood has been established. The climate is right. Success can only be measured if the challenge is met. Take the risks!

17 Developing teachers' language resources

Robert Keith Johnson

The traditional responsibilities of language teaching specialists in teacher education, particularly in situations where language teachers are not native speakers of the target language, involve methodology and instruction in the second language to raise the level of teachers' second language proficiency. A further responsibility, the subject of this chapter, should be to help all teachers to use the language resources that they have as effectively as possible in the classroom. Access to the knowledge, attitudes, and skills embodied in the various subject area curricula is gained with the aid of written and spoken discourse or not at all. If this essential component in the educational enterprise is missing or nonfunctional, nothing happens. A course that focuses on the effective use of language in the classroom should therefore form an important part of the training of any teacher, whether of a first or second language; but it is crucial where a second language is the medium of instruction, since in this case the vital connection is most at risk.

This chapter outlines the underlying theory and the methodological approach adopted in a program entitled 'Classroom Language', which focuses upon language across the curriculum in a context where English is widely used as the medium of instruction. The various kinds of exercises and communication tasks used in the program are also described and illustrated.

The 'Classroom Language' programme

Classroom Language is a compulsory unit within a basic professional training programme for secondary school teachers in all subject areas.[1] It consists of fifteen contact hours, which are divided between language laboratory and discussion sessions. Its aim is to make students aware of the role language plays in the classroom, and although teachers are expected to apply what they learn within their subject areas, the course is not subject-specific. Similarly the course is not language-specific. The

---

1 'Classroom Language' is a component of the Postgraduate Certificate of Education programme of the Faculty of Education, Hong Kong University. I would like to acknowledge the work of Penny Cameron, Rose Chan, and Cecilia Shek, who have all made major contributions to the programme since its inception.

programme is conducted through English for teachers in English-medium schools and in Chinese/Cantonese for teachers of Chinese and Chinese History, and for teachers from Chinese-medium schools. The discourse functions and principles introduced are assumed to be universal.

The teaching and learning approach

Most students enter the programme expecting to be taught English. When it is clear that this is not our aim, there is the problem of differentiating our work from that of the subject area specialists and others concerned with methodology. Our colleagues, who do not have the advantage of doing the course, find our intentions even more obscure. They tend to believe that, whatever we may say, what we really do is remedial language teaching; and if we don't, then we should. The concept of language across the curriculum, in second language teacher education or elsewhere, still has a long way to go. We have to admit too that our own understanding of our role has not always been as certain as it is now. This gradual increase in confidence in what we are doing has been reflected in a general movement away from the exploratory, almost discovery-based approach with which we began, towards one which uses models and examples and offers conclusions as well as experiences and learning opportunities.

'Foundations' courses in the philosophy, sociology, and psychology of education as well as specialists in methodology, general or subject-related, are concerned in various ways with the role of the teacher, as a person, as a member of society, within the school, and in the classroom. The ideas presented in these courses interact with and are accommodated to each teacher's personality, experience, and preconceptions, and result in a teaching style or a plan of action which the teacher seeks to implement in the classroom. As language specialists we do not attempt to influence the teachers' intentions, or aims; rather we help them to evaluate the relationship between intentions and their realisation in discourse. If a teacher's aim is to terrify his or her pupils into silence, we might, as fellow educators, urge reasons for reconsideration, but in doing so we would be moving beyond our primary role. The problem is usually in the other direction. Teachers claim that their intention is to promote an open, responsive, learner-centred, 'democratic' classroom learning environment, but the language they use explicitly or implicitly reinforces their authority and discourages learners from taking the initiative. The analysis of what is (and what is not) said in the classroom makes concrete and specific an area which is usually discussed only in general and abstract terms – that is, at the level of intention rather than realisation.

In relation to content, we are less likely to be tempted to go beyond our role. We are not experts in the various subject areas, and we must rely on the teachers (our students) and the subject area specialists for their advice on what should be taught and how. Our aim is to make teachers aware that having the appropriate knowledge and intentions is one thing; communicating them effectively through language is another.

The language of the learner is not dealt with formally in our programme. 'Pupil talk' is presented in the modelled interactive exchanges, and teachers role-play the parts of students in simulation exercises, but our focus is normally on the language used by the teacher, which in the context of our course can be modified, and not that of the pupil, which cannot.

We also spend more time on spoken than on written language. Teachers spend far more time speaking than they do writing; and as academically oriented people, teachers' skills in relation to written texts are often more highly developed than those relating to speech. Nevertheless we are paying more attention now than in the past to the language of textbooks or course books in particular, and to the ways in which information is realised in written discourse in general. We feel that the more aware teachers are of written discourse structure, the better they will be at helping their pupils to process and produce it themselves.

The use of the language laboratory

Of the fifteen contact hours in the course, six are spent in the language laboratory, with students engaged in various tasks. The remaining hours are spent in discussion of issues raised by these tasks and the applications of conclusions to particular subject areas.

The language laboratory exercises are necessarily artificial and contrived, but they have the advantage that thirty teachers can be engaged simultaneously and intensively in what we hope are interesting and challenging activities; and the language laboratory booths, though a totally different environment from that of the classroom, serve to focus attention very narrowly upon linguistic aspects of teaching.

The laboratory, a standard National model, has been modified so that booths can be paired. This permits quite a wide range of communicative and analytical tasks which would otherwise be impossible, and the teaching materials are organised to take maximum advantage of this facility. Students receive copies of one of two versions of the course booklet, A or B, so that an information gap can be created and exploited where appropriate. The types of organisation of tasks in the language laboratory are summarised here:

1. *Individualised work.* With each booth under the control of the individual concerned, students can record, rerecord, replay, and re-

peat as they feel appropriate: for example, in preparing a set of instructions, or following and evaluating the instructions prepared by their partners. (Most tape preparation is done outside scheduled contact hours.)

2. *Classwork.* Some of the tasks are conducted in a lockstep fashion, with the lecturer controlling all booths from the console and using a master tape as stimulus material. (In this mode of operation, students are usually paired so that they can discuss what they hear and conduct a joint evaluation.)

3. *Pair work.* Pair work includes role play and simulation exercises, problem solving, communication gap activities, and periods for discussion and evaluation which may be as short as a few seconds or as long as several minutes.

The existence of the language laboratory preceded that of the course, and the (political) need to make use of it was initially more obvious than any educational advantages. We have come to feel, however, that without it the course would be less focused and less 'data-driven' than it is at present.

The design of the teaching materials

In broad terms each exercise or task follows the stages of development, practice, and application outlined here:

1. *Development.* Particular teaching acts are identified and communication tasks are prepared which depend crucially for their success upon the effective performance of those teaching acts.

2. *Practice.* Teachers complete the communication tasks and evaluate their performances.

3. *Application.* Teachers identify general principles governing the effective completion of such tasks and discuss ways of applying those principles to their own teaching subjects.

The content of the teaching materials

When the course began, we intended to develop separate sets of materials for the various subject areas. We still recognise the importance of demonstrating to teachers the relevance of the programme to their needs, but for many purposes the use of subject-specific material simply does not work. In setting tasks in which communication is likely to break down, we are attempting to simulate the situation which exists between the teacher, who knows, and the learner, who does not. On tasks where two 'knowers' are working together, communication does not break down, and the message that emerges for the teachers is that there is no problem. As a result, we attempt to stay well clear of expert knowledge our teachers may share, so that the success of the communication tasks depends upon the effective use of language, and not on 'triggering' knowledge which the hearer or reader already possesses. The danger is that some teachers see the activities as 'mere' games, irrelevant to their professional interests and lacking serious content or purpose. This makes the third design stage (Application) essential, not only for the transfer of learning, but for the credibility of the course as a whole.

The aspects of classroom language

We discuss classroom language under three major headings: one, the *physiological* aspect, is obligatory, obviously enough, for any spoken utterance, but each utterance may express either the *interpersonal* or *pedagogical* intentions of the teacher, or both.

The physiological aspect

Despite advances in technology and current trends in educational theory, the teacher's voice is likely to remain a major educational resource. It is minimally necessary for teachers to speak loudly and clearly enough to be understood by large numbers of pupils in often noisy environments and to produce their voices in a way which avoids physical and psychological stress. Optimally, the teacher's voice should be as rich and as varied an instrument as an actor's.

The physiological aspect of teacher talk used to receive more attention than it now does, for several possible reasons. 'Elocution' has become unfashionable, an anachronism in a world in which non-standard accents and different varieties of English have gained considerable acceptance. Linguistic interest has shifted away from articulation and towards cognition; and in teacher education, there has been a shift in emphasis from teacher-centred to learner-centred approaches, with the teacher as a manager of resources and facilitator of learning. Focusing upon the teacher's voice may seem almost reprehensible from these perspectives.

The decline in interest in voice production is regrettable, however laudable the changes which have brought it about. There is evidence from Hong Kong and elsewhere that many teachers suffer from vocal strain, that this affects their teaching and their general health, and that they would welcome assistance (Cameron 1983). This is one of the areas in which applied linguists with the appropriate expertise have a great deal to offer to teachers across the curriculum.

The interpersonal aspect

The interpersonal aspect of classroom discourse is divided into three modes: control, organisation, and motivation. In crude terms, control and organisation functions are realised in such utterances as 'Stand up!', 'Sit down', 'Why are you late?', and 'Move into your discussion groups'. Motivational functions are realised by such utterances as 'Well done' and 'That was a good try'. The areas are not clearly differentiated: 'Get your homework in on time or there will be trouble' could be regarded as motivating, organising, or exercising control over a pupil. However, 'managing' the classroom and creating a classroom climate in which students are willing and eager to learn are clearly important aspects of a teacher's work. What seems particularly interesting and revealing is the inverse relationship which exists in the data between the overt manifestation of these functions in the teachers' language and the reality of the situation − that is, repeated attempts to motivate indicate that motivation is poor; continuous attempts to control indicate poor discipline; and the amount of time the teacher spends on management is a fair indication of how effective the teacher is as a manager. (For example, when 'O.K., move into groups' is sufficient, we know we are dealing with a well-organised classroom. When we hear 'O.K., move into groups. No, don't move your desk. No, Johnny, there's no need to move your desk. No more than four in a group. Your group is too big. *Don't move your desks . . .* ', we know there will be very little effective time-on-task in that classroom.)

One of the greatest difficulties faced by a new teacher, or an unsuccessful one, is the lack of overt linguistic realisations in 'good' classrooms which the teacher could use as a model. The effective teacher says, 'Move into your groups' and it happens. The new teacher does exactly the same thing and chaos breaks out. In motivational terms too, precisely what teachers say and how they say it are not necessarily important. Some ogres (judged on verbal behavior) are not just respected but loved by their students. Actions in this context speak louder than words. Nevertheless, talking is one way of showing, and the teacher whose pupils moved into groups without problems did so because at some point clear instructions were given by the teacher and were understood and accepted by the pupils. Similarly, the belief amongst pupils that their efforts are appreciated may not depend solely on the words of the teacher, but that belief is certainly reinforced by those words. Discussion of classroom language data, aided by transcriptions, helps to develop teachers' awareness and understanding of these issues, even though what is important may be revealed more by what is not said than by what is.

The pedagogical aspect

Unlike the interpersonal aspect, in the pedagogical aspect of classroom language, what you say is what you do. If a question is poorly expressed, the most highly motivated students will not be able to answer it. Likewise, the fact that the teacher is known to have the best interests of the students at heart may make a poorly expressed instruction easier to tolerate, but it does not make it easier to understand and follow.

Each of the three pedagogical modes, operative, interactive, and informative, is discussed in turn with examples of the types of tasks and exercises used.

THE OPERATIVE MODE

The operative mode has three phases: framing, mediating, and evaluating, with the boundaries between the phases marked by the teacher's 'directive' and by the students' 'performance'. In the model we use, the intention(s) of each utterance can be analysed functionally using a modified version of the Sinclair and Coulthard (1975) and Sinclair and Brazil (1982) frameworks for analysing classroom discourse.

The exercises here follow the general pattern described earlier fairly closely: A problem is set; students attempt to solve the problem; they evaluate the outcome and derive general principles which they then apply to their subject area.

In one task, the students in each pair prerecord a set of instructions for organising cards to form a given pattern. In the laboratory, group A and group B teachers exchange tapes. Each teacher has a set of cards to work with when following their partners' instructions. The task is a difficult one, and very few complete it successfully. Teachers then continue, in pairs, seeking clarification from their partners in order either to complete the pattern-making task or to check that the task has been completed satisfactorily. Again, and more surprisingly perhaps, very few teachers succeed, establishing the point that giving complex instructions is difficult, even in situations where interaction and feedback are possible.

We then provide a taped model. In this case most teachers are able to complete the task satisfactorily after listening to the tape only once. The five cards the teachers have and the pattern they are supposed to construct are given in Figure 1.

The points which usually come out of the discussion are the following:

1. A very high proportion of the text in complex instructions is 'framing' as opposed to 'directive'.

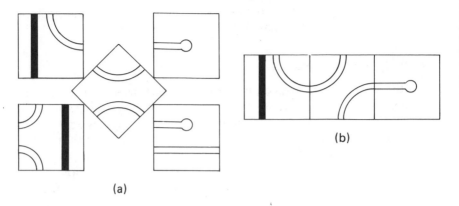

Figure 1   *Pattern-making Task (a) Original cards (b) Solution*

2. Instructions need to be broken down into stages.
3. The order of the steps within each stage can be crucial.

The task is of course an unrealistic one in that a diagram or pattern should be presented visually, not orally, but its purpose is achieved in that teachers see the necessity to reevaluate their strategies.

The teachers are asked as their final task to prepare a set of instructions for a complex task within their subject area. They are also asked to monitor their performance in class in using the operative mode through tapes of recorded lessons. As every teacher and classroom observer is uncomfortably aware, instructions are rarely given at the beginning of a task in a way which enables students to complete it without further interruption. Too often, there is a succession of interjections from the teacher along the lines of 'Class, just pay attention for a moment, . . . ', 'Listen for a moment please . . . ', or 'Er, there seems to be a problem with . . . ', as one deviation from the teacher's intention after another is discovered as the teacher moves round the class. The teachers are urged to regard all such 'repair strategies' as evidence of failure in the original formulation of the instructions, to go back to the wording of those instructions (hence the need for a recording), and to see how they could have been improved by anticipating and eliminating the difficulties which resulted. Here obviously it is not just the wording of the directive or the framing that precedes it which is important. It may be necessary to incorporate into the discourse the informative mode – to give examples, models, illustrations – and the interactive mode – to determine whether or not the information has been understood. These informative and interactive exchanges may be seen as 'embedded' within the framing phase of the operative mode, which provides the overriding pedagogical objective at this stage in the lesson.

THE INTERACTIVE MODE

Like the operative mode, the interactive mode has three phases (framing, mediating, and evaluating), with boundaries marked in this case by an elicitation by the teacher (which may not be a question) and a reply by a student.

Units and exercises on the interactive mode also follow the pattern outlined earlier. Teachers listen to taped exchanges and role-play or engage in simulation tasks in order to identify problem areas and discuss means for achieving solutions. The emphasis is upon the language used, and teachers are discouraged from making statements like 'The question needs to be reworded'. Instead they are asked to propose a rewording which would achieve a more satisfactory outcome. The following exercises are presented and discussed briefly as illustrations.

Classroom exchanges for evaluation. The exchanges are almost all taken from tapes recorded as part of a previous research project on classroom language (Johnson 1983). However, to protect the teachers concerned about their voices being recognised, and to improve the quality of the sound, the exchanges were rerecorded. Where the point being made is more a question of timing or attitude than content, and fairly simple, teachers are not given a transcription to follow: for example, where the teacher prompts a hesitant student four or five times, finally answering the question without leaving the student time to reply, or where an inadequate question is simply repeated three or four times until an equally inadequate response is obtained.

For more complex exchanges, teachers are given a transcript:

(1) Teacher: What food does an amoeba eat, John?
(2) Pupil 1: Algae.
(3) Teacher: Does it eat solid food or liquid food, Mary?
(4) Pupil 2: Er, solid.
(5) Teacher: Solid food particles. Some examples, please. Tom?
(6) Pupil 3: Algae, sir.
(7) Teacher: Algae. Any more examples?

Comments included the dismissive treatment of John, who had given a correct answer (as we later discover) but not the answer the teacher had in mind at the time; and secondly, the switch to a binary choice question (3) in order to get the required answer. Proposed solutions included the following as an improvement for (5).

Teacher: Solid food particles. Yes. And we have had one example already from John. That was algae. Any more examples?

The movement from nonbinary to binary questions (3) raises the important issue of the prevalence and functions of binary questions in classroom discourse.

One problem associated with the taped extracts and transcripts is the apparent ineptitude of some teachers. It is very easy to sit back and criticise, without the pressures of class control, lesson content, and above all the need to do something *immediately* which the classroom teacher is always under. It helps that the evaluators do not just criticise, but have to propose more effective responses. However, the greatest aid to achieving a constructive and suitably humble approach to the data is the requirement that teachers record, transcribe, and evaluate sections of their own lessons.

Role-play exercises. In one role-play exercise, the 'teachers' attempt to extract answers from reluctant 'pupils'. Feelings of superiority, following evaluation of the classroom extracts, do not survive the replaying of these recorded exchanges; or those of an equally revealing exercise which involves the partners in 'Socratic' questioning exchanges. Teachers prepare positions or conclusions which they intend their partners to reach. They then seek to bring their partners to those conclusions by means of questioning. Again the exchanges are recorded, replayed, and evaluated.

Handling students' replies. One of the most difficult tasks for any teacher is handling students' replies. Supplying continuity between a correct response and the next phase of a lesson is comparatively easy; moving a student from a wrong or partly wrong answer towards a better one requires very considerable mental agility, and it is often at this point in an interactive exchange that teachers appear least adept.

As an exercise to bring out the problems and to help teachers to develop strategies for dealing with this situation, we provide sets of partly matching questions and answers: for example, the question might relate to the causes of traffic problems, while the answer offers a possible solution. Each question and reply is therefore prescribed, but from then on the teacher has to take over and 'handle' the reply. The exchanges are recorded and evaluated, and proposals for improvements or alternative strategies are considered.

THE INFORMATIVE MODE

The third mode of the pedagogical aspect that we deal with is the informative mode. In this case an approximately equal amount of time is given to oral and written text. The three-phase model can also be applied here (framing, informing, consolidating), but it has proved less satisfactory, primarily because there is no objective basis for marking the divisions between the phases, particularly that between framing and informing, which would require the analyst to distinguish between what is 'given' and what is 'new' information, which might in any case differ from pupil to pupil. There is also a difference of scale. A lesson has pedagogical goals which are normally stated in terms of knowledge and skills to be acquired. Interactive and operative modes will be embedded within the structure of the lesson, and may dominate it in terms of time spent, but the overall lesson framework has a macrostructure of stages, topics, themes and subthemes, just as a course book in geography or physics has chapters and sections, headings and subheadings. The pedagogical approach and the teaching style adopted influence the proportion of lesson time spent in interaction and on tasks as opposed to reading or listening for information, but the overall aim of all teaching and learning is in some broad sense to inform.

In dealing with the informative mode, we focus on content rather than intention and show teachers that any learning unit within the curriculum exists within a 'macro' information structure which can be mapped out hierarchically in headings and subheadings, categories, subcategories, and so on. The term *microstructure* is used to refer to the information within a particular unit of connected discourse.

In dealing with this very complex area, teachers are asked to distinguish between 'information structure' (the 'facts' their discipline deals with and the inherent structure of those facts) and discourse structure, which is that knowledge translated from abstract and nonlinear forms to concrete and linear realisation in linguistic strings. Our aim is to explore this relationship between information structure and discourse structure in order to determine what makes a discourse, particularly one in the informative mode, more or less effective. The conclusion that we promote is a somewhat simplistic one, but it is one which we feel is well adapted to the needs of a second language situation. We feel that the more clearly the discourse reflects and signals the underlying information structure, the more effective the discourse is likely to be; that is, we are arguing for a very high level of predictability in pedagogical discourse. Less simplistically we argue that the 'expert' in a given area brings to a discourse a highly developed presuppositional base which 'new' information is checked against. The expert also has a set of discourse schemata or expectations about the manner in which that information will be presented. The structure of the discourse is therefore of less importance for the expert than for the neophyte. Further, a major goal for students of any subject is that they should internalise those schemata which are so important for effective communication, and we argue that the student is helped to achieve this goal more rapidly and effectively if the schemata which are to be internalised are realised explicitly in the discourse which students experience.

The following illustrate the kinds of exercises on the informative mode.

1. (a) The teachers hear two discourses which contain the same content. They take notes and decide which discourse is more effective.
   (b) With the transcriptions in front of them, the teachers discuss and agree on reasons why one discourse is more effective than the other. They usually point to the higher level of organisation and more effective use of discourse markers in one of the texts.
   (c) A tree diagram is used to show the structure of the information in the discourses (in this case, situation, problem, solution), and a comparison is made between the two transcriptions and the information structure. This shows that the more effective discourse 'reveals' the information structure, where the other tends to obscure it.
2. Recent models of the information structures underlying academic discourse are introduced. We use models based on Davies and Greene (1984) and Lunzer and Gardner (1984), both sets of models being derived from a Schools Council project in Great Britain. The teachers then 'map' various written discourses from textbooks in their subject areas onto these models and use their knowledge and expertise to decide
   (a) what improvements should be made in the information structure or content of the discourse, and
   (b) what improvements should be made in the discourse so that it makes the information more accessible to the reader and inducts the reader more effectively into this particular style of discourse – that is, assists the reader to internalise the schemata appropriate to reading and writing this type of text.
3. Text reconstruction.
   (a) Teachers identify a passage in a textbook within their subject area, 200–300 words in length, which they feel is inadequate in both content and presentation.
   (b) They complete a content analysis of the passage by presenting the information in a tree diagram or a table.
   (c) They modify the information structure.
   (d) They rewrite the passage, which must be of the same length and level as the original.

Conclusion

A recent evaluation exercise showed that we still have a long way to go in the practical details of running the programme, and improvements are needed as well as the more theoretical level. Nevertheless, my main worry, that teachers would perceive the programme as irrelevant or at best peripheral to their needs, seems unfounded. Recording their own lessons proved popular and useful, and it was suggested that there should be a before and after tape and transcription to see what differences emerged. We had felt that the task of transcribing and analysing even quite short sections of lessons would be unpopular because it is time consuming, and because discourse analysis is not something teachers of science or history could be expected to find immediately appealing. The value of discourse analysis per se remains an open question, but teachers found that transcription and analysis were helpful and resulted in new insights into their performance in the classroom. We are at present revising our programme, but do not expect that this will be the final version. With all the work that is currently being carried out in classroom research and on discourse by linguists and psycholinguists, we expect to continue to revise and develop the programme in the years ahead. Our goal for next year is to spend as much time as possible recording and observing in classrooms in order to test the validity of the models we have developed so far and to extend the range of authentic examples that we can use for illustration and evaluation.

In conclusion, we feel that there is a long way to go, but the direction is right. We are convinced that a programme of this kind should be a component in any foreign or second language teacher preparation programme, but feel that it may be of particular relevance to second language teacher education, where English has a role to play across the curriculum.

18 An ethnographic approach to inservice preparation: the Hungary file

Fraida Dubin and Rita Wong

In this chapter, we present a view about inservice programs for nonnative teachers that we have come to foster through our involvement with teacher preparation activities in a variety of locales where English is taught as a foreign and second language. Realizing that the role of the outside specialist is tenuous, at best, we suggest that teacher educators must strive to understand the context of teaching through their particinants' perspective, a goal that is more significant, we believe, than bringing the latest word about theory or practice to teachers in the trenches. We call this view "an ethnographic approach," borrowing from social science research models which stress qualitative rather than quantitative data collection. The first part of the chapter focuses on inservice training in general; the second part is a case study of a program for Hungarian teachers in which we participated as teacher educators over five summers in the 1980s. The two parts are interconnected: Part 2 illustrates the motivation for adopting the general approach that is presented in Part 1.

Part 1. Background to inservice training

There are several ways in which inservice training (IST) and preservice training (PST) contrast. From the start, it is vital to emphasize that the two domains are not mirror images of each other. There is far more to their dissimilarity than whether the participants have blank or full slates, so to speak. Certainly, IST is not well characterized by simply turning PST inside out.

IST usually takes place for a specific purpose, even if that purpose is not evident on the surface; therefore, gathering information at the outset in order to produce a meaningful needs analysis is crucial. In addition, IST programs usually have focused requirements that are different from PST. For example, a practicum component may be called for in IST for quite different reasons than it would be in PST. Experienced teachers in IST may benefit from actually trying out new methods in a simulated situation before taking them back to their classrooms. But their need for practice is directed toward other matters than it would be for inexperienced teachers.

282

At first, it may seem appealing to apply the distinction to IST and PST that has been made between training and education (Campbell 1967; Larsen-Freeman 1983), handing over to PST the distinction of "educating" future teachers, while designating IST to take up more "situation-oriented-concerns" (Larsen-Freeman 1983). In this view, PST education provides the breadth and scope of the various disciplines, which become teachers' background knowledge. IST, on the other hand, pinpoints specific areas by offering a repertoire of techniques to use in a known situation. In Larsen-Freeman's view, PST should give teachers sufficient knowledge to be able to make their own choices and training to develop skills.

Although in a general sense this distinction is valid, in the real world it falls short of illuminating some of the more fundamental differences between PST and IST. More significant for second language (L2) IST is the issue of the teacher educator's practical knowledge of the teachers' teaching situation. Does the program staff have firsthand experience with the educational system and institutions of the teachers? How conversant are the teacher educators with the teachers' first language and culture? How much time do the teacher educators have to acquaint themselves with various aspects of the student teachers' culture? What access do they have to these kinds of information?

A model for IST that has been proposed for another educational field (L1 reading) assumes that information about staff or student teachers' needs is easily accessible, and in fact already in the teacher educators' possession. The model contains the following steps (Siedow, Memory, and Bristow 1985); (1) assess staff needs; (2) determine inservice objectives; (3) plan content; (4) choose methods of presentation; (5) evaluate IST effectiveness; (6) provide follow-up assistance and reinforcement.

However, carrying out the first step, the needs analysis, may not be immediately possible in many English language IST programs. Teacher educators may not be familiar with the student teachers' teaching situation. In fact, the student teachers may not be fluent speakers of the English language. Moreover, the teacher educators may have very little information about the resources of the training site.

Teacher educators working within a particular school district, who are members of the same community from which the teachers are drawn, come closest to the model suggested by Siedow et al. (1985), since they are probably well acquainted with the issues that have motivated a teacher preparation program. Even programs provided by national and international agencies, such as Peace Corps and VISTA, can be built around quite specific requirements, since there is likely to be ongoing feedback from teachers in the field to teacher educators. Another type of IST, often overlooked, is the professional convention, which provides training for practicing teachers (Gardiner 1987). The higher-education units or credits that attendees can obtain are based on a wide choice of conference offerings, although frequently without any specific check on what understandings or insights resulted from attendance.

All of the kinds of teacher education discussed so far presuppose that the providers of IST understand the teachers' classroom and institutional situations. Or, on a scale of low to high, they represent a fairly high degree of acquaintanceship with the teachers' work world. Within second language IST over the past few decades, there has been a good deal of activity at the low-understanding end of the scale. An example of low understanding sometimes occurs when academic specialists provide programs for teachers in parts of the world where English is a foreign language. The possibility that the specialists might have intimate knowledge and understanding of the teachers' situation always exists, but the opposite is also the case.

Although the U.S. government and American educational institutions have been prominent in the worldwide activity of providing IST for second language teachers in the recent period, organizations such as the British Council paved the way before them. Britten (1985b) outlined IST programs from the viewpoint of British efforts. He mentioned that the "commonest need [in such programs] is for language improvement [for the trainees]" (p. 234).

Early (1983), in a personal narrative, recounted his experiences with the British Council in Yugoslavia. He provided a wealth of background information about the country and its educational institutions. It is not clear, however, whether he possessed such knowledge before he undertook setting up programs for the British Council. Britten also describes IST as typically short-term, employing outside experts in the field. Indeed, teacher educators emerge like village elders. Early sums up his experience with the British Council in Yugoslavia by noting, too, "that the process is . . . a subtler one than the mere importation of ready-made educational solutions. It involves dialogue, interaction between outside 'experts' and native practitioners" (p. 151).

An American academic specialist/"village elder" is likely to fall into doing IST programs abroad by receiving an unexpected telephone call: "Are you able to go to . . . in . . . for . . . weeks/months?" Being adventurous by nature, with a penchant for exotic travel, the American responds positively. In some cases details of the assignment may have been well defined. More typically, the responsibility of delineating the goals and objectives of the program falls into the hands of the selected teacher educators. At this point in the design of the program, the specialists need to start the information-gathering process by asking questions that will help in their preparation.

Preparatory questions

1. *Define target audience.* Will the teachers be novices or experienced? What levels do they teach – elementary through tertiary? Will the group be composed exclusively of teachers or will it include supervisors and inspectors, too?

2. *Secure information regarding sponsors.* Who suggested holding the program? What are the sponsors' goals for the program? How will the sponsors evaluate the program? Will the sponsors' representative be present at the program? What role do the sponsors have in the organization of the program? How have past programs, if any, been evaluated?

3. *Secure archival information.* Are there reports from previous programs? Where are they filed? Can the writers be contacted?

4. *Define time factors.* What are the starting and ending dates? Do the dates include travel time to and from the program site? When does the program occur in relation to the teachers' school year? Are the teachers using their vacation or holiday time to attend the program? In a residence program, how will the teachers spend their free time (evenings and weekends)? Will they travel home? How much of each day will be devoted to organized classes, recreational activities, individual study and reading, or free time?

5. *Survey program site and its resources.* Where will the teachers live? Where will the staff live? Where will meals be provided? Will the staff have some or all of their meals with the teachers? Where are the classrooms in relation to where the teachers and teacher educators live? What are the physical characteristics of the classrooms? What audiovisual equipment is available? What support services (typing, copying, etc.) are available? What are the characteristics of the environment: Are there historical, cultural, or recreational attractions?

6. *Determine composition of the teaching staff.* What are the institutional affiliations and areas of expertise represented? How will responsibilities be shared among the group? Will one person serve as a coordinator? Are there opportunities for the teaching team to meet together before the program begins?

7. *Survey language competence and expectations of participants.* What exposure have the teachers had to native varieties of English? Have they attended previous IST programs, American or British? Have they attended IST programs abroad? Do they expect a lecture format exclusively? Do they expect hands-on experiences? Will they be comfortable in participatory activities?

8. *Define broad goals and specific objectives.* Will the program concentrate on techniques or on background enrichment? What will be the

mix of professional topics, language, and pedagogy, as well as other components? How important is the goal of improving the teachers' own language competence?

9. *Design a syllabus schedule.* How will the syllabus incorporate the overall goals? How will the teacher educators assume responsibilities for various components of the syllabus? Will all of the trainers take part in all of the activities? How much of the day will be devoted to planned activities?

10. *Specify, locate, and secure materials.* Will the program provide textbooks, audio- and videotapes, and other materials? What is the budget for these materials? Who is responsible for ordering materials and getting them to the program site? Are there locally produced materials that should be utilized?

11. *Prepare program materials.* What materials can be prepared before the program starts (course handouts, questionnaires, evaluation instruments, visual aids, background materials for films, and so on)?

Ongoing questions

Information-gathering must go on throughout the program. It is not sufficient simply to prepare a syllabus on the basis of the prepatory questions, even though they serve to get the program underway. The answers to ongoing questions help teacher educators understand the participants' teaching situations from the outlook of the local culture. They also add to the data base for future staff. Getting beneath the surface of the host culture may present barriers that go beyond English language teaching. They may impinge upon political constraints, religious beliefs, or other culture-based elements. Asking direct questions may not be the most effective way. In fact, the teacher educators need to exercise tact and diplomacy; the need for cross-cultural sensitivity is vital.

In many ways, endeavoring to understand as much as possible about the teachers' own views of their needs and expectations brings teacher educators into touch with an ethnographic approach to IST. In ethnography, the investigator seeks to understand members of a culture from an insider's viewpoint. The goal is far more difficult to achieve than it appears on the surface. But at least having the goal as an ideal can help staff avoid making serious misjudgments in the planning and executing of an IST program. Many of the customary techniques ethnographers use in the field may be cumbersome to carry out in IST (interviews, questionnaires, surveys, participant observations, etc.). Nevertheless, all attempts to understand the belief systems that motivate behavior in the host culture serve the overall goal.

The following list of questions suggests the kind of information educators-as-ethnographers seek about the participants' work world and about themselves as a teacher-education team. We have formulated it with the benefit of hindsight. Our realization that these kinds of questions need to be asked evolved as a result of gaining more and more experience with the circumstances of a particular country's educational system.

1. *The curriculum for English language instruction.* Does the government have a mandated curriculum? To what extent is it followed? Has it been recently updated or revised?

2. *The role of countrywide examinations.* Is there a logical connection between the curricula and the examinations? Are there countrywide English language examinations? Under whose auspices are they administered? What is the approach to language pedagogy underlying the examination? Do these examinations serve as screening instruments for university applicants?

3. *Textbooks in use.* What are the textbooks in use? Are they produced locally or imported from abroad? How are they selected? Are the teachers satisfied with them? Do the textbooks have a range of ancillary materials: workbooks, tapes, teacher's manuals, visual aids? Are there unofficial books in use? How do teachers procure them? What other materials, both visual and audio, do teachers have access to?

4. *Teachers' preservice preparation.* What kind of preservice preparation did the teachers undertake: university or teacher education college? Are there status differences between graduates of these institutions? What were their fields of concentration: literature, language, pedagogy, others? Who becomes an English language teacher in the particular country?

5. *Teaching assignments and conditions.* What is a typical teaching load: the average number of pupils per class, the number of hours teachers teach? What other subjects do teachers teach? Do they have supervisors who support their efforts? Do they have more than one job? Do they tend to be the sole supporters of families? What is the general status of teachers?

6. *Teachers' personal sensitivities.* How comfortable are they in using English with their peers? Are they reticent in expressing opinions in front of peers? Are they willing to display their teaching abilities before their peers?

7. *Teachers' benefits and liabilities from attending the IST program.* Are all the participants' tuition and expenses at the program provided by the sponsoring agency? Have they been allowed time off from their regular positions to attend? How have they arranged for substitutes both at school and at home? Why have they come: to learn, to rest, to socialize, to have a vacation, to speak English?

8. *Teacher educators' views.* Can the staff work well together as a team? As individuals, do they want to expend the time and energy

287

required for ongoing planning and exchanging of information during the program? Are they curious and interested to learn about the host country and its language, culture, political/economic life? Do they tend to view the activity of teacher education as that of bringing "wisdom" to local teachers or as participating in others' growth and development?

Part 2. The American IST course in Hungary

Our own affirmative responses to telephoned invitations from Washington, D.C., to go to Hungary as teacher educators – we were there both separately and at the same time – were certainly motivated by the typical language teaching specialist's enthusiasm for travel. We also sensed the opportunity to gain new professional experience. In our earliest encounters with the Hungary program, it scarcely occurred to us to ask many of the questions outlined in Part 1. The fact that there was a program in existence seemed to imply that issues of needs analysis/ course planning had been settled. Actually, it was from venturing into a program that we as teacher educators knew little about that we came to recognize the importance of an ethnographic approach. In this section we sketch out some of the details of the IST course in Hungary, in effect answering many of the questions posed in Part 1.

The American Course (the name apparently was supplied by the host country) began in the early 1980s, a time when the Hungarian government was reaching out to the United States. One result was an agreement to jointly sponsor a course for Hungarian teachers of English. The agreement called for the Hungarian government to select the participants; provide in-country facilities, including housing and a living stipend for the American specialists; and to provide a recreation program. The American government, through the U.S. Information Agency, selected the team of academic specialists who became the teacher educators and provided for their travel and compensation.

The program was generally modeled on one the British Council had provided for many years. It took place during the teachers' summer holiday period, usually quite soon after they had finished the school year. The site was a provincial town that had accommodations for a live-in, three-week program at a school, college, or cultural center. The teachers came from locations throughout the country.

From its inception, the program has had a syllabus that combines language pedagogy and American literature. Although never explicitly articulated, at least three goals have coexisted. One has been the academic specialists' presumed goal of enhancing the participants' professional skills. The second has been the U.S. government's goal of promoting American culture, since the agency after all is in the "public information" business. A third goal has been the participants' own need to develop their individual English language proficiency. Since the program has received minimal guidance from its American and Hungarian sponsors, it has rested with each team to work out a reasonable balance among the three goals. During the early years, a new team was chosen each time. More recently, at least one person has been invited to go back the following year to effect continuity.

From the perspective of the TEFL (teaching English as a foreign language) academic specialists, the program goal has been to present current findings in language acquisition and pedagogy. For example, there have been significant developments in communicative language teaching to which Hungarian teachers have had little exposure. As each year's team has come to grips with the program syllabus, there has been a tendency, of course, for each teacher educator to select material she or he is currently most interested in or familiar with.

The promotion of American culture, the U.S. government's goal, has been realized in various ways: through lectures on the latest developments in American literature (e.g., a survey of black women writers); discussions of contemporary poetry and short stories; showings of classic and current American films; a library of current magazines and newspapers for free-time reading. Since many of the participants' preservice education at the university was primarily through literature courses, this component has been well received. Each year, at least one academic specialist has had an English department affiliation at an American university.

As for the participants, they have been more apt to see the program as an opportunity to improve their English language skills. Many of them live and teach in provincial towns, and have little or no contact with English speakers. They look to IST programs, both American and British, as a chance for intensive self-improvement. Indeed, those with well-developed social skills endeavor in every way to interact with the teacher educators, both in and outside of class.

Through the life of the program, however, there has been a tendency for some academic specialists, from both literature and TEFL, to be unobservant of any of these goals. They have come prepared only to repeat the lectures they delivered on their own campuses in the United States, assuming that the content would be suitable for a Hungarian audience. Also, different teams have tended to work out the conflict of goals in various ways, from avoidance (never discussing overall program goals) to implicit acceptance that each trainer would have a block of time to present his or her specialty, with little or no attempt made to integrate program content. As a result, in some programs there has been an undercurrent not unlike a popularity contest among the staff, each with a small group of teachers as strong loyalists.

The fact that different teams of teacher educators are selected each year, at times with members not knowing each other before coming, has made planning difficult. Some continuity has resulted from bringing back a member of the previous year's team to serve as "coordinator." Even so, the role of the coordinator has not been specified in much detail; thus a great deal is left up to the particular teacher educators for each year's program. The degree to which the educators are able to work together as a team is a matter of chance. The selection of staff takes place through the U.S. Information Agency in Washington, D.C. Academic specialists have had a minimum of input to the process.

In the first few years of the program there was little attempt at coordination or preprogram planning. Initial communication among the staff occurred when they first met each other in a Budapest hotel lobby. There was an assumption that someone else had planned the program and that the staff would be given a copy of the schedule. They were surprised to find that there was none.

Although the TEFL specialists, at least, have all come with considerable experience living and working in other cultures, very few of them over the years of the program have had firsthand knowledge of Hungary. As outsiders, teacher educators have had a tendency to assume unconsciously that the Hungarian teacher participants would all be cut from the same economic slice of life. Through participant observation, however, the often deep differences among them have become apparent. One teacher educator has recounted the variety of opinions that were expressed when she used a *New York Times* clipping about a famous shopping street in Budapest as the basis for class activities. Some deplored the article, saying that the area was strictly for tourists; they could never afford to shop there. Others found the article engrossing; they were eager to read what an American correspondent had written about their city, and they didn't disparage the subject matter in any way.

Along with the social class differences among them, the teachers have come from a wide spectrum of teaching situations. Although the Ministry of Education has primarily selected teachers from the secondary level ("gymnasium" teachers, who also teach Russian, a required subject in the country), there have also been teachers from other organizations, such as technical, elementary, and various institutions; the Hungarian airlines; a ballet school.

Participants' language proficiency has been relatively high given their limited exposure, particularly to spoken American English. Their interest level and enthusiasm has been noted to be particularly keen; they attend the course because they want to be there (the selection process seems to be clouded in bureaucratic mystery for them, as well); many make personal sacrifices and complex arrangements to be away from home.

With a group of forty to fifty teacher participants (typically females have outnumbered males two to one), a training team of three or four academic specialists, and a site away from the trainees' own cities and towns, the three-week program has had certain characteristics in common with a summer camp experience for adults. The teachers themselves have been interested to explore the local sights; at the same time, they have always graciously extended themselves to be guides, translators, and hosts to their American "tutors."

While Hungarians insist that their language is not learnable by non-natives, the slightest attempt on the part of staff to use the local language has not only had the functional advantage of making it easier to ask for directions, order in a restaurant, and so on, but it has also communicated their deeper interest in the culture and the people. The effort, when it has been put forth, has helped to mitigate the image of teacher educators as experts who appear from overseas, drop their pearls of wisdom, and vacate as soon as the program is over.

Hungarian teachers have access to British textbooks in significant numbers; there are materials sponsored by the Ministry of Education, and a growing number of independently produced books published in Hungary for English language instruction. Hungarians have had highly limited, if any, contact with American-produced materials, except those brought into the country by Fulbright lecturers. Although a library of American books exists in the U.S. Embassy in Budapest, most teachers do not avail themselves of this resource because they believe that to do so might put them in jeopardy with the internal political bureaucracy. Many have aspirations to travel abroad; they are planning to apply for visas or scholarships. Thus the American course has been one of the few opportunities for teachers to use materials that otherwise would not be accessible.

The American IST course is the new show in town, so to speak. Many who have been attending British Council programs for English language teachers over the years cannot resist comparing the efforts of the two Western countries. The British Council IST program in Hungary most recently has concentrated on the elementary level. But over the more than twenty years that the British Council has been providing IST in Hungary, teachers from a variety of settings and levels have been accommodated. A sprinkling of teachers at the American course have often mentioned their attendance at short-term programs in the United Kingdom. In fact, for many Hungarian teachers an invitation to attend a seminar abroad is the most realistic possibility for travel to the West.

Summary

Over the years we have been involved in the American IST course in Hungary (1983–7), we have learned how important preplanning and ongoing information-gathering can be in providing a program with a high degree of relevance to the local situation. We have also come to appreciate how necessary it is for teacher educators to work together as a team. In addition, we have been able to draw generalizations from the experience that we believe are applicable to a wide variety of inservice programs. Not only is teaching English in exotic places exhilarating, but providing inservice training courses in other cultures is highly rewarding.

19 Observing classroom behaviours and learning outcomes in different second language programs

Nina Spada

This chapter reports on the use of a second language (L2) classroom observation instrument in a variety of L2 programs over a five-year span. It has been used in regular English and French as a second language (ESL and FSL) programs for children, in intensive ESL programs for children and adults, and in extended French and French immersion programs for children and adolescents. These programs vary in their approach to second language teaching, the time devoted to the teaching of the second language, and the characteristics of the L2 environment learners may have access to outside the classroom setting. In all six instructional contexts, the observation scheme has been used for process-oriented research purposes. That is, the scheme has been used as a descriptive tool to provide information about what actually goes on between teachers and students in pedagogical and, in some cases, linguistic interactional terms. Furthermore, in two of these programs, the observation scheme has been used for both process- and product-oriented research purposes. In other words, it has been used to describe instructional differences in an attempt to relate those differences to learning outcomes.

The chapter begins with a description of how this observation scheme was used in the six instructional settings. Next is a discussion of the results that have been obtained in terms of (1) differences in instruction across various L2 programs (i.e., process-oriented studies) and (2) relationships between instructional differences and learning outcomes (i.e., process-product studies). Before the studies are discussed, both the observation scheme and the instructional programs in which it has been used will be described.

Observation instrument: the COLT scheme

The observation instrument, referred to as COLT (Communicative Orientation of Language Teaching), was originally developed within the context of a large-scale study investigating questions related to the nature

The author is grateful to Patrick Allen, Maria Fröhlich, Fred Genesee, and Patsy Lightbown for their comments and useful discussion in the preparation of this chapter.

293

of language proficiency and its development in educational contexts for children learning a second language (Allen et al. 1982, 1983; Harley et al. 1987). The scheme consists of two sections. Part A, which contains categories derived primarily from issues in the communicative language teaching literature, describes classroom activities in organizational and pedagogical terms; Part B, which contains categories to reflect issues in first and second language acquisition research, describes aspects of the verbal interactions that take place between teachers and students within activities. (For a complete description of the COLT scheme and rationale for Part A and Part B categories, see Allen, Fröhlich, and Spada 1984.)

Part A contains five major categories: Activity Description, Participant Organization, Content, Student Modality, and Materials (see Appendix 1). These categories and their subsections were designed to capture those aspects of classroom instruction that are more or less typical within a "communicative language teaching" approach. For example, classroom organization that is student-focused, with an emphasis on meaning-based practice and the use of authentic materials in which extended texts predominate, is considered to be more communicatively oriented than a classroom that is teacher-centered, where language itself is the focus of instruction and where most materials are pedagogical, with little extended text.[1]

Part B (see Appendix 1) is used to analyze classroom activities at the level of verbal interaction. This section of the scheme measures such features as the extent to which learners are given opportunities to produce the second language without teacher-imposed linguistic restrictions, to engage in sustained speech, to exchange unknown or relatively unpredictable information, and to initiate discourse. Part B also measures teacher talk to determine, for example, the extent to which teachers ask genuine versus pseudo questions,[2] and how they respond to students' utterances in terms of comments, repetitions, paraphrases, and incorporations. (See Fröhlich, Spada, and Allen 1985 for details regarding the coding procedures for COLT.)

The programs

Four studies have reported using COLT in one or more of the six L2 instructional programs described here. Two of these studies have focused on describing and comparing classroom behaviors either between dif-

---

1 Part A is a "real-time" section of the coding scheme used during the classroom observation sessions by one or two observers. Part B is used in post-hoc analyses of the classroom observation data from audiotaped recordings.
2 Genuine questions are those to which the teacher and/or student does not already know the answer. Pseudo questions are those to which the answer is already known.

ferent L2 programs (Fröhlich et al. 1985) or within the same L2 program (Lightbown and Spada 1987). The other two have used the COLT scheme to capture differences in instruction between individual classes within the same L2 program in an attempt to relate differences in instruction to learning outcomes (Allen et al. 1987; Spada 1987). The six instructional program types represented in this research can be briefly distinguished as follows:

1. *ESL for children.* The ESL program was in an anglophone environment, in an English-speaking school where grade 7 students spent all or most of the day with their ESL teacher. In addition to English language instruction, students also received varying amounts of subject-matter instruction.
2. *Intensive ESL for children.* The intensive ESL program was in a French-medium school in a francophone environment where grade 5 and 6 students spent all day with their ESL instructor for half of the school year and the rest of the year doing their regular academic subjects in French. In the intensive ESL classes, no curriculum-based subject-matter instruction was provided.
3. *Core French for children.* The core French program was one in which grades 7 and 11 students received approximately 30–40 minutes of French language instruction a day. This program was in an English-speaking school in an anglophone environment.
4. *French immersion for children.* In the French immersion program, French was used as the medium of instruction in subject-matter classes at the grade 7 level. This program was in an anglophone environment.
5. *Extended French for children.* In the extended French program, grade 7 students were taught one school subject in French in addition to their regular core French program. This program was in an English-medium school in an anglophone environment. The observations were carried out in the subject-matter classes of this program.
6. *Intensive ESL for adults.* The intensive ESL program was one in which intermediate-level students received approximately 5 hours of instruction per day in English over a 6-week period. This program was located in an English university in an anglophone environment.

The discussion of the studies that have used the COLT scheme begins with the two process-oriented studies and later turns to those which were process–product-oriented.

Process-oriented studies

Thirteen classes spread across four different L2 programs were observed in a study by Fröhlich et al. (1985) to determine whether the COLT scheme was capable of capturing instructional features in a variety of L2 programs with different pedagogical orientations. All four programs were school-based (at the grade 7 level); those represented were core French (4 classes), extended French (2 classes), French immersion (2 classes), and ESL (5 classes). Classes lasted from 30 to 100 minutes, and each class was visited twice by two observers. The data were analyzed using both Part A and Part B of the COLT scheme.

The COLT scheme was designed to capture differences in the communicative orientation of L2 instruction. That is, the occurrence or nonoccurrence of a cluster of specific features on the scheme is interpreted as representing a more or less communicative orientation to L2 instruction. With this distinction in mind, the investigators had a number of expectations concerning the main characteristics of the four types of programs under investigation. These expectations were based on some preliminary observations of classes in the various programs, discussions with teachers and program consultants regarding the methodological approach used in their program, and a review of textbooks and other teaching materials. Based on this information, the investigators predicted that the core French program, with its strong emphasis on form-based practice, would probably emerge as the least communicative on the COLT scheme. The extended French program, with its presentation of some subject matter, was predicted to emerge as more communicative than the core French program. French immersion was predicted to be even more communicatively oriented than both extended and core French because of its complete focus on French-medium subject-matter instruction. With regard to the ESL program, the investigators predicted that although teachers would "use class time to practice various aspects of the language code, they would seek to introduce communicative enrichment material from the 'real world' outside the classroom whenever possible," since the ESL learners were learning their second language in an English-speaking environment (Fröhlich et al. 1985: 31). According to these predictions, the four programs were viewed as being placed along a communicative continuum in the following order: core French at the "least communicative" end and French immersion at the "most communicative" end, with extended French and ESL in between.

The results of the analyses of the Part A and Part B features for all classes within each of these four programs generally confirmed the predictions made about the relative communicative orientation of one program compared with another, although some specific features were exceptions.[3] For example, as predicted, the core French program was found to be highly teacher-centered, but so were the other French L2 programs, which was not predicted. The ESL program was considerably

3 For a detailed description of the results, see Fröhlich et al. (1985).

less teacher-centered than the other groups, but this did not turn out to mean that the ESL students were involved in more group interaction, as anticipated, but rather that they were involved in a considerable amount of individual seat work. Also, as predicted, the core French program focused more heavily on code-related features of the second language than did the immersion and extended French programs, which were considerably more meaning-based. However, the ESL program was again found to be the exception in that it was the most heavily oriented toward explicit language instruction, with comparatively little time spent on meaning-based instruction.[4]

The Part B features analysis also confirmed some of the investigators' predictions. It revealed that although teachers in all programs rarely asked genuine questions, the proportion of genuine questions increased by program in the predicted order: core French, extended French, French immersion, and ESL. This order was also found for the amount of sustained speech used by teachers in these programs. That is, teacher turns in core French classes were rarely sustained; whereas in the extended French, French immersion, and ESL classes, sustained discourse on the part of the teacher was greater. An analysis of the teachers' spoken reactions to student utterances (i.e., the use of such strategies as repetition, paraphrase, expansions, and elaborations) revealed that in all programs teachers rarely expanded and elaborated upon students' utterances, although when such teacher behaviors did occur, they tended to be in the extended and immersion programs.

The Part B analysis of the students' speech revealed that students in the core French program produced significantly fewer unpredictable responses than those in the other programs. This had been predicted, since it was felt that a focus on subject matter in the extended French and immersion programs would lead to more opportunities for unpredictable speech on the part of the learner. Also as predicted, in the core French program, the students' speech was the most restricted in linguistic form as well as the most minimal in length of utterance. Much less restricted speech and more sustained discourse were found in the speech of learners in the extended French, immersion, and ESL programs.

In the second process-oriented study, Lightbown and Spada (1987) used a modified version of the COLT scheme (see Appendix 2) in a study of experimental intensive ESL programs in the elementary schools in Quebec. They used COLT to investigate whether there were instructional differences between classes in which intensive instruction was being offered. For each of two five-month intensive sessions, four classes

---

4 The investigators suggested that a possible reason for the heavy code focus in these ESL classes was because learners had considerable opportunities for informal acquisition of the second language outside the classroom setting and needed to focus on code in the classroom.

TABLE I. PARTICIPANT ORGANIZATION: MEAN PERCENTAGES OF OBSERVED
TIME BY PROGRAM

	Core	Extended	Immersion	ESL	Intensive ESL
Teacher-centered	58.49	70.48	60.90	21.28	53.67
Student-centered	2.72	17.20	17.32	11.05	13.11
Choral	14.40	0	2.73	1.28	0
Group	5.01	0	0	10.00	12.48
Individual	19.38	12.32	19.05	43.02	14.76
Group/Ind.	0	0	0	13.37	5.98

were observed four times each. This represented a total of thirty-two observation sessions, which lasted approximately five hours each. The data collected from these sessions were analyzed using the Part A features of the scheme.[5] The results of these analyses indicated that the classes were similar to each other. Instruction was teacher-centered for about half the time for all classes, with the remaining time spent in group, individual, and student-centered ways. Also, all classes spent very little time focusing on the linguistic aspects of the second language, emphasizing topic and meaning-based instruction instead.[6] Classes were also similar in their focus on skills-based practice and materials use. This is not to imply that there were no class differences. For example, one of the classes tended to be more form-focused than the others, and another class tended to use materials in which the texts were more extended than others. However, these differences were slight, and overall the eight intensive classes observed can be described as exhibiting similar characteristics of communicative language teaching.

It is interesting to examine how the five programs described in these two studies compare in terms of the Part A features analysis of COLT. Tables 1–4 present these findings. Before a comparison of these results is presented, it is important to emphasize that the results were obtained from a small sample of classes in the five programs under investigation. Therefore, these data do not reflect instructional characteristics of all classes in all programs. Nonetheless, the general characteristics of classroom instruction captured by the COLT scheme are probably typical of the classes in these different L2 programs.

Table 1 shows that there are differences in participant organization

5 This research is continuing, and the investigators plan to carry out a Part B features analysis of these data.
6 It is important to note that Quebec law prevents the instruction of academic subject matter in any language other than the official language, French, in French-medium schools. Therefore, when we refer to topic and content coverage in intensive instruction, we are not referring to regular subject areas such as mathematics, science, etc., but rather to such topics as housing, sports, music, family, etc.

TABLE 2. CONTENT: MEAN PERCENTAGES OF OBSERVED TIME BY PROGRAM

	Core	*Extended*	*Immersion*	*ESL*	*Intensive ESL*
Management	2.37	9.45	4.75	5.85	22.33
Language	58.44	25.10	25.47	66.43	13.75
Other topics	27.89	40.55	62.53	16.52	50.00

Note: The content category on Part A of the COLT scheme is divided into several subcategories. Because the studies used slightly different versions of these categories, only the major ones are used for comparison purposes here. These percentages do not add up to 100 because only exclusive focus on the three content areas is presented in this table. The remaining time was spent on a combination of language and other topics.

TABLE 3. MODALITY: MEAN PERCENTAGES OF OBSERVED TIME BY PROGRAM

	Core	*Extended*	*Immersion*	*ESL*	*Intensive ESL*
Listening	7.46	13.70	12.87	2.85	9.08
Speaking	1.09	0	0	0	.56
Reading	0	1.08	1.37	.84	3.34
Writing	1.66	0	2.25	3.52	1.93
List./Speak.	38.30	19.52	32.50	24.33	46.27
List./Speak./Read.	24.78	44.40	29.57	4.17	2.67

Note: Only the most frequently occurring categories across all programs are presented here. Many more combinations for modalities occurred in all programs.

TABLE 4. TYPE OF MATERIALS: MEAN PERCENTAGE OF TIME OBSERVED IN PROGRAMS

	Core	*Extended*	*Immersion*	*ESL*	*Intensive ESL*
Text					
Minimal	43.08	35.11	31.20	52.29	12.87
Extended	11.31	38.19	50.90	34.73	17.79
Audio	.68	3.75	0	0	.72
Visual	18.23	5.28	4.10	1.08	14.15

Note: These figures do not add up to 100 because materials were not used at all times during instruction.

across programs. For example, the ESL program is the least teacher-centered, and extended French is the most teacher-centered. In terms of group-work opportunities, the two ESL programs are the highest, with French immersion and extended French having no group work. Table 2 indicates that French immersion programs focus on topics other than language more than any other program (which is to be expected) and that core French and ESL focus most heavily on explicit language instruction. Of more interest perhaps is the greater amount of time that the intensive ESL classes spent on topics other than language compared with the other two programs that were language-based (i.e., core French and ESL). Table 3 shows that in all programs students spent most of their time engaged in a combination of modality practice rather than in isolated practice of the four skills. The most frequently occurring modalities involve combinations of listening and speaking, with listening/speaking/reading occurring most frequently in French immersion and extended French programs. Table 4 indicates that programs differ somewhat in the type of materials used. Not surprisingly, materials in which extended text predominates are most often used in immersion classes, followed by extended French and ESL. Presumably this is because subject-matter instruction is provided (in varying amounts) in these three programs, and students have higher proficiency levels. Materials used in the other two programs (core French and intensive ESL), which are language-based as opposed to subject matter-based, have less extended text.

What is particularly interesting about the profiles that emerge from an analysis of these five L2 programs is not so much the differences between them, but rather the similarities. For example, the Part A analysis revealed that all programs tend to be based on a high degree of teacher-fronted activities, with little group and/or pair interaction. This is striking, since several of these L2 programs have been described as communicative in nature, yet they provide limited opportunities for students to practice communicating with each other. Since opportunities for the negotiation of meaning and creative language use in interactions among nonnative speakers are thought to enhance second language learning (Long 1981, 1982; Long and Porter 1985), it is surprising (even considering the small nature of the sample) that more opportunities for such language practice are not represented in the classroom data for the five L2 programs represented in these studies. The Part B analysis of four of these programs also revealed some interesting similarities. Learners were found to rarely initiate discourse and were seldom asked questions to which teachers did not already have the answer. Even in the program described as being the most communicative (French immersion) learners were quite restricted in their language use opportunities, and teachers rarely elaborated upon students' utterances.

The two process-oriented studies were conducted for very different purposes: to validate the COLT observation scheme and to compare instruction within one program (i.e., intensive ESL) to prepare the ground for later process–product-oriented research. As such, they were necessary and valid. However, descriptive process studies of this type are of limited value. The crucial question remains as to whether instructional differences contribute to differences in learning outcomes. The two studies presented next address this question.

Process–product-oriented studies

Spada (1984, 1987) used COLT in three classes of an adult communicatively based ESL program. This was a six-week intensive summer program in which each class was observed for five hours a day, once a week, for four weeks. The study was motivated by an interest in finding out how different teachers interpreted theories of communicative language teaching in their actual classroom practices and to determine whether differences in the implementation of communicative language teaching principles had any effect on learning outcomes.

A pre- and posttest design was used for the study. Intermediate-level learners were given the same battery of proficiency tests during the first and last weeks of classes. This included the Comprehensive English Language Test (1970); the Michigan Test of English Language Proficiency (1977) a communicative reading, writing, and speaking test developed by those working in the ESL program; and a multiple-choice sociolinguistic and discourse test.[7]

The classroom observation data were analyzed both qualitatively and quantitatively using the Part A features of the COLT scheme. Because these data are numerous, it is not possible to report all of them here. Instead, the discussion will be limited to a summary of those findings where qualitative and quantitative differences emerged. (See Spada 1984 and 1987 for details of the observation analyses and findings.) Before a description of these class differences is provided, it is important to emphasize that all three classes were communicatively based (they provided opportunities for spontaneous language use in group work and teacher-fronted activities, focused on code and meaning, included integrated skills practice, etc.). However, classes differed in some ways, particularly in the amount of time spent on explicit language practice.

The qualitative analysis, which involved an examination of the types of activities, revealed that one of the classes (class A) was different from the other two (classes B and C) in the following ways: class A spent considerably more time on form-based activities (with explicit focus on grammar), while classes B and C spent more time on meaning-based activities (with focus on topics other than language). Classes B and C also had many more authentic activity types than class A. Furthermore, the classes differed in the way in which certain activities were carried

7 The sociolinguistic and discourse tests are revised versions of tests developed within the context of the Development of Bilingual Proficiency Project (Allen et al. 1982, 1983; Harley et al. 1987), Ontario Institute for Studies in Education.

out, particularly listening activities. For example, in classes B and C, the instructors tended to start each listening activity with a set of predictive exercises. These were usually followed by the teacher reading comprehension questions to prepare students for the information they were expected to listen for. The next step usually involved playing a tape-recorded passage and stopping the tape when necessary for clarification and repetition requests. In class A, however, the listening activities usually proceeded by giving students a list of comprehension questions to read silently; they could ask teachers for assistance if they had difficulty understanding any of them. A tape-recorded passage was then played in its entirety, usually twice, while students answered comprehension questions.

Some of the quantitative analyses of the remaining categories on Part A of the scheme confirmed these class differences. For example, in the content category, class A spent almost twice as much time as class C on explicit form-based practice and triple the amount of time that class B spent in this way. Since the distinction between form-based and meaning-based practice is central to the debate on communicative language teaching, these differences in relative code focus between class A and classes B and C led the investigator to examine whether relative degrees of form and meaning-based instruction contributed differently to various aspects of learners' L2 proficiency.

To investigate this question, two comparison groups were formed: one that compared the means of class A to those of classes B and C combined (C1), and another that compared the means between classes B and C (C2). These groups were compared in analysis of covariance (ANCOVA),[8] in which the seven posttest proficiency measures were separately analyzed to determine whether learners in one class improved more on these measures than learners in another. The results of this ANCOVA indicated that type of instruction accounted significantly for differences in improvement on the listening and speaking tests in the first comparison (i.e., class A compared with classes B and C) and on the discourse test in the second comparison (i.e., class B compared with class C). Further analyses indicated that learners in classes B and C improved significantly more than learners in class A on the listening test. Also, learners in class B improved more than learners in class C on the discourse test. In addition, while learners in classes B and C improved on the speaking test (although not significantly for class C), learners in class A got worse.[9] There were no other measures that were significantly

8 An ANCOVA was used so that any initial differences in the subjects' pretest performance that might have confounded differences between the groups as revealed in their posttest scores could be statistically controlled.
9 A closer examination of the speaking test data revealed that the results were probably due to differences in pre- and posttest evaluators' assessment of learners' performance

related to instructional differences. It is important to note, however, that there was a difference between the means of class A and classes B and C on the grammar test, indicating higher scores for class A. This did not reach statistical significance.

In interpreting the different performance of learners on the listening test, the investigator examined both quantitative and qualitative differences in the listening practice offered in the three classes. The quantitative results revealed that class A spent considerably more time in listening practice than the other two classes, yet class A improved the least. However, because the listening practice in this class did not prepare learners for the listening input as carefully as the listening comprehension instruction did in classes B and C, the investigator concluded that qualitative rather than quantitative differences in instruction seemed a more plausible explanation for significantly more improvement in listening comprehension in classes B and C.

It was more difficult to interpret the differential performance of learners on the discourse test, since class B, which improved significantly more than class C, spent very little time focusing on this particular aspect of language. However, this class did spend more time than class C focusing on code (this included grammatical and functional aspects of code). This additional time spent on various code-related aspects of language, combined with the fact that the discourse test had items on it that measured both grammatical and discoursal aspects of language, may have contributed to these findings. However, as the investigator points out, improvement in discourse competence may be more related to such factors as the amount of reading and writing learners do outside the classroom, which was not considered in the study.

Because the differences in performance on the speaking test were confounded by differences in the evaluators' assessments from pre- to posttest administration in class A, it was not possible to establish direct relationships between performance on this measure and differences in instructional treatment. However, separate *t*-test analyses of the pre- and posttest speaking scores indicated a significant improvement for class B but not for class C. When a closer examination of the speaking activities in these classes was made, it was discovered that while learners in class B were encouraged to focus on both code and meaning in their speaking practice, learners in class C were rarely asked to focus their attention on code. This was interpreted as support for the argument that a focus on both code and meaning is required for the development of oral communication skills. (See Spada 1984 for a further discussion of the speaking test data.)

---

rather than to the effects of differences in instruction. That is, the posttest evaluator was a "harder marker" than the pretest evaluator.

In a second study using COLT to investigate relationships between instructional input and learning outcomes, Allen and his colleagues (1987) observed eight grade 11 core French classes and analyzed the observation data using both Part A and Part B of the COLT scheme. These classes were selected because they had been described by teachers and schoolboard personnel as representing different approaches to instruction. That is, while some classes were described as "analytical or structurally oriented," others were described as "experiential or functionally oriented." The investigators used COLT to determine: (1) whether and how these different orientations to instruction were manifested in classroom teaching behaviors and (2) whether different instructional orientations would lead to different learning outcomes.

Each class was observed four times over the regular school year. In addition, students were given a battery of proficiency tests that included a multiple-choice grammar test, a written exercise (writing an informal request in a note), another written exercise (writing a formal letter of request), and a listening comprehension test. In addition to these tests, a randomly selected sample of students participated in an oral interview. All tests were administered on a pre- and posttest basis.

Based on the findings of the Part A and Part B features analysis, the investigators rank-ordered the eight classes on an experiential-analytical scale and divided them into two distinct groups: experiential (Type E) and analytical (Type A).[10] Two classes fell into the Type E group, and the remaining six into the Type A group. The results of the Part A analysis in which statistically significant differences were found revealed that Type A classes spent more time than Type E classes on topics. controlled by the teacher and on activities involving the use of minimal written text. In addition, there was a tendency (not statistically significant) for Type A classes to spend more time focusing exclusively on form, whereas Type E classes spent more time focusing on topics other than language. There were minimal differences in terms of participant organization, although contrary to expectations, the Type E classes tended to spend more time in whole-class interaction than Type A classes. Therefore, while there were a few categories on Part A of the scheme where statistically significant differences were found, categories such as participant organization, explicit focus on language, student modality, and source of materials did not yield significant differences. The investigators concluded that "none of the classrooms correspond to a prototypic Type A program (i.e. one in which only analytic activities are used), or to a prototypic Type E program (i.e. one in which only ex-

---

10 Classes were categorized as Type E or Type A by taking the total percentage of time spent on each of the experiential features in Parts A and B of COLT (e.g., group work, unpredictable language use, sustained speech, focus on topics/meaning, reaction to message), adding them together for each class, and ranking the individual class totals.

periential activities are used). The classrooms in this sample fall somewhere in between the two extremes" (Allen et al. 1987: 65).

The Part B analysis revealed several categories where statistically significant differences emerged. For example, students in Type E classes spent a greater amount of time producing sustained speech, reacting to message, and expanding each other's utterances than students in Type A classes. In addition, students in Type E classes were less restricted in language use than students in Type A classes. Finally, while teachers in Type A classes reacted significantly more to code than message, teachers in Type E classes did the reverse.

The analysis of the possible effects of these instructional differences on learning outcomes was done in three stages. First, the performance of learners in the eight classes that formed the two instructional groups ("experiential" and "analytical") was compared in an analysis of covariance using learners' pretest scores as the covariate. The results of this analysis indicated that there were no significant differences between the two groups on any of the proficiency measures. The only measure that came close to discriminating between the two groups (but failed to reach statistical significance) was the grammar test. In the second stage of the analysis, the performances of learners in only the two most extreme classes from each end of the experiential and analytical continuum were compared. The results indicated significant differences between groups on the grammar test, with Group A showing more improvement than Group E. There were no significant differences between groups on any other measure. In the third stage of the analysis, the investigators correlated the adjusted posttest class means on each proficiency measure with all categories of Parts A and B of the COLT scheme. Since these data are numerous, only a summary is provided. It is important to emphasize that few of the correlations between the COLT categories and proficiency measures reached statistical significance. However, as the investigators point out, their intention was to look for patterns of consistency in these correlations, in order to identify possible areas of investigation for future studies.

The correlational analyses between Part A of COLT and the proficiency measures revealed that "the profile of a successful classroom is one where the teacher does relatively more talking compared with individual students to the class as a whole; relatively more time is spent on classroom management; more time is spent on form-focused activities than on general discussion; the students themselves spend relatively little time speaking; and visual aids and L2 materials are used relatively often" (Allen et al. 1987: 89) The findings based on correlational analyses of the Part B features and proficiency measures indicated that genuine questions, reaction to message, and topic incorporation were positively related to improvement, whereas sustained speech by students, predictable questions, and reaction to code were negatively related. These results imply that learners benefited from both the analytical and experiential aspects of instruction.

A comparison of the results of the process–product-oriented studies reveals both differences and similarities. In the two studies, learners received instruction that provided both form and meaning-based practice. However, classes differed in the degree to which each was provided. For example, in Spada's study, the Part A features analysis of COLT confirmed that all three classes were communicatively oriented, with meaning-based instruction provided in both group and teacher-centered ways. However, the classes differed in the degree to which instruction focused explicitly on the linguistic aspects of the second language. In the Allen et al. study, the classes were also found to differ in the relative amount of time spent on form and meaning-based instruction. However, classes were also found to differ in other ways based on a combined Part A and Part B features analysis of the type of instruction in these classes. Although this permitted a more detailed analysis of classroom behaviors, it also resulted in some rather mixed profiles for analytical and experiential classes. For example, one class which spent over 60% of the time focusing on code was not placed into the analytical category because it scored sufficiently high on a number of other experiential categories (i.e., use of extended text, sustained speech, reaction to message, student initiations, etc.) to permit it a place in the experiential group. This presents problems regarding the placement procedures for classes in these categories and raises the important question as to whether certain features of analytical and experiential instruction should be weighted more heavily than others. Nonetheless, there were two classes in the Allen et al. study that differed most greatly in the amount of form and meaning-based practice provided. These classes were the ones that represented the extreme analytical and experiential profiles (the analytical class spent 70% of time on form; the experiential class spent 60% of time on meaning). It is these classes which best permit a comparison with those in Spada's study regarding the contributions of relative form and meaning-based instruction to L2 proficiency.

It will be recalled that when the ANCOVAs were carried out in these studies, Allen and his colleagues found an advantage for grammatical ability when the instruction was *primarily* form-based, and no advantage for communicative ability when the instruction was *primarily* meaning-based. In Spada's study, in which learners were receiving essentially meaning-based instruction with varying amounts of code-related practice, somewhat different results were obtained. That is, while there was a tendency for learners who received more form-based instruction to perform better on the grammatical test, learners receiving less form-based instruction did not obtain significantly lower scores on this measure and, furthermore, performed better on some of the other measures (e.g., discourse speaking and listening). These results are discussed further in the Conclusion.

Conclusion

The results of the studies using COLT confirmed that there are indeed measurable differences in the way in which instruction is carried out both within and across different L2 programs. The results have also indicated that there are similarities in the kinds of instruction provided in these programs. This should not come as a surprise because as classroom teachers, we know that different language teaching methodologies overlap to different degrees in their instructional characteristics. Clearly, it is this overlap of complex teacher and learner behaviors that makes it difficult to directly relate specific instructional behaviors to learning outcomes.

Nonetheless, the two process-product studies that used COLT to capture instructional variation in different L2 programs both found that there were considerable between-class differences to show that the type of instruction was either more form-based or meaning-based. What is interesting to note, however, is that the two studies obtained different results regarding the contributions of form and meaning-based instruction to L2 learning. The Allen et al. study indicated that primarily form-focused instruction led to the development of higher grammatical abilities than primarily meaning-based instruction. However, instruction that was primarily meaning-based did not lead to higher levels of communicative ability. This latter finding is not consistent with the results of other studies, which have reported that learners receiving more meaning-based instruction perform significantly better on communicative measures and no differently on grammatical measures than learners receiving more form-based instruction (Savignon 1972; Thomas 1987). Indeed, these results are more consistent with the findings of Spada's study, where a focus on form within meaning-based instruction led to similar levels of grammatical ability and higher levels of communicative ability on some measures. Perhaps an explanation for these different findings is that the experiential classes in the Allen et al. study did not provide as much or the same kind of meaning-based instruction as the other studies. This is possible, particularly since the classes in the other studies were in adult L2 programs that were experimenting with innovations in communicative L2 teaching, whereas the classes in the Allen et al. study were in a more traditional program.

Although more research is needed to determine how form and meaning-based instruction can contribute to different aspects of learners'

L2 abilities, it seems reasonable to conclude on the basis of the studies reviewed here that neither an extreme form-focused nor meaning-focused approach leads to the development of both grammatical and communicative abilities. Furthermore, there is evidence to suggest that instruction that is primarily meaning-based but provides opportunities for "grammatical consciousness raising" (Rutherford 1987) or explicit focus and attention to code, particularly at times when the apparent need arises (Long, 1987), probably works best. One implication of these findings for current teacher education programs in ESL is that continued training in the development of communicative methodologies, materials, and instructional techniques should be encouraged. However, perhaps a more important implication is that such teacher training programs must not lose sight of the necessity to provide effective instruction and guidance in how to incorporate the teaching of code within a communicative framework.

Appendix 1: COLT scheme

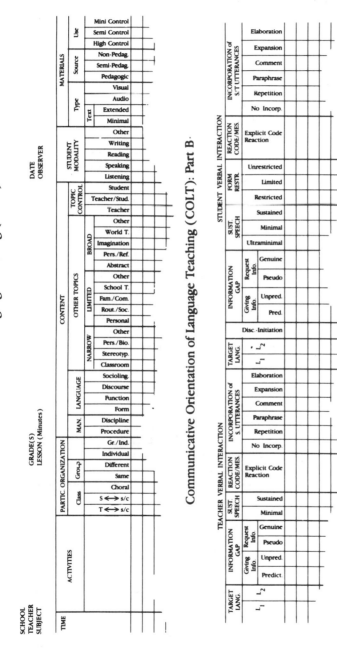

Communicative Orientation of Language Teaching (COLT): Part A

Communicative Orientation of Language Teaching (COLT): Part B

Reprinted with the permission of TESOL and the authors from P. Allen, M. Frölich, and N. Spada, "The communicative orientation of language teaching; an observation scheme" in J. Handscombe, R.A. Orem, and B.P. Taylor (eds.), *On TESOL '83* (Washington, D.C.: TESOL, 1984).

Nina Spada

Appendix 2: Modified version of the COLT scheme: Part A

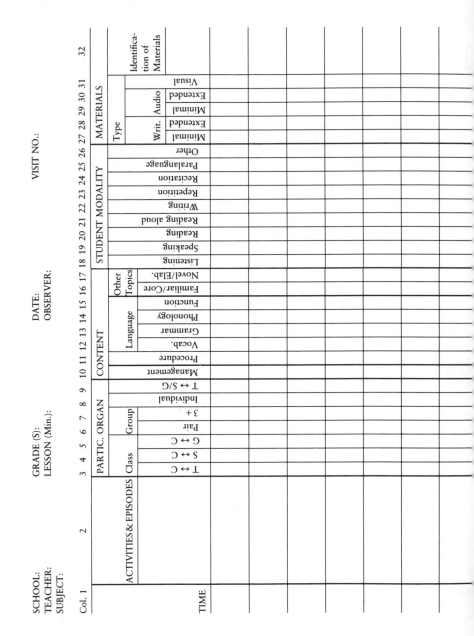

Questions and tasks

Chapter 16 (Lange)

1. Summarize the characteristics of effective teachers outlined by Lange. In what ways is his treatment of teacher effectiveness similar to / different from that of Richards in Chapter 1?

2. Compare Lange's statement on the effective teacher with that of Bartlett in Chapter 13.

3. Analyze a teacher education program you are familiar with. To what extent does it deal with the five areas of knowledge and practice that characterize reflective teaching? To what extent does it incorporate the nine core features of teacher education programs?

4. Why does Lange suggest that the base discipline for the preparation of second language teachers should be education, not linguistics?

5. In what ways are the various principles outlined by Lange reflected in the postbaccalaureate program of teacher development at the University of Minnesota?

Chapter 17 (Johnson)

6. What does Johnson mean by the term *language across the curriculum?*

7. Could Johnson's language awareness course be usefully incorporated into teacher preparation programs aimed at native speakers? If so, what modifications would you make to the program as outlined?

8. Record or otherwise obtain samples of language corresponding to Johnson's "operative," "interactive," and "informative" modes. Analyze these. What insights do they provide? How might such a task be carried out with teachers-in-preparation?

Chapter 18 (Dubin and Wong)

9. What, according to Dubin and Wong, are the major differences between pre- and inservice teacher education that need to be taken into account in planning inservice programs?

10. Using the questions in Part 1 of the Dubin and Wong chapter as a point of departure, develop a needs analysis instrument for an inservice context you are familiar with. Use the instrument to carry out a needs analysis.

11. To what extent are the issues raised in Part 1 of Dubin and Wong's chapter reflected in Part 2?

Chapter 19 (Spada)

12. What are some of the ways in which observation schemes can be incorporated in teacher preparation programs?

13. In what ways does Spada's chapter complement that by Day (Chapter 4)?

14. Analyze part of a live or recorded lesson using part of the COLT scheme. What difficulties did you experience? What insights did you obtain into the lesson you analyzed that were not immediately apparent from a casual, unstructured observation?

References

Abbot, G., and P. Wingard (eds.). 1981. *The Teaching of English as an International Language.* Glasgow: Collins.

Abbott, S., and R. M. Carter. 1985. Clinical supervision and the foreign language teacher. *Foreign Language Annals* 18: 25–9.

Abbs, P. 1986. The poisoning of the Socratic idea. *The Guardian* (January 13).

Abramson, L. V., M. E. P. Seligman, and J. D. Teasdale. 1978. Expectancy changes in depression and schizophrenia. *Journal of Abnormal Psychology* 87: 102–9.

Abramson, L. V., M. E. P. Seligman, and J. D. Teasdale. 1978. Learned helplessness in humans: critique and reformulation. *Journal of Abnormal Psychology* 87: 49–74.

Acheson, K., and M. D. Gall. 1980/1987. *Techniques in the Clinical Supervision of Teachers: Preservice and Inservice Applications.* New York: Longman. (Second edition published in 1987.)

Adams, R., and B. Biddle. 1970. *Realities of Teaching: Explorations with Videotape.* New York: Holt, Rinehart & Winston.

Alinsky, S. D. 1971. *Rules for Radicals: Practical Primer for Realistic Radicals.* New York: Random House.

Allen, J. B. P., E. Bialystock, J. Cummins, R. Mougen, and M. Swain. 1982. The development of bilingual proficiency: interim report on the first year of research. Unpublished manuscript. Ontario Institute for Studies in Education, Toronto.

Allen, J. B. P., S. Carroll, J. Burtis, and V. Gaudino. 1987. The core French observation study. In Allen et al. (eds.), The Development of Bilingual Proficiency: final report. Volume II: Classroom treatment. Unpublished manuscript. Ontario Institute for Studies in Education, Toronto.

Allen, J. P. B., J. Cummins, R. Mougen, and M. Swain. 1983. The development of bilingual proficiency. Second year report. Unpublished manuscript. Ontario Institute for Studies in Education, Toronto.

Allen, P., M. Fröhlich, and N. Spada. 1984. The communicative orientation of language teaching: an observation scheme. In J. Handscombe, R. A. Orem, and B. P. Taylor (eds.), *On TESOL '83.* Washington, D.C.: TESOL.

Allwright, D. 1983. Classroom-centered research on language teaching and learning: a brief historical overview. *TESOL Quarterly* 17(2): 191–204.

1988. *Observation in the Language Classroom.* London: Longman.

Allwright, D., and K. M. Bailey. 1990. *Focus on the Language Classroom: An Introduction to Classroom Research for Language Teachers.* Cambridge: Cambridge University Press.

References

Apple, M. 1975. Scientific interests and the nature of educational institutions. In W. Pinar (ed.), *Curriculum Theorizing*. Berkeley, Cal.: McCutchen.

Asher, A. L. 1983. Language acquisition diaries: developing an awareness of personal learning strategies. Unpublished master's thesis. School for International Training, Brattleboro, Vermont.

Atkinson, M. J., and J. Heritage (eds.). 1986. *Structures of Social Action: Studies in Conversation Analysis*. New York: Cambridge University Press.

Bailey, K. M. 1980. An introspective analysis of an individual's language learning experience. In R. Scarcella and S. Krashen (eds.), *Research in Second Language Acquisition: Selected Papers of the Los Angeles Second Language Research Forum*. Rowley, Mass.: Newbury House.

————. 1983. Competitiveness and anxiety in adult second language learning: looking *at* and *through* the diary studies. In H. W. Seliger and M. H. Long (eds.), *Classroom Oriented Research in Second Language Acquisition*. Rowley, Mass.: Newbury House.

————. 1985. Classroom-centered research on language teaching and learning. In M. Celce-Murcia (ed.), *Beyond Basics: Issues and Research in TESOL*. Rowley, Mass.: Newbury House.

Bailey, K. M., and R. Ochsner. 1983. A methodological review of the diary studies: windmill tilting or social science? In K. M. Bailey, M. H. Long, and S. Peck (eds.), *Second Language Acquisition Studies*. Rowley, Mass.: Newbury House.

Bailey, L. G. 1977. Observing foreign language teaching: a new method for teachers, researchers, and supervisors. *Foreign Language Annals 10:* 641–8.

Barnes, D. 1976. *From Communication to Curriculum*. New York: Penguin.

Bateson, G. 1972. *Steps to an Ecology of Mind*. New York: Ballantine.

Bellack, A., H. M. Kliebard, R. T. Hyman, and F. L. Smith. 1966. *The Language of the Classroom*. New York: Teachers College Press.

Berliner, D. C. 1984. The half-full glass: a review of research on teaching. In P. L. Hosford (ed.), *Using What We Know about Teaching*. Alexandria, Va.: Association for Supervision and Curriculum Development.

————. 1985. Effective classroom teaching: the necessary but not sufficient condition for developing exemplary schools. In G. R. Austin and H. Garber (eds.), *Research on Exemplary Schools*. New York: Academic Press.

————. 1988. Facets of pedagogical expertise: developing our understanding of ignorance and expertise in pedagogy. Paper presented at the annual meeting of the American Association of Colleges for Teacher Education, New Orleans, La.

Bernhardt, E. B., and J. Hammadou. 1987. A decade of research in foreign language teacher education. *Modern Language Journal 71:* 289–99.

Berreman, G. D. 1962. *Behind Many Masks: Ethnographic and Impression Management in a Hymalayan Village*. Monograph No. 4. The Society for Applied Anthropology.

Birkmaier, E. M. 1973. Research on teaching foreign languages. In R. Travers (ed.), *Second Handbook of Research on Teaching*. Chicago: Rand-McNally.

Blair, R. W. 1982. *Innovative Approaches to Language Teaching.* Rowley, Mass.: Newbury House.

Blass, L., and M. Pike. 1981. Dear diary: enhancing language learning and teaching. *CATESOL Newsletter* (January).

Blatchford, C. H. 1976. The silent way and teacher training. In J. Fanselow and R. Crymes (eds.), *On TESOL '76.* Washington, D.C.: TESOL.

Blum, R. E. 1984. *Effective Schooling Practices: A Research Synthesis.* Portland, Ore.: Northwest Regional Educational Laboratory.

Bogdan, R., and S. J. Taylor. 1975. *Introduction to Qualitative Research Methods.* New York: Wiley.

Borg, W. R., M. Kelley, P. Langer, and M. Gall. 1970. *The Mini-course: A Microteaching Approach to Teacher Education.* Beverly Hills, Cal.: Collier-Macmillan.

Bowers, R. 1987a. Theory and practice in English language teaching. Paper presented at the 21st annual TESOL Convention, Miami Beach, Florida, April 21–25.

Bowers, R. (ed.). 1987b. *Language Teacher Education: An Integrated Programme for EFL Teacher Training.* ELT Documents 125. Basingstoke, England: Modern English Publications/Macmillan.

Breen, M. P. 1985. The social context for language learning: a neglected situation? *Studies in Second Language Acquisition* 7(2): 135–58.

British Council. 1981. *ELT Documents 110.* London: British Council.

No date. *Teaching and Learning in Focus.* London: British Council.

Britten, D. 1985a. Teacher training in ELT: Part 1. *Language Teaching 18:* 112–28.

1985b. Teacher training in ELT: Part 2. *Language Teaching 18:*220–38.

Bronowski, J. 1956. *Science and Human Values.* New York: Harper & Row.

Brown, C. 1985. Two windows on the classroom world: diary studies and participant observation differences. In P. Larsen, E. Judd, and D. Messerschmitt (eds.), *On TESOL '84: A Brave New World for TESOL.* Washington, D.C.: TESOL.

Brown, G. 1975. *Microteaching.* London: Methuen.

Brumfit, C. 1984. *Communicative Methodology in Language Teaching.* Cambridge: Cambridge University Press.

Butler-Wall, B. 1979. Diary studies. In E. Arafa, C. Brown, B. Butler-Wall, and M. Early, Classroom Observation and Analysis. Unpublished manuscript, Applied Linguistics Ph.D. Program, University of California, Los Angeles.

Cameron, P. H. 1983. Speech and the teacher. Unpublished master's of education dissertation. University of Hong Kong.

Campbell, R. 1967. On defining the objectives of a short-term training program. *TESOL Quarterly, 1*(4): 44–51.

Candlin, C., and C. Edelhoff. 1982. *Challenges: Teacher's Handbook.* Harlow: Longman.

Candlin, C. N., and D. F. Murphy (eds.). 1987. *Language Learning Tasks.* Englewood Cliffs, N.J.: Prentice-Hall.

Carnegie Forum on Education and the Economy. 1986. *A Nation Prepared: Teachers for the 21st Century.* New York: Carnegie Education Foundation.

References

Carney, R. 1986. A critic in the dark. *The New Republic* (June 30).
Carnine, D., and J. Silbert. 1978. *Direct Instruction Reading*. Columbus, Oh.: Merrill.
Carr, W., and S. Kemmis. 1983. *Becoming Critical: Knowing through Action Research*. Geelong, Australia: Deakin University Press.
    1986. *Becoming Critical: Education, Knowledge, and Action Research*. Geelong, Australia: Deakin University Press.
Carroll, J. B. 1963. Research on teaching foreign languages. In N. L. Gage (ed.), *Handbook of Research on Teaching*. 1st ed. Chicago: Rand-McNally.
Chaudron, C. 1988. *Second Language Classrooms: Research on Teaching and Learning*. New York: Cambridge University Press.
Clifford, R. T., H. L. Jorstad, and D. L. Lange. 1977. Student evaluation of peer-group microteaching as preparation for student teaching. *Modern Language Teaching* 61: 229–36.
Cogan, M. 1973. *Clinical Supervision*. Boston: Houghton-Mifflin.
Cohen, L., and L. Manion. 1980. *Research Methods in Education*. London: Croom Helm.
Committee of Inquiry into Reading and the Use of English. 1975. *A Language for Life (The Bullock Report)*. London: Department of Education and Science.
Comprehensive English Language Test for Speakers of English as a Second Language. 1970. New York: McGraw-Hill.
Cooper, J. M. 1983. Basic elements in teacher education program evaluation: implications for future research and development. In K. R. Howey and W. E. Gardner (eds.), *The Education of Teachers: A Look Ahead*. New York: Longman.
Cooper, M. H. 1986. The ecology of writing. *College English* 48(4): 364–75.
Copeland, M. 1980. Affective dispositions of teachers in training towards examples of supervisory behaviour. *Educational Research* (74): 37–42.
Copeland, W. D. 1982. Student teachers' preference for supervisory approach. *Journal of Teacher Education* 33(2):32–6.
Coulthard, M., and M. Montgomery (eds.). 1981. *Studies in Discourse Analysis*. London: Routledge & Kegan Paul.
Crawford-Lange, L. M., and D. L. Lange. 1984. Doing the unthinkable in the second language classroom: a process for the integration of language and culture. In T. V. Higgs (ed.), *Teaching for Proficiency: The Organizing Principle*. Lincolnwood, Ill.: National Textbook Co.
Crippendorf, K. 1980. *Content Analysis: An Introduction to Its Methodology*. Beverly Hills: Sage Publications.
Cruickshank, D. R. 1984. Helping teachers achieve wisdom. Manuscript. College of Education, Ohio State University, Columbus, Ohio.
    1985. Uses and benefits of reflective teaching. *Phi Delta Kappa* 66: 704–6.
Cruickshank, D. R., and J. H. Applegate. 1981. Reflective teaching as a strategy for teacher growth. *Educational Learership* 38: 553–4.
Cruickshank, D. R., Holton, J., Fay, D., Williams, J., Kennedy, J., Myers, B. and J. Hough. 1981. *Reflective Teaching: Instructor's Manual*. Bloomington, Ind.: Phi Delta Kappa.

316

Curran, C. 1976. *Counseling-Learning in Second Languages.* Apple River, Ill.: Apple River Press.
      1978. *Understanding: A Necessary Ingredient in Human Belonging.* Apple River, Ill.: Apple River Press.
Danielson, D. 1981. Views of language learning from an "older learner." *CA-TESOL Newsletter* (January).
Darling-Hammond, L., A. E. Wise, and S. R. Pease. 1983. Teacher evaluation in the organizational context: a review of the literature. *Review of Educational Research 53*(3): 285–328.
Davies, F., and T. Greene. 1984. *Reading for Learning in the Sciences.* Edinburgh: Oliver & Boyd.
de Bono, E. 1970. *Lateral Thinking: Creativity Step by Step.* New York: Harper & Row.
Deen, J. 1987. A teacher's diary study of an experiment in project-based language learning. Unpublished manuscript. TESL master's program, University of California, Los Angeles.
Dewey, J. 1933. How we think. In W. B. Kolesnick, 1958, *Mental Discipline in Modern Education.* Madison: University of Wisconsin Press.
Doff, A., C. Jones, and K. Mitchell. 1984. *Meanings into Words,* Intermediate. Cambridge: Cambridge University Press.
Dowling, G., and K. Sheppard. 1976. Teacher training: a counseling focus. In J. Fanselow and R. Crymes (eds.), *On TESOL '76.* Washington, D.C.: TESOL.
Doyle, W. 1977. Paradigms for research on teacher effectiveness. In L. S. Shulman (ed.), *Review of Research in Education,* Vol. 5. Itasca, Ill.: Peacock.
Duckworth, E. 1986. Teaching as research. *Harvard Educational Review 56*(4): 481–95.
Dulay, H., M. Burt, and S. Krashen. 1982. *Language Two.* New York: Oxford University Press.
Dunkin, M., and B. J. Biddle. 1974. *The Study of Teaching.* Washington, D.C.: University Press of America.
Early, P. 1983. Inservice teacher training in Yugoslavia: A memoir. In J. E. Alatis, H. H. Stern, and P. Strevens (eds.), *Applied Linguistics and the Preparation of Second Language Teachers: Towards a Rationale.* Washington, D.C.: Georgetown University Press.
Early, P., and R. Bolitho. 1981. Reasons to be cheerful for helping teachers to get problems into perspective: a group counseling approach to the inservice teacher training of foreign teachers of English. *Recherches Echanges 6*(1): 13–33.
Elliot, J. 1980. Implications of classroom research for professional development. In E. Hoyle and J. Megary (eds.), *World Yearbook of Education 1980: Professional Development of Teachers.* New York: Nichols.
Ellis, R. 1985. *Understanding Second Language Acquisition.* Oxford: Oxford University Press.
Emig, J. 1978. Writing as a mode of learning. *College Composition and Communication 28*(2): 122–8.
Evertson, C. M., L. M. Anderson, and J. E. Brophy. 1978. *The Texas Junior*

References

High School Study: Report of Process-Product Relationships. Austin: University of Texas, Research and Development Center for Teacher Education.

Fanselow, J. 1977a. Beyond Rashomon: conceptualizing and observing the teaching act. *TESOL Quarterly 11*(1): 17–41.

1977b. The treatment of error in oral work. *Foreign Language Annals 10*(5): 583–92.

1981. What kind of flower is that? An alternative model for discussing lessons. Paper presented at the Paris Seminar on Interaction Analysis, The Goethe Institute, Paris.

1983. Over and over again. In J. E. Alatis, H. H. Stern, and P. Strevens (eds.), *GURT '83.* Washington, D.C.: Georgetown University Press.

1987a. Do *me* a favor? Don't do *me* a favor. Do *yourself* a favor. Unpublished manuscript. Teachers College, Columbia University, New York.

1987b. *Breaking Rules: Generating and Exploring Alternatives in Language Teaching.* White Plains, N.Y.: Longman.

Fanselow, J., and R. L. Light. 1977. *Bilingual, ESOL, and Foreign Language Teacher Preparation: Models, Practices, Issues.* Washington, D.C.: TESOL.

Filmore, L. W., and C. Valadez. 1986. Teaching bilingual learners. In M. C. Wittrock (ed.), *Handbook of Research on Teaching.* 3rd ed. New York: Macmillan.

Fisher, C. W., Filby, N. N., Marliave, R. S., Cahen, L. W., Dishaw, M. M., Moore, J. E., and D. C. Berliner. 1978. *Teaching Behaviors, Academic Learning Time, and Student Achievement.* Final report of phase III-B, beginning teacher evaluation study. San Francisco: Far West Laboratory for Educational Research and Development.

Fisher, C. W., D. C. Berliner, N. N. Filby, R. S. Marliave, L. S. Cahen, and M. M. Dishaw. 1980. Teaching behaviours, academic learning time and academic achievement: an overview. In C. Denham and A. Lieberman (eds.), *Time to Learn.* Washington, D.C.: U.S. Department of Education, National Institute of Education.

Flanders, N. A. 1960. *Interaction Analysis in the Classroom: A Manual for Observers.* Ann Arbor: University of Michigan.

1970. *Analyzing Teaching Behaviour.* Reading, Mass.: Addison-Wesley.

Flower, L. S., and J. R. Hayes. 1977. Problem-solving strategies and the writing process. *College English 39*(4): 449–61.

Frake, C. O. 1980. *Language and Cultural Description: Essays by Charles O. Frake.* Stanford, Cal.: Stanford University Press.

Freeman, D. 1982. Observing teachers: three approaches to in-service training and development. *TESOL Quarterly 16*: 21–8.

1983. Teacher observation: process and choice. Paper presented at the 17th annual TESOL Convention, Toronto, Canada.

1987. Moving from teacher to teacher-trainer: some thoughts on getting started. *TESOL Newsletter 21*(3).

1989. Teacher training, development and decision-making. *TESOL Quarterly 23*(1): 27–45.

Freire, P. 1970. *Pedagogy of the Oppressed.* New York: Seabury Press.

1972. *Pedagogy of the Oppressed.* Harmondsworth, England: Penguin.

1973. *Education for Critical Consciousness.* New York: Seabury Press.

Fröhlich, M., N. Spada, and J. B. P. Allen. 1985. Differences in the communicative orientation of L2 classrooms. *TESOL Quarterly 19:* 51–62.

Gage, N. L. (ed.). 1963. *Handbook of Research on Teaching.* 1st ed. Chicago: Rand-McNally.

Gaies, S. J. 1983. The investigation of classroom processes. *TESOL Quarterly 17(2):* 205–17.

Gall, M. D. 1970. The use of questions in teaching. *Review of Educational Research 40:* 707–21.

Gallagher, J. J., and M. J. Aschner. 1963. A preliminary report on analyses of classroom interaction. *Merrill-Palmer Quarterly of Behavior and Development 9(3):* 183–94.

Gardiner, J. 1987. Associations as instructional resources. In *ASHE Handbook on Teaching and Instructional Resources.* Stillwater: Oklahoma State University.

Garfinkel, H. 1967. *Studies in Ethnomethodology.* Englewood Cliffs, N.J.: Prentice-Hall.

Gebhard, J. G. 1985. Activities in a teacher preparation practicum: providing and blocking opportunities for change. Unpublished doctoral dissertation. Teachers College, Columbia University, New York.

1986. Multiple activities in teacher preparation: opportunities for change. Paper presented the the 20th annual TESOL Convention, Anaheim, California.

Gibb, J. 1964. Is help helpful? *Forum* (February): 25–7.

Good, T. L. 1979. Teaching effectiveness in the elementary school. *Journal of Teacher Education 30(2):*52–64.

1981. Teacher expectations and student perceptions: a decade of research. *Educational Leadership 38:* 415–23.

Good, T. L., and T. M. Beckerman. 1978. Time on task: a naturalistic study in sixth grade classrooms. *Elementary School Journal 78:* 193–201.

Good, T. L., and J. E. Brophy. 1987. *Looking in Classrooms.* New York: Harper & Row.

Gore, J. 1987. Reflecting on reflective teaching. *Journal of Teacher Education 37:* 33–9.

Gore, J., and V. L. Bartlett. 1987. Pathways and barriers to reflective teaching. Paper presented at the Australian Curriculum Studies Association Conference, Sydney, July.

Gower, R., and S. Walters. 1983. *Teaching Practice Workbook.* London: Heinemann.

Graesser, A., and J. B. Black (eds.). 1985. *The Psychology of Questions.* Hillsdale, N.J.: Erlbaum.

Gremmo, M., and D. Abe. 1984. Teaching learning: redefining the teacher's role. In P. Riley (ed.), *Discourse and Learning.* Harlow, England: Longman.

Harley, B., J. B. P. Allen, J. Cummins, and M. Swain. 1987. The development of bilingual proficiency: final report. Vol. II: Classroom treatment. Unpublished manuscript. Ontario Institute for Studies in Education, Toronto.

Harmer, J. 1983. *The Practice of English Language Teaching.* London: Longman.

References

Haskell, J. 1987. A bare-bones bibliography bookshelf. *TESOL Newsletter* 21(2).

Hatch, E. M. 1978. *Second Language Acquisition: A Book of Readings*. Rowley, Mass.: Newbury House.

Hawley, W. D., S. J. Rosenholtz, H. Goodstein, and T. Hasselbring. 1984. Good schools: what research says about improving student achievement. *Peabody Journal of Education* 61(4): 1–178.

Ho Fong Wan Kam, B. 1985. A diary study of teaching EFL through English and Chinese to early secondary school students in remedial English classrooms. Unpublished master's thesis. Division of English, Chinese University of Hong Kong.

Hoetker, J. 1968. Teacher questioning behaviour in nine junior high school English classes. *Research in the Teaching of English 2:* 99–106.

Hoetker, J., and W. P. Ahlbrand. 1972. The persistence of the recitation. *American Educational Research Journal* 6(2): 145–67.

Holden, S. (ed.). 1979. *Teacher Training*. London: Modern English Publications.

Holly, M. L. 1984. *Keeping a Personal-Professional Journal*. Geelong, Australia: Deakin University Press.

Hook, C. 1981. *Studying Classrooms*. Victoria, Australia: Deakin University Press.

Hopkins, D. 1985. *A Teacher's Guide to Classroom Research*. Harlow, England: Longman.

Hubbard, P., H. Jones, B. Thornton, and R. Wheeler. 1983. *A Training Course for TEFL*. Oxford: Oxford University Press.

Huebner, D. 1987. The vocation of teaching. In F. S. Bolin and J. McConnell Falk (eds.), *Teacher Renewal: Professional Issues, Personal Choices*. New York: Teachers College Press.

Jackson, P. W. 1986. *Life in Classrooms*. New York: Holt, Rinehart & Winston.

Jarvis, G. A. 1968. A behavioural observation system for classroom foreign language skill acquisition activities. *Modern Language Journal* 52(2): 335–41.

1972. They're tearing up the street where I was born. *Foreign Language Annals* 6:198–205.

1976. Teacher education: they're tearing up the street where I was born. In J. Fanselow and R. L. Light (eds.), *Bilingual, ESOL and Foreign Language Teacher Preparation: Models, Practices and Issues*. Washington, D.C.: TESOL.

Johnson, R. K. 1983. Bilingual switching strategies: a study of the modes of teacher-talk in bilingual secondary school classrooms in Hong Kong. *Language Learning and Communication* 2(3): 267–85.

Jones, B., A. S. Palinscar, D. S. Ogle, and E. G. Carr (eds.). 1987. *Strategic Teaching and Learning: Cognitive Instruction in the Content Areas*. Elmhurst, Ill.: North Central Regional Educational Laboratory in cooperation with Association for Supervision and Curriculum Development.

Jordan, R. (ed.). 1983. *Case Studies in ELT*. Glasgow: Collins.

Joyce, B., and B. Showers. 1981. Teacher training research: working hypothesis for program design and directions for future study. Paper presented at the annual meeting of the American Educational Research Association, Los Angeles.

Joyce, B., and W. Weil. 1972. *Perspectives for Reform in Teacher Education.* Englewood Cliffs, N.J.: Prentice-Hall.

1980. *Models of Teaching.* Englewood Cliffs, N.J.: Prentice-Hall.

Keith, M. J. 1987. We've heard this song... Or have we? *Journal of Teacher Education* 38(3): 20–5.

Kelley, L. G. 1969. *25 Centuries of Language Teaching.* Rowley, Mass.: Newbury House.

Kemmis, S. 1986. Critical reflection. Unpublished manuscript. Deakin University, Geelong, Australia.

Kemmis, S., and R. McTaggart. 1982. *The Action Research Planner.* Victoria, Australia: Deakin University Press.

Lambert, R. D. 1987. The case for a national foreign language center: an editorial. *Modern Language Journal 71:* 1–11.

Lange, D. L. 1979. Suggestions for the continuing development of pre- and in-service programs for teachers of second language, In J. D. Arendt, D. L. Lange, and P. M. Myers (eds.), *Foreign Language Learning, Today and Tomorrow: Essays in Honour of Emma M. Birkmaier.* New York: Pergamon.

1983. Teacher development and certification in foreign languages: where is the future? *Modern Language Journal 67:* 374–81.

1987a. The nature and direction of recent proposals and recommendations for foreign language education: a response. *Modern Language Journal 71:* 240–9.

1987b. Teacher development: building the future on the past. Paper presented at a policy conference on foreign language education, Retrospect Prospect, Ohio State University.

Langer, J. 1986. A sociocommunicative view of literacy learning. Plenary presentation, CATESOL Convention, Oakland, Cal.

Lanier, J. E., and J. W. Little. 1986. Research on teacher education. In M. C. Wittrock (ed.), *Third Handbook of Research on Teaching.* New York: Macmillan.

Larsen-Freeman, D. 1983. Training teachers or educating a teacher. In J. E. Alatis, H. H. Stern, and P. Strevens (eds.), *Georgetown University Round Table on Language and Linguistics.* Washington, D.C.: Georgetown University Press.

1986. *Techniques and Principles in Language Teaching.* New York: Oxford University Press.

Leinhardt, G., and D. Smith. 1984. Expertise in mathematics instruction: subject matter knowledge. Paper presented at the annual meeting of the American Educational Research Association, New Orleans.

Lightbown, P., and N. Spada. 1987. Learning English in intensive programs in Quebec schools: report on first year of research. Unpublished manuscript. Concordia University, Montreal.

Long, M. H. 1980. Inside the "black box": methodological issues in classroom research on language learning. *Language Learning 30:* 1–42.

References

1981. Input, interaction and second language acquisition. In H. Winitz (ed.), *Native and Foreign Language Acquisition*. New York: New York Academy of Sciences.

1982. Native speaker non-native speaker conversation in the second language classroom. In M. Clarke and J. Handscombe (eds.), *On TESOL '82*. Washington, D.C.: TESOL.

1983. Training the second language teacher as a classroom researcher. In J. E. Alatis, H. H. Stern, and P. Strevens (eds.), *GURT '83: Applied Linguistics and the Preparation of Second Language Teachers*. Washington, D.C.: Georgetown University Press.

1987. Task-based language teaching and second language acquisition. Plenary presentation at the TESL Canada Summer Institute Forum, Concordia University, Montreal.

Long, M. H., C. Brock, G. Crookes, C. Deike, L. Potter, and S. Zhang. 1984. The effect of teachers' questioning patterns and wait-times on pupil participation in public high school classes in Hawaii for students of limited English proficiency. Technical Report No. 1. Honolulu: University of Hawaii, Social Science Research Institute, Center for Second Language Classroom Research.

Long, M. H., and G. Crookes. 1986. Intervention points in second language classroom processes. Paper presented at the RELC Regional Seminar, Singapore, April.

Long, M. H., and P. Porter. 1985. Group interlanguage talk and second language acquisition. *TESOL Quarterly* 19: 207–28.

Lortie, D. C. 1975. *Schoolteacher: A Sociological Study*. Chicago: University of Chicago Press.

Lunzer, E., and K. Gardner. 1984. *Learning from the Written Word*. Edinburgh: Oliver & Boyd.

McDermott, R. L. 1980. Profile: Ray L. Birdwhistell. *The Kinesis Report* 2(3): 1–16.

McDermott, R. L., K. Gospodinoff, and J. Aron. 1978. Criteria for an ethnographically adequate description of concerted activities and their contexts. *Semiotica* 24(3/4): 245–75.

McDermott, R. L., and D. Roth. 1978. The social organization of behaviour: interactional approaches. *Annual Review of Anthropology* 7: 321–45.

McIntyre, D. 1980. The contribution of research to quality in teacher education. In E. Hoyle and J. Megary (eds.), *World Yearbook of Education 1980: Professional Development of Teachers*. New York: Nichols.

McTaggert, R., and S. Kemmis. 1983. *The Action Research Planner*. Geelong: Deakin University Press.

Marzano, R. J., R. S. Brandt, C. S. Hughes, B. F. Jones, B. Z. Presseinsen, S. C. Rankin, and C. Suhor. 1988. *Dimensions of Thinking: A Framework for Curriculum and Instruction*. Alexandria, Va.: Association for Supervision and Curriculum Development.

Matsumoto, K. 1987. Diary studies of second language acquisition: a critical overview. *JALT Journal* 9(1): 17–34.

Mayher, J. S., N. B. Lester, and G. M. Pradl. 1983. *Learning to Write / Writing to Learn*. Upper Montclair, N.J.: Boynton/Cook.

Medley, D. M. 1979. The effectiveness of teachers. In P. L. Peterson and H. J. Walberg (eds.), *Research on Teaching: Concepts, Findings and Implications*. Berkeley, Cal.: McCutchan.

Mehan, H. 1979. *Learning Lessons: Social Organization in the Classroom*. Cambridge, Mass.: Harvard University Press.

Meredith, N. 1984. The murder epidemic. *Science 84* (December): 43–8.

Michigan Test of English Language Proficiency. 1977. Ann Arbor: University of Michigan.

Mohlman, G., J. Kierstead, and M. Gundlach. 1982. A research-based inservice model for secondary teachers. *Educational Leadership 40*:16–19.

Montessori, M. 1967. *The Discovery of the Child*. New York: Ballantine.

Moore, T. 1977. An experimental language handicap (personal account). *Bulletin of the British Psychological Society 30*:107–10.

Moskowitz, G. 1971. Interaction analysis: a new modern language for supervisors. *Foreign Language Annals 5*(2): 211–21.

Mulkeen, T. A., and T. J. Tetenbaum. 1987. An integrative model of teacher education and professional development. *Educational Horizons* (Winter): 85–7.

Murray, D. A. 1968. *A Writer Teaches Writing*. Boston: Houghton Mifflin.

National Commission on Excellence in Education. 1983. *A Nation at Risk: The Imperative for Educational Reform*. Report to the nation and the Secretary of Education, United States Department of Education. Washington, D.C.: Government Printing Office.

Nunan, D. 1988. *The Learner-Centred Curriculum*. Cambridge: Cambridge University Press.

1989. *Understanding Language Classrooms: A Guide for Teacher Initiated Action*. London: Prentice-Hall.

O'Brien, T. 1981. The E-R-O-T-I model: a stimulating guide for teacher training. In G. Marsh (ed.), *Focus on the Teacher*. ELT Documents 110. London: British Council.

Ochsner, R. 1979. A poetics of second language acquisition. *Language Learning 29*: 53–80.

Oller, J. W., Jr., and P. A. Richard-Amato (eds.). 1983. *Methods That Work: A Smorgasbord of Ideas for Language Teachers*. Rowley, Mass.: Newbury House.

O'Malley, J. M., A. U. Chamot, and C. Walker. 1987. Some applications of cognitive theory to second language acquisition. *Studies in Second Language Acquisition 9*: 287–306.

Orem, R. 1981. TESOL entering the eighties: some professional perspectives. *TESOL Newsletter 15*.

Orlich, D., R. Harder, R. Callahan, C. Kravas, D. Kauchak, R. Pendergass, and A. Keoge. 1985. *Teaching Strategies: A Guide to Better Instruction*. 2nd ed. Lexington, Mass.: D.C. Heath.

Ornstein, A. C. 1985. Research on teaching: issues and trends. *Journal of Teacher Education 36*(6): 27–31.

Paquette, F. A. 1966. Guidelines for teacher education programs in modern foreign languages: an exposition. *Modern Language Journal 50*: 323–425.

Peck, R. F., and J. A. Tucker. 1973. Research on teacher education. In R. M. W.

References

Travers (ed.), *Second Handbook on Research on Teaching*. New York: Macmillan.

Pennington, M. C. 1985. Review of the teacher/learner interaction series. *TESOL Quarterly* 19(2): 353–6.

1989. Faculty development for language programs. In R. K. Johnson (ed.), *The Second Language Curriculum*. Cambridge: Cambridge University Press.

Perl, S. 1979. The composing process of unskilled college writers. *Research in the Teaching of English* 13(4):317–36.

Peterson, P. L., and H. J. Walberg. 1979. *Research on Teaching: Concepts, Findings and Implications*. Berkeley, Cal.: McCutchan.

Philips, S. 1982. The language socialization of teachers: acquiring the "cant." In G. Spindler (ed.), *Doing the Ethnography of Schooling: Educational Ethnography in Action*. New York: Holt, Rinehart & Winston.

Pica, T., and C. Doughty. 1985. Input and interaction in the communicative language classroom: a comparison of teacher-fronted and group activities. In S. Gass and C. Madden (eds.), *Input in Second Language Acquisition*. Rowley, Mass.: Newbury House.

President's Commission on Foreign Language and International Studies. 1980. Strength through wisdom: a critique of U.S. capability. *Modern Language Journal* 64:9–57.

Quality schooling and professional education: a critical relationship: planning for tomorrow's schools. 1988. Proposal to the Ford Foundation, submitted on behalf of the Holmes Group through the Office of the Dean, College of Education, Michigan State University.

Ramani, E. 1987. Theorizing from the classroom. *ELT Journal* 41(1):3–11.

Rardin, J. 1977. The language teacher as facilitator. *TESOL Quarterly* 11(4):383–7.

Redfield, D. L., and E. W. Rousseau. 1981. A meta-analysis of experimental research on teacher questioning behaviour. *Review of Educational Research* 51:237–45.

Richards, J. C. 1990. *The Language Teaching Matrix*. New York: Cambridge University Press.

Richards, J. C., and G. Crookes. 1987. The practicum: a survey of research and current practices. Paper presented at the 21st annual TESOL Convention, Miami Beach, Florida.

Richards, J. C., and N. Hino. 1983. Training ESL teachers: the need for needs assessment. In J. E. Alatis, H. H. Stern, and P. Strevens (eds.), *GURT '83: Applied Linguistics and the Preparation of Second Language Teachers*. Washington, D.C.: Georgetown University Press.

Richards, J., and T. Rodgers. 1986. *Approaches and Methods in Language Teaching*. New York: Cambridge University Press.

Riley, P. 1984. *Discourse and Learning*. Harlow, England: Longman.

Rogers, C. 1951. *Client-Centered Therapy*. Boston: Houghton-Mifflin.

1961. *On Becoming a Person*. Boston: Houghton-Mifflin.

Peterson and H. J. Walberg, *Research on Teaching: Concepts, Findings and Implications*. Berkeley, Cal.: McCutchan.

Rosenthal, R., and L. Jacobson. 1968. *Pygmalian in the Classroom: Teacher*

Expectations and Pupils' Intellectual Development. New York: Holt, Rinehart & Winston.

Rowe, M. B. 1973. *Teaching Science as Continuous Inquiry.* New York: McGraw-Hill.

——— 1974. Wait time and rewards as instructional variables: their influence on language, logic and fate control. Part 1: Fate control. *Journal of Research in Science Teaching 11:* 81–94.

——— 1986. Wait time: slowing down may be a way of speeding up. *Journal of Teacher Education 37:* 43–50.

Rutherford, W. 1987. *Second Language Grammar: Learning and Teaching.* London: Longman.

Savignon, S. 1972. *Communicative Competence: An Experiment in Foreign Language Teaching.* Philadelphia: Center for Curriculum Development.

Scheflen, A. E. 1973. *Communicational Structure.* Bloomington: Indiana University Press.

Schenkein, J. 1978. *Studies in the Organization of Conversational Interaction.* New York: Academic Press.

Schmidt, R. W., and S. N. Frota. 1986. Developing basic conversational ability in a second language: a case study of an adult learner of Portuguese. In R. R. Day (ed.), *Talking to Learn: Conversation in Second Language Acquisition.* Rowley, Mass.: Newbury House.

Schubert, W. H. 1986. *Curriculum: Perspective, Paradigm, and Possibility.* New York: Macmillan.

Schumann, F. E. 1980. Diary of a language learner: a further analysis. In R. Scarcella and S. Krashen (eds.), *Research in Second Language Acquisition: Selected Papers of the Los Angeles Second Language Research Forum.* Rowley, Mass.: Newbury House.

Schumann, F. E., and J. H. Schumann. 1977. Diary of a language learner: an introspective study of second language learning. In H. D. Brown, R. H. Crymes, and C. A. Yorio (eds.), *On TESOL '77: Teaching and Learning English as a Second Language – Trends in Research and Practice.* Washington, D.C.: TESOL.

Schwab, J. 1983. The practical 4: something for curriculum professors to do. *Curriculum Enquiry 14:* 239–65.

Seelye, H. N. 1984. *Teaching Culture.* Skokie, Ill.: National Textbook Co.

Sergiovanni, T. J., and R. J. Starratt. 1983. *Supervision: Human Perspectives.* New York: McGraw-Hill.

Shapiro-Skrobe, F. 1982. Interaction in elementary school ESL reading lessons before and after teacher workshops. Unpublished doctoral dissertation. Teachers College, Columbia University, New York.

Short, E. C. 1987. Curriculum decision making in teacher education: policies, program development, and design. *Journal of Teacher Education 38(4):* 2–12.

Shulman, L. 1987. Knowledge and teaching. *Harvard Educational Review 56:* 1–22.

Siedow, M. D., D. Memory, and P. S. Bristow. 1985. *Inservice Education for Content Area Teachers.* Newark, Del.: International Reading Association.

References

Simpson, R. L., and J. J. Galbo. 1986. Interaction and learning: theorizing on the art of teaching. *Interchange 17:* 37–51.

Sinclair, J. McH., and D. Brazil. 1982. *Teacher Talk*. Oxford: Oxford University Press.

Sinclair, J. McH., and M. Coulthard. 1975. *Towards an Analysis of Discourse*. Oxford: Oxford University Press.

Smith, F. 1971. *Understanding Reading: A Psycholinguistic Analysis of Reading and Learning to Read*. New York: Holt, Rinehart & Winston.

1975. *Comprehension and Learning: A Conceptual Framework for Teachers*. New York: Holt, Rinehart & Winston.

1987. A critical pedagogy of classroom practice. Paper presented at the Curriculum Theorizing and Classroom Practices Conference, Bergamo, Ohio, November.

Soltis, J. F. (ed.). 1987. *Reforming Teacher Education: The Impact of the Holmes Group Report*. New York: Teachers College Press.

Spack, R., and C. Sadow. 1983. Student-teacher working journals in ESL freshman composition. *TESOL Quarterly 17(4):* 575–93.

Spada, N. 1984. The interaction between type of instruction, informal contact, learner opinions and second language proficiency. Unpublished dissertation. University of Toronto.

1987. Instructional differences and learning outcomes: a process-product study of communicative language teaching. *Applied Linguistics 8:*137–61.

Spradley, J. P. 1980. *Participant Observation*. New York: Holt, Rinehart & Winston.

Sprinthall, N. A., and N. Thies-Sprinthall. 1983. The need for theoretical frameworks in educating teachers: a cognitive developmental perspective. In K. R. Howey and W. E. Gardner (eds.), *The Education of Teachers: A Look Ahead*. New York: Longman.

Stallings, J. A., and D. H. Kaskowitz. 1974. *Follow through Classroom Observation Evaluation 1972–1973*. Menlo Park, Cal.: Stanford Research Institute.

Stenhouse, L. 1975. *An Introduction to Curriculum Research and Development*. London: Heinemann.

Stern, H. H. 1983. Toward a multidimensional foreign language curriculum. In R. G. Mead, Jr. (ed.), *Foreign Languages: Key Links in the Chain of Learning*. Reports of the Northwest Conference on the Teaching of Foreign Languages. Middlebury, Vt.: Northeast Conference.

Stevick, E. 1980. *Teaching Language: A Way and Ways*. Rowley, Mass.: Newbury House.

Swaffar, L. K., K. Arens, and M. Morgan. 1982. Teacher classroom practice: redefining method as task hierarchy. *Modern Language Journal 66:* 24–33.

Tarone, E. 1980. Communication strategies, foreigner talk, and repair in interlanguage. *Language Learning 30:* 417–31.

Taylor, B. P. 1979. Exploring community language learning. In C. Yorio, K. Perkins, and J. Schachter (eds.), *On TESOL '79*. Washington, D.C.: TESOL.

Telatnik, M. A. 1977. The intensive journal as a self-evaluative instrument for the ESL teacher. Unpublished master's thesis, University of California, Los Angeles.

——— 1978. The intensive journal as a self-evaluative instrument. Paper presented at the 1978 annual TESOL Convention, Mexico City.

Tetenbaum, T. J., and T. A. Mulkeen. 1986. Designing teacher education for the twenty-first century. *Journal of Higher Education* 57: 621–36.

Thomas, J. 1987. Comparing traditional and communicative approaches to the teaching of French. *TESOL Newsletter: Applied Linguistics Interest Section.* Washington, D.C.: TESOL.

Tikunoff, W. J. 1983. *Utility of the SBIF Features for the Instruction of Limited English Proficiency Students.* Report No. SBIF-83-R 15/16 for NIE Contract No. 400-80-0026. San Francisco: Far West Laboratory for Educational Research and Development.

——— 1985. *Developing Student Functional Proficiency for LEP Students.* Portland, Ore.: Northwest Regional Educational Laboratory.

Tikunoff, W. J., D. C. Berliner, and R. C. Rist. 1975. *Special Study A: An Ethnographic Study of Forty Classrooms of the Beginning Teacher Evaluation Study Known Sample.* Report No. 75-1-5. San Francisco: Far West Laboratory for Educational Research and Development.

Tomorrow's Teachers: A Report of the Holmes Group. 1986. East Lansing, Mich.: Holmes Group.

Travers, R. (ed.). 1973. *Second Handbook of Research on Teaching.* Chicago: Rand-McNally.

Tripp, D. 1987. *Theorising Practice: The Teacher's Professional Journal.* Geelong, Australia: Deakin University Press.

Ullmann, R., and E. Geva. 1982. *The Target Language Observation Scheme (TALOS).* New York Board of Education, Core French Evaluation Project. Ontario Institute for Studies in Education, Toronto.

van Lier, L. 1984. Discourse analysis and classroom research: a methodological perspective. *International Journal of the Sociology of Language* 49:111–33.

——— 1988. *The Classroom and the Language Learner: Ethnography and Second-Language Classroom Research.* London: Longman.

Van Manen, M. 1977. Linking ways of knowing with ways of being practical. *Curriculum Inquiry* 6: 205–28.

Walberg, H. J., D. Schiller, and G. D. Haertel. 1979. The quiet revolution in educational research. *Phi Delta Kappa* 61:179–83.

Walker, R. 1985. *Doing Research: A Handbook for Teachers.* London: Methuen.

Webb, N. M. 1980. A process-outcome analysis of learning in group and individual settings. *Educational Psychologist* 15: 69–83.

Widdowson, H. G. 1984. The incentive value of theory in teacher education. *ELT Journal* 38(2).

Wieder, L. D. 1974. *Language and Social Reality: The Case of Telling the Convict Code.* Paris: Mouton.

Williams, E. 1985. *Reading in the Language Classroom.* Basingstoke: Macmillan.

Willis, J. 1983. *Teaching English through English.* London: Longman.

References

Winne, P. H. 1979. Experiments relating teachers' use of higher cognitive questions to student achievements. *Review of Educational Research* 49:13–50.

Wittrock, M. C. (ed.). 1986. *Handbook of Research on Teaching.* 3rd ed. New York: Macmillan.

Wragg, E. C. 1970. Interaction analysis in the foreign language classroom. *Modern Language Journal* 54:116–20.

Wright, T. 1987. *Roles of Teachers and Learners.* Oxford: Oxford University Press.

Zeichner, K. M. 1981–2. Reflective teaching and field-based experience in teacher education. *Interchange 12:* 1–22.

    1983. Alternative paradigms for teacher education. *Journal of Teacher Education 34:* 3–9.

Zeichner, K. M., and D. P. Liston. 1985. An inquiry-oriented approach to student teaching. Paper presented at the Practicum Conference, Geelong, Australia, January 1985.

Zeichner, K. M., and K. Teitlebaum. 1982. Personalized and inquiry-oriented teacher education: an analysis of two approaches to the development of curriculum for field-based experiences. *Journal of Education for Teaching* 8: 95–117.

Zigarmi, P. 1979. Teacher centers: a model for staff development. In A. Lieberman and L. Miller (eds.), *Staff Development: New Demands, New Realities, New Perspectives.* New York: Teachers College Press.

Zimpher, N. L., and E. A. Ashburn. 1985. Studying the professional development of teachers: How conceptions of the world inform the research agenda. *Journal of Teacher Education* 6:16–26.

Zumwalt, K. K. 1982. Research on teaching: policy implications for teacher education. In A. Lieberman and M. W. McLaughlin (eds.), *Policy Making in Education.* Chicago: University of Chicago Press.

Index

Page numbers in italics indicate material in tables or figures.

elicitation (teacher preparation activity), 33

elocution, 273

engaged time, *see* time-on-task (engaged time) concept

English as a foreign language (EFL)
  Egyptian case study and, 173–81
  ethnographic approach and, 282, 289, 290
  Yugoslavian case study and, 171–3

English as a second language (ESL)
  COLT and, 293, 295, 296, 297, 299, 300, 301, 308
  ethnographic observation example and, 45, 54–7
  journal use analysis and, 232, 237
  SCORE and, 49–53
  teacher development and, 251–4, 262, 264
  teaching practicum study and, 118, 119, 124, 129

errors
  analytical skills development and, 145
  feedback (supervisory) and, 185, 192
  student teacher practicum study and treatment of, 123–5

ethnographic approach
  American course in Hungary and, 288–91
  English as a second and foreign language and, 282
  inservice training and, 282–4
  local culture and IST participant's teaching situation and, 286–8
  preparatory information-gathering process and, 285–6
  teacher observation and, 44, 45–6, 47
  teacher observation example and, 54–7
  see also cultural awareness (teacher development program); cultural environment (SLA)

evaluation
  AMEP program and, 75
  AMEP program and teacher-dominated lesson, 67–8
  AMEP program and teacher talk and behavior, 72–3
  classroom exchanges, 277–8
  of classroom language program, 280–1
  clinical supervision and, 172, 177
  as different from assessment, 62
  journal use and, 238, 240
  reflective teaching and peer, 248
  self-evaluation, 63, 74
  of teacher, 4–5
  of teacher development program, 266–8
  see also supervision

Evertson, C.M., 11

experimental teacher preparation practices, 26–7, 36
  see also teacher preparation activities

experimentation, teacher development and, 255, 257

Fanselow, J., 16, 18, 19, 21, 120, 124, 129, 158–9, 163, 165

Far West Laboratory for Education Research and Development, 6

feedback, 226, 237
  AMEP program and, 68–9, 71
  effective teaching and, 7
  of errors (student teacher practicum study), 124
  role relationships analysis and, 87
  supervision and, 185, 187
  teacher development program and, 265
  video viewing and role playing exercise and, 150

Fisher, C.W., 11

Flanders, N.A., 19, 163, 179

Flanders's sign system, 19

FOCUS (Foci in Communication Used in Settings), 19, 116, 163, 165, 189